Bows and Arrows of Antiquity

Edmund Bulanda

Bows and Arrows of Antiquity

2024

* * *

Research on the bow and its accessories has been carried out many times from a general, cultural-historical point of view, because the different varieties of this weapon, which are widespread almost all over the world, seem to be a particularly suitable means of distinguishing different ethnic groups on the one hand, and defining their mutual influences and relationships in particular eras, on the other.

In these studies, which cover a wide area, the ancient bow has been taken into account only to a small extent, and the few works dealing only with the Greek bow have focused exclusively on one era, without examining the development of the bow in the broader context in which it had to be placed – so, their results are neither comprehensive nor flawless in detail[1].

The intention of this study is to present as fully as possible data on both the peoples of the ancient East and the Greeks based on written sources and monuments, in order to provide an overview of the history of archery and arrow forms in the ancient world.

I owe my first suggestion regarding dealing with this material to Prof. Peter R. v. Bieńkowski, and the dissertation on the ancient bow, which included a study on Odysseus's masterful shot, which has since been published in the magazine „Eos", vol. in Kraków in 1908.

I then continued these studies at the Vienna Archaeological and Epigraphic Seminary and while traveling around Italy and Greece, which enabled me to obtain friendly support from the Imperial and Royal Ministry of Culture and Education, thanks to which I was able to complete the material substantively. By presenting the work in a significantly expanded and completely revised form, I feel obliged to thank my archaeological teachers in Krakow and Vienna, in particular for their various support and suggestions. I am very grateful to Professor Flinders Petrie for information on Egyptian horn bows and for tablets from museums and libraries in Vienna, Rome, Naples and Athens. Finally, I would like to thank my friends and colleagues C. Praschniker, A. Schober and O. Walter who helped me while working or printing.

Vienna, February 1913
Edmund Bulanda

---

[1] D. N. Anuczin, Über antike Bogen und Pfeile in den Arbeiten des 5. archäologischen Kongresses in Tyflis 1881, Moskau 1887, p. 33 f. (Russisch.) Fr. Ratzel, Die afrikanische Bogen, ihre Verbreitung und Verwandtschaften, Abhandlungen der Königl. phil.-hist. Klasse, Bd. XIII, Nr. 3. A. Hansard, The book of achery, London 1845 C. J. Longmann and Col. Walrond, Achery, London 1894. M. Jähns, Entwicklungsgeschichte der alten Trutzwaffen mit einem Anhänge über die Feuerwaffen, Berlin 1899.

Contents

Basic forms of bows and arrows

It is difficult to answer the question of when and where the bow was first used and how prehistoric man invented this invention[2]. The arrow appears to be derived from a javelin[3], for it is in fact nothing more than a small spear; the bow stores the energy of the arm and requires the accumulation of various forces to then discharge it[4]. So the question of how prehistoric man invented the bow is obviously not solved, especially since the bow consists of two elements: a bending bow that stores the energy of the arms, and a string. Where did the inventor of the bow get them? There is still not enough information on this topic. We also cannot answer the question of when the bow was invented. In the oldest Stone Age, the bow was probably still unknown[5]. By the Neolithic period, we already have good evidence that the bow was used throughout Europe, as well as in Asia and North Africa[6]. From this era we have several bows from Western Europe[7], all made of yew wood[8]. Although no bows are known from Northern Europe to date, we find sure and vivid evidence of their existence in drawings by prehistoric man and countless arrowheads[9]. Bows have also not yet been found in southern Europe, and the presence of arrowheads must suffice as evidence of their use[10]. The fact that the oldest bow in

---

[2] See H. Schurtz, Urgeschichte der Kultur, 1900, p. 344-346. D. N. Anuczin, a. a. O. p. 339-341. M. Jahns, a. a. O. p. 280-281. M. Hoernes, Natur- und Urgeschichte des Menschen, 1909, Bd. II, p. 197.

[3] H. Schurtz, a. a. O. p. 347. D. N. Anuczin, a. a. O. p. 339-340.

[4] H. Schurtz, a. a. O. p. 344. A. Schaumberg, a. a. O. p. 2.

[5] D. N. Anuczin, a. a. O. p. 341 and 351. M. Hoernes, Natur- und Urgeschichte des Menschen, Bd. II, p. 195 f. M. Jahns, a. a. O. p. 279.

[6] J. de Morgan, Les premieres civilisations, Paris 1909, p. 144, A. J. Reinach, La flèche en Gaule, ses poisons et ses contrepoisons, in L'Anthropologie, Bd. XX, p. 68. Sophus Müller, Urgeschichte Europas, L. Jiriczek, 1905, p. 18.

[7] R. Munro, Les stations lacustres d'Europe aux âges de la pierre et du bronce, trad. frang. par Dr. P. Rodet, Paris 1908, p. 18 (Wollishoffen), p. 30 (Sutz), p. 115 (Clairvaux), p. 125 (Châlain), p. 130 (Robenhausen), p. 236 (Péuil). Vgl. auch J. Dechelette, Manuel d'Archéologie, Paris 1908, Bd. I, p. 367 (Clairvaux), p. 536 (Robenhausen). de Nadaillac, Moeurs et monuments des peuples préhist. Paris 1888, p. 75 (Sutz); G. und A. de Mortillet, Musée préhistorique, Paris 1903, Taf. XLIX, No. 523 (Robenhausen). A. J. Reinach, a. a. O. in L'Anthropologie, Bd. XX, p. 68. M. Jähns, a. a. O. p. 296 ff. Zeitschrift für Ethnologie, Bd. V (1873), p. 109.

[8] V. Hehn, Kulturpflanzen und Haustiere, VIII. Aufl. von O. Schräder, Berlin 1911, p. 15 and a note on this, p. 531. A. J. Reinach, a. a. O. in L'Anthropologie, Bd. XX, p. 68, Anmerkung 3.

[9] J. de Morgan, a. a. O. p. 146. O. Montelius, Die Kultur Schwedens, deutsch von C. Appel. II. Aufl., Berlin 1885, p. 69. G. und A. Mortillet. a. a. O. Taf. XLVII-XLVIII. A. Schaumberg, a. a. O. p. 4.

[10] Albert Dumont, Mélanges d'archéologie et d'épigraphie, Paris 1892, p. 23 f. H. Schliemann, Mykenae, Leipzig 1878, p. 311-313.

Europe was made of yew wood (*taxus*) is also proven by comparative linguistic studies[11].

We have already mentioned that a bow consists of two main components, the actual flexible bow and the string. All bows, from the oldest known to us to the modern ones, if we ignore minor local differences[12], can be divided into simple and complex[13].

Simple bows are those made of only one material, tree branches or other pieces of wood. This type of bow is undoubtedly the most original and oldest. It is actually a European and African bow; a type that reached its highest development in the Middle Ages in Western Europe[14].

Compound bows are those that have survived to this day (in the case of, for example, Russian Bashkirs, Arabs, Persians, Eskimos, etc.), made of several materials, such as wood, horn, bone, animal fibers or the like[15]. These individual parts are very closely connected to each other by glue or other means and externally covered with bark, varnish or other material so thoroughly that the individual elements are not recognizable[16]. Composite bows also include those that consist of two mountain goat horns and are connected in the middle with a different material[17]. We call them horn bows.

In its simple form, the arrow is pointed at the front and cut straight or notched at the back. It is a stick that is thrown from a bow as a projectile. Only over time was the arrow technically improved through particularly careful design of the tip and radius. First, the arrow shaft at the bottom received fletches and a base notch. To prevent further splitting of the ray, it was often wrapped just above the notch. The feathers should ensure a more stable flight of the arrow, and the notch, in turn, allows for safer positioning on the string[18]. In some countries of the ancient world, the arrowhead was poisoned to make it more effective[19].

---

[11] O. Schrader, Sprachvergleichung und Urgeschichte, Jena 1906 -1907, III. Aufl , Bd. II, p. 104. O. Schrader, Reallexikon der indogermanischen Altertumskunde, Straßburg 1901, p. 620. A. Schaumberg, a. a. O. p. 68 f.

[12] In the case of straight bows, these differences are mainly limited to the type of wood they are made of and the way they are made, and in the case of composite bows, to the choice of materials and their composition and processing.

[13] v. Luschau, Über einen zusammengesetzten Bogen aus der Zeit Rhamses II., in Zeitschrift für Ethnologie, Bd. XXV (1893), Verhandlungen p. 269. Derselbe, Über den antiken Bogen, in Festschrift für O. Benndorf, Wien 1898, p. 189; see also Berliner philologische Wochenschrift 1899, p. 411 f.; Zeitschrift für Ethnologie, Bd. XXXI (1899), Verhandlungen p. 232 ff. H. Balfour, On the structure and affinities of the composite bow, in Journ. of the Anthr. Inst Bd. XIX (1890), p. 220 ff. Einige Gelehrte nehmen auch als eine dritte Abart des Bogens die Armbrust an. See darüber D. N. Anuczin, a. a. O. p. 342, und H. Schurtz, a. a. O. p. 347.

[14] M. Jähns, a. a. O. p. 282. D. N. Anuczin, a. a. O. p. 342.

[15] H. Balfour, Journal of the Arthr. Inst. Bd. XIX (1890), p. 220-246. v. Luschau, a. a. O. M. Jähns, a. a. O. p. 287-289. G. Klemm, Allgemeine Kultur-Geschichte der Menschheit, Leipzig 1843, Bd. II, p. 281, und Bd. VII (Leipzig 1849), p. 334 f. A. Schaumberg, a. a. O. p. 8.

[16] M. Jähns, a. a. O. p. 287.

[17] D. N. Anuczin, a. a. O. p. 351, reports that the Indians of North America use similar bows.

[18] H. Schurtz, a. a. O. p. 347.

[19] A. J. Reinach, a. a. O. in L'Anthropologie Bd. XX, p. 53 ff.

8

The inevitable need to carry several arrows, both in war and in hunting (which was very inconvenient to carry in the hand, especially poisoned arrows), led man to the invention of the quiver. This was even more understandable since the quiver not only allowed the archer to take several arrows with him, but also gave him a free hand when shooting.

I. Bow and arrow among the peoples of the ancient East

1. Egyptians

Original ancient bows from Egypt, they are both simple and complex. The straight ones have the shape of a round, slender rod evenly tapering at both ends (Fig. 1) and resemble modern African bows, especially those from Wanyamwesi[20].

Fig. 1

F. v. Luschan, Zeitschrift für Ethnologie, Bd. XXV, Verhandlungen, S. 266, Fig. 1

Of the composite ones, only three slightly better preserved ones have been discovered so far: one, found in a niche grave in Thebes from the time of Rhamses II (13th century B.C.), is now in Berlin under number 4712 of the Egyptian department, the other, also found in Thebes, comes from the 26th Dynasty and is currently kept in the University Museum in Oxford. The third bow from the times of Amenhotep II (18th dynasty)[21] has been preserved in very poor condition and is currently in the Cairo Museum. These three bows are undoubtedly of Asian origin; v. Luschan[22] believes that the Berlin bow came to Egypt with the Hittites, and with H. Balfour[23] attributes the second one to the Assyrians; whether it is right, we cannot say, because relations between the peoples of the ancient world, according to recent research, have been so vivid

---

[20] v. Luschan, a. a. O. in Zeitschrift für Ethnologie, Bd. XXV, Verhandlungen p. 266. See H. Balfour, On a remarkable ancient bow and arrows believed to be of Assyrian origin, in Journ. of the Anthr. Inst. Bd. XXVI (1897), p. 211. G. Wilkinson, Manners and Customs of the ancient Egyptians, II. Aufl. von P. Birch, London 1878, Bd. I, p. 202, fig. 31. M.. Jähns, a. a. O. p. 300. Heuzey, Bull, de la Soc. des antiquaires de France 1890, p. 182.

[21] Catalogue général d. Mus., Fouilles de la vallée des rois, Taf. XIX, n. 24.120.

[22] v. Luschan, a. a. O. in Zeitschrift für Ethnologie, Bd. XXV, Verhandlungen p. 270. v. Luschan, a. a. O. in Festschrift für O. Benndorf, p. 193, C. J. Longman, Archery (Badminton Series), London 1894, p. 63 ff. See dazu Anmerkung M. Jähns, a. a. O. p. 301.

[23] H. Balfour, in Journ. of the Anthr. Inst. Bd. XXVI, p. 215 ff.

since ancient times[24] that in such transmissions only in the rarest cases can a person's nationality be determined with certainty. These may have been Hittites and Assyrians, as well as Chaldeans, Babylonians, or other Asian peoples who used compound bows. The fact that compound bows did not come to Egypt with the Hittites is evidenced by hieroglyphs, among which the bow was present from ancient times, in various signs. We can divide these signs into two main groups, representing composites and simple bows[25]. The Egyptians must have encountered the compound bow from the earliest times[26]. But the fact that in the old list of peoples all known nations[27] have composite bows suggests that the Egyptians used a different one, i.e. a simple bow. Evidence of what has been said can be found in the oldest representations of bows on the so-called scorpion vase[28] and on pallets with hunting scenes[29]. Without a doubt, we are dealing here with a simple bow that was already used in the oldest graffiti[30] – the same one that is already known to us from the prehistoric period in Europe[31]. It is quite strange that in ancient times it was never considered a weapon of war, but only of hunting; only when the pharaohs were forced, due to the non-warlike nature of the Egyptians[32], to maintain large forces of Nubian mercenaries, did the bow spread as an evident weapon of war[33]. Moreover, we see the bow in the hands of the gods[34] – this is testimony to us that it was known from ancient times, because all the peoples of antiquity credited the gods with the invention of objects of special importance to them, and therefore also the bow, which they used since prehistoric times. Thus, if the bow was already known in the old empire[35], then since the Middle Kingdom we find it in the hands of people from almost all classes, from pharaohs[36] to the lowest warriors[37].

---

[24] J. de Morgan, Les premières civilisations, Paris 1909, passim. G. Maspero, Histoire ancienne des peuples de l'orient classique, Paris 1905, passim. W. Max Müller, Asien und Europa nach altägyptischen Denkmälern, Leipzig 1893, p. 2 ff.

[25] R. Lepsius, Der Bogen in der Hieroglyphik, in Zeitschrift für ägyptische Sprache und Altertumskunde, Leipzig 1872, p. 79 ff.; auch E. Meyer, Geschichte des Altertums, Bd. I2, p. 48 (§ 167).

[26] M. Jähns, a. a. O. p. 301.

[27] E. Meyer, a. a. O. Bd. I2, p. 153 ff. (§ 227) W. M. Müller, a. a. O. p. II ff.

[28] J. E. Qurbell, Hierakonpolis, London 1900, Bd. I, Taf. XIX, XX.

[29] Jean Capart, Primitive Art in Egypt, translated by A. p. Griffith, London 1905, fig. 170, p. 230 ff. See Mon. Piot X, p. 112, fig. 5. H. Schurtz, a. a. O. p. 345, which describes the pallet as „Assyrian".

[30] Jean Capart, a. a. O. fig. 161, p. 211.

[31] A. T. Reinach, a. a. O. in L'Anthropologie, Bd. XX, p. 69.

[32] A. Erman, Ägypten und ägyptisches Leben, Tübingen, p. 686 ff.

[33] J. H. Breasted, Geschichte Ägyptens, deutsch von H. Ranke, Berlin 1910, p. 348. E. Meyer, a. a. O. Bd. P, p. 254 ff. (§ 287).

[34] Lepsius, Denkmäler aus Ägypten, Berlin 1849, IV, 49. A. Erman, Die ägyptische Religion, II. Aufl. Berlin 1909, p. 17.

[35] Lepsius, Denkmäler, II, 108. The relief comes from the second tomb of Saniet-el-Meitin, from the VI Dynasty. See also wooden bows from the period between the old and middle kingdoms, which are now preserved in the Berlin collection of Egyptian antiquities. Detailed List of Egyptian Antiquities, II. Aufl. Herausgegeben von der General Verwaltung, Berlin 1899, p. 74, Nr. 8662; p. 103, Nr. 13 741 usw.

[36] Lepsius, Denkmäler, III, 126, 127, 128, 130, 188 usw.

[37] Lepsius, Denkmäler, III, 153, 154.

At all times, it remained the noblest and most popular weapon of the Egyptians[38]. He was, if we can use Jähns' expression, a royal weapon[39]. Its size reached 1 m, and sometimes even much more[40], as shown by Egyptian monuments from the Middle[41] and New Kingdom[42]. Depending on the owner, it was more or less decorated. The ordinary warrior was content with simple weapons, while dignitaries, especially pharaohs, had extremely beautifully decorated, complex bows, some of which were covered with gold fittings and also reinforced or covered with various types of wood.[43]

We already mentioned two types at the beginning of our discussion of Egyptian bows – the simple and the compound, and we described the latter type of bow as not being of Egyptian origin. On monuments you can almost always see with certainty what type the bows depicted belong to, since we find two types. The main shapes – those that correspond to a simple, modern arch[44], and the second; which appears as an angular[45] shape. We consider the latter to be a variant of the composite bow, and will treat it as such throughout our discussion. The Assyrian bow will be explained in more detail.

In Egyptian representations of bows, we find a third form that corresponds to the Greek horn bow[46], known from finds[47]. Fragments of this type come from a private tomb in Abydos, which was located next to the tomb of Den Setui (1st Dynasty)[48] (Fig. 2). Prof. WM Flinders Petrie writes about this find: » A group of bows and arrows was found in one of the private graves west of the Den. The bows consist of two long straight oryx horns, held together by a conical handle of wood; undoubtedly the binding around the corners protected the wood from splitting. The wooden connector is visible just below the top two corners. Since this find is of great importance for the study of the Greek horn bow – especially that mentioned in Homer – we will return to it in the following discussion.

The bowstring, as with all other peoples of the ancient and modern world, was prepared from raw (boiled white) skin, intestines, animal or plant tissue[49]. To strengthen it, it was customary to screw several pieces together, this can be

---

[38] G. Maspero, a. a. O. Bd. I. p. 58.

[39] M. Jähns, a. a. O. p. 302.

[40] A. Erman, Ägypten und ägyptisches. Leben, p. 332. See also the dimensions of the straight bows of the Berlin Egyptian Museum, especially in Verzeichnis der ägyptischen Altertümer p. 74, 103. A. Schaumberg, a. a. O. p. 22.

[41] Lepsius, Denkmäler, III, 141. Newberry, Beni-Hasan, London 1891-1892, Bd. I, Taf. XIV, XVI. A. Schaumberg, a. a. O. p. 21.

[42] Lepsius, Denkmäler, III, 81. G. Maspero, a. a. O. Bd. II, p. 215-225.; A. Schaumberg, a. a. O. p. 23 ff.

[43] W. Max Müller, a. a. O. p. 204. G. Wilkinson, a. a. O. Bd. I2, p. 203.

[44] G. Maspero, a. a. O. Bd. I, p. 309; Bd. II, p. 387, 399, 469 usw.

[45] We see these two forms in a relief from the time of Amenhotep IV (XVIII dynastia), see A. Moret, Stele de la XVIIIC Dynastie, in Revue bow. Bd. XXXIV (1899), p. 237.

[46] Lepsius, Denkmäler, II, 136. G. Maspero, a. a. O. Bd. I, p. 104, 213.

[47] W. M. Flinders Petrie, The royal tombs of the first Dynasty, London 1900, Bd. II, p. 26, Taf. VIIa n. 7.

[48] We owe the photograph of these bows to Prof. Flinders Petrie. In the attached letter, the scholar emphasizes once again that the bows date back to the time of the First Dynasty „from the tomb of the Den Setui dynasty I w Abydos".

[49] G. Wilkinson, a. a. O. Bd. I, p. 205.

12

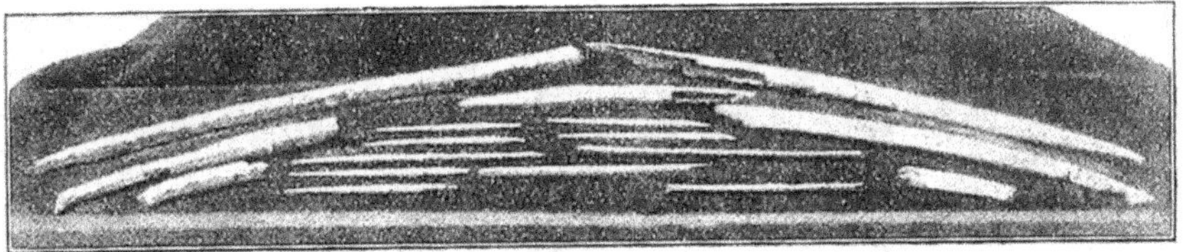

Fig. 2

Based on the photo von Prof. W. M. Flinders Petrie

clearly seen in the representations[50]. At one end of the bow the string was always attached, often very ingeniously, by lacing or tying. Since the string did not find sufficient support at the smooth ends of the bow, even when wrapped or tied very tightly, it must have been given special support, either by notches or perhaps by horn hooks[51]. To attach the string to the other end of the bow, archers rested one end of the bow on the ground and pressed their knee against the inside of the bow while sitting or standing; then they pressed the other end of the bow to their chest with their left hand and attached the free end of the string to it with their right hand[52] (Fig. 3). There was also another type of nocking, with the bow resting on the shoulder and the archer bending it with his left hand and trying to attach the string with his right (Fig. 4). Although we rarely see a depiction of a drawn bow, we can assume that it was re-strung each time it was used, so that both the bow and the string did not lose their elasticity due to constant tension[53].

When drawing the bow, the Egyptians used the thumb and index finger or the second and third fingers[54], where the thumb lightly presses on the arrow[55]. Morse also rightly noted the „Mediterranean grip" (v. Lushan) in Egyptian archers[56] (Fig. 5), i.e. the string is pulled with the three middle fingers, the arrow rests lightly between the index and middle fingers on the string, while the thumb remains completely inactive. However, this does not exhaust all tensioning methods, because Egyptian paintings show various variations in many cases[57]; however, the representation of a given method is so insufficient in that neither one nor the other tensioning method can be identified with certainty.

---

[50] G. Maspero, a. a. O. Bd. I, p. 59. J. Rosellini, Monumenti dell' Egitto della Nubia, Pisa 1832-1834, Bd. II, Taf. CXVII, I, 2, 8; Taf. CXVIII, I.

[51] G. Wilkinson, a. a. O. Bd. I2, p. 202. M. Jähns, a. a. O. p. 291.

[52] Cf. the illustrations in Rosellini, a. a. O. Bd, II, Taf. CXVII, I, 2, 6. Auch G. Maspero, a. a. O. Bd. I, p. 309. See also: M. Jähns, a. a. O. p. 301. A. Schaumberg, a. a. O. p. 28 f.

[53] Herodot II, 173.

[54] On the different methods of stringing the bow, cf. E.Morse, Ancient and modern methods of arrowre-lease, in Bulletin of the Essex Institute, Bd. XVII (1885), p. 123 ff. Excerpts repeated by F.v. Luschana, Über das Bogenspannen, in Zeitschrift für Ethnologie, Bd. XXIII (1891), Verhandlungen p. 670 ff. und M. Jähns, a. a. O. 292 f.

[55] G. Wilkinson, a. a. O. Bd. I2, p. 204.

[56] E. Morse, a. a. O. p. 171 (»Mediteirariean release«).

[57] See E. Morse, a. a. O. fig. 34-41. Lepsius, Denkmäler, III, 36b.

Fig. 3

G. Wilkinson, Manners and Customs, Bd. I2, Fig. 32

Fig. 4

G. Wilkinson, a. a. O. Bd. I2, Fig. 33

By the way, we would like to note here that the Egyptians held the bow
with their left hand when shooting. To protect this hand from the blow of the
returning string, which could cause a painful wound, archers had special protective devices, as seen, for example, in our Fig. 6[58]. The bows were stretched
so much that the bow formed almost a semicircle, and the string reached either

---

[58] G. Wilkinson, a. a. O. Bd. I2, fig. 34 and 35, p. 203. Preserved protective element leather cuff Lieutenant L. Borchardt, Kunstwerke aus dem ägyptischen Museum zu Cairo, Cairo-Dresden, Taf. 37.

14

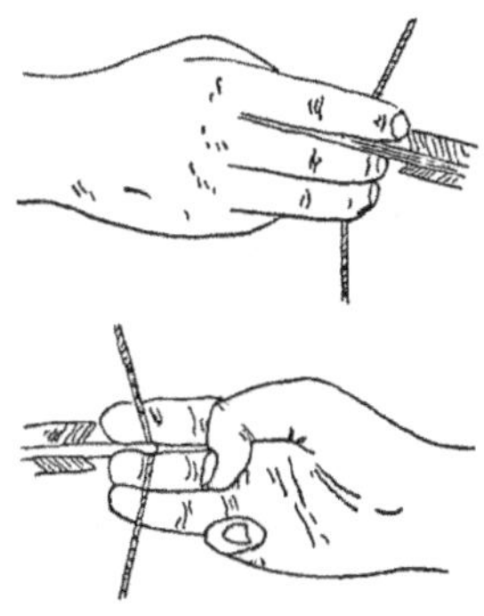

Fig. 5

E. Morse, Bulletin of the Essex Institute, Bd. XVII (1885), Fig. 8, 9

Fig. 6

G. Wilkinson, a. a. Q. Bd. I2, Fig. 35

the ear (Fig. 7) or the chest[59]. We can observe this strong tension especially in war bows[60]; on the other hand, in a hunting bow, which did not have to be drawn so tightly, the string when taut reached only a little beyond the elbow or at most to the chest[61].

The arrows, the length of which ranged from 80 to 90 cm[62], were made of solid wood or reed[63]; of course, the lowest end of the beam, as elsewhere, was

---

[59] Lepsius, Denkmäler, III, 127a, 132, 160, 166.

[60] Lepsius, Denkmäler, III, 126,127. See also: G. Maspero, a. a. O. die Figuren auf p. 387, 399, 452, 453, 473 usw.

[61] Lepsius, Denkmäler, III, 131, 132. G. Wilkinson, a. a. O. Bd. I2, fig. 34, 35.

[62] See, for example, p. 103 of the above-mentioned catalogue of the Egyptian Museum in Berlin.

[63] G. Wilkinson, a. a. O. Bd. I, I, p. 205, fig. 37.

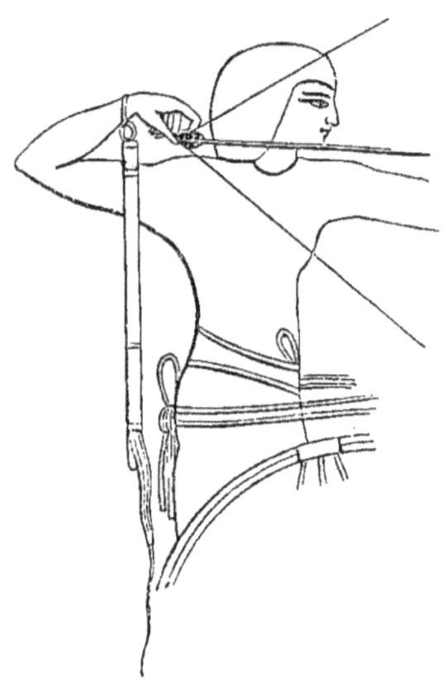
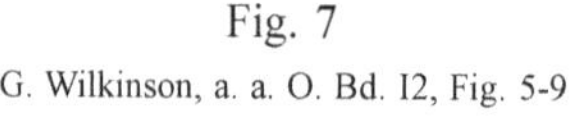

<table>
<tr><td style="text-align:center">Fig. 7
G. Wilkinson, a. a. O. Bd. 12, Fig. 5-9</td><td style="text-align:center">Fig. 8
H. Balfour, Jour. of the Anthrop. Institute, Bd. XXVI
(1897), Taf. X, 8, 9</td></tr>
</table>

equipped with a notch (Fig. 8), with which the arrow was attached to the string. There were always three colored feathers above this notch at the lower end of the ray. There was always an arrowhead attached to the upper end of the shaft; only on those arrows that were used for hunting birds can we notice a thickening at the upper end[64]. For reed arrows, a solid wood stick was used in which the arrowhead was attached. In the illustrations we see arrowheads almost always with wide edges[65], but excavations have brought us a variety of shapes, from thin needles to wide triangular ones with barbs. Wood, bone, stone and metal were used as materials. The flint arrowheads in particular are crafted with extreme delicacy, almost completely uniform, thinly worked and sharply hewn. They continued to be used even in later periods when metal-working[66] had been invented; it should only be emphasized that arrowheads from the prehistoric period are much more carefully developed than those that were used at the same time as metal ones.

The development of arrowhead forms[67] has long been developed and we repeat it briefly after the work of Flinders Petrie and Quibell. The simplest

---

[64] L. Borchardt, a. a. O. Taf. 37, Text. p. 16.

[65] See Rosellini, a. a. O. Bd. II. Taf. CXVII, 1, 2, 6; also W. M. Müller, a. a. O. p. 7.

[66] Sir J. Evans, The ancient stone implements of Great Britain, II ed. London 1897, p. 9. M. Jähns, a. a. O. p. 298.

[67] On the work on Egyptian arrowheads, see: W. M. Flinders Petrie, T. E. Quibell, Naqada and Bailas, London 1896, p. 21, 46, 56, Taf. XLI, LXXII, LXXIII; Flinders Petrie, Medum, London 1892, Taf. XXIX. Flin- ders Petrie, Diospolis parva, London 1901, p. 23, Taf IV. J. E. Quibell, Hierakonpolis, I, Taf. XXIV. Flinders Petrie, The royal tombs of the first dynasty, London 1900, Bd. I, p. 28, Taf. XXXVII; Bd. II, Taf. IV,

16

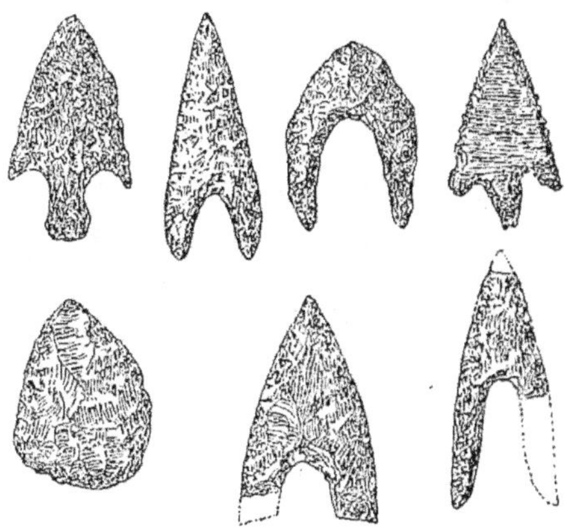

Fig. 9

J. de Morgan, Recherches sur les Origines de l'Égypte, Bd. I, Fig, 183, 185, 189, 190, 196, 199, 201

forms are wooden tips in the shape of a club and a wedge. The same shapes can also be found in those made of flint. Then came leaf-shaped and then diamond-shaped points, which were attached to a radius with one end. Arrowheads with barbs and a socket for insertion (fig. 9) make quite a big step forward. Similarly, several forms can be distinguished in metal arrowheads. Particularly noteworthy are leaf-shaped tips with or without a sleeve and an insertion socket, as well as triangular tips with the same attachment to the radius. Of course, the most dangerous were metal arrowheads with barbs. A selection of all these forms can be found in Fig. 10 after „Tanis" by Flinders Petrie.

Regarding the use of the quiver by the Egyptians, the following can be said: on the monuments of the ancient empire, we do not see the quiver anywhere. Although we do not find any depictions of war from this era at all, the quiver does not appear as a hieroglyphic sign either[68]. Most likely, as G. Maspero rightly argues,[69] it was only during the Middle Kingdom that the quiver came to Egypt from Asia. However, it is commonly found in the period of the Middle Kingdom, at a time when the bow was already a kind of national weapon[70].

VI, p. 22, 23, 34, 35. E. A. Budge Wallis, Egypt in the Neolithic and archaic periods, London 1902, Bd. I, p. 84. Flinders Petrie, Tanis, London 1883, Bd. II, Taf. XXXIX, 8-16, 20. J. de Morgan, Recherches sur les Origines de l'Égypte, Paris 1896, Bd. I, p. 127 bis 132, 209-210, fig. 138 238; Bd. II (1897), p. 81-84, fig. 196-225.

[68] B. Lepsius, Denkmäler, 11,20-22. – Flinders Petrie, Medum, Taf. IX usw.

[69] G. Maspero, Notes au jour le jour, in Proceedings of the Society of biblical archeology, Bd. XIV (London 1892), § 18 (S. 184-187).

[70] Zob. Lepsius, Denkmäler, II, 131-133; Rosellini, a. a. O. Bd. I. Taf. XXVI-XXVIII (From the Middle Kingdom).

17

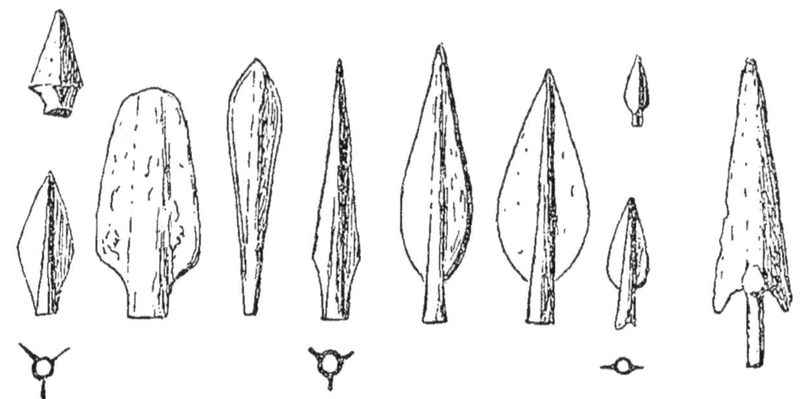

Fig. 10

W. M. Flinders Petrie, Tanis II, Taf. XXXIX, Nr. 8-16, 20

Previously, it was probably customary to simply carry arrows in the right hand[71] (see Fig. 6), and sometimes, e.g. when drawing a bow, they were also placed on the ground[72].

In later times, every Egyptian archer was provided with a quiver in which he could carry a sufficient supply of arrows. The quiver was usually worn on a strap that ran over the right shoulder and chest so that it hung on the left side of the body[73], and this was probably the custom among infantry troops during battle. We also often find a quiver worn on the right shoulder[74]. Pharaohs who shot arrows from chariots usually had quivers attached to the outside of the vehicle's casing[75]. Quivers were mostly made of leather and often decorated with beautiful decorations or paintings[76]; those most valued in the army, as well as bow containers, had gilded decorations and colorful enamelled images. Each quiver was equipped with a cover which, like the quiver itself, was sometimes exquisitely decorated. Instead of an actual bow case, infantry archers, or low-class warriors,[77] used a special bow case that covered only the center of the bow.

This leather bag was, of course, much cheaper than the beautifully decorated bow case and, according to Anuchin, it was intended to protect the bow not so much from rain, but from hand sweat[78].

---

[71] Lepsius, Denkmäler, II, 132, 136.

[72] Rosellini, a. a. O. Bd. II, CXVII, 1, 2, 6. Newberry, Beni Häsan, Bd. I, Taf. 14. Auch G. Maspero, a. a. O. Bd. I, p. 309 and 452.

[73] G. Wilkinson, a. a. O. Bd. I2, p. 207, fig. 85. Rosellini, a. a. O. Bd. I, Taf. LXXXIII. Lepsius, Denkmäler, III, 127, 130, 166.

[74] Lepsius, Denkmäler, III, 160.

[75] v. Bissing-Bruckmann, Denkmäler ägyptischer Skulptur, Taf. 91, 92. D. N. Anuczin, a. a. O. fig. 29.

[76] A splendid leather quiver with a lid by Lieutenant L. Borchardt, a. a. O. Taf. 37, Text. p. 16.

[77] Rosellini, a. a. O. Bd. II, Taf. CXXI, 23, 26.

[78] D. N. Anuczin, a. a. O. p. 362, fig. 25. G. Wilkinson, a. a. O. Bd. I2, fig. 18.

18

Generally speaking, Egyptian archers never used a shield. However, they could be shielded by their companions. However, this was probably used only in the case of pharaohs, who almost always fired from chariots[79]. We do not need to mention here the fact that fighting using chariots began only from the times of the Hyksos, with whom horses came to Egypt[80].

2. Ethiopians

The influence of Egyptian culture on Ethiopia is a well-known fact[81]. However, it seems to us doubtful whether the Ethiopian bow was also subject to this influence, since it was a simple wooden bow, and, on the contrary, perhaps in Egypt it was in general use only by Nubian mercenaries[82]. According to the unanimous testimony of Herodotus, Diodorus and Strabön[83], the Ethiopian bow was very large, because its length was 4 cubits, i.e. 1,776 m[84], which is also visible in paintings[85]. It was made of solid wood or reed, very similar to the modern African one. Strabo's message says that the Ethiopians used to give the bow the necessary flexibility by heating it over a fire[86].

The arrows were made of reed, with feathery fletches above the notch and fitted with stone tips[87]. When stringing, the Ethiopians mainly used the Mediterranean method, although of course there are various deviations from it[88]. The quiver is generally rare in Ethiopia, most of the time the shooters held the arrows in their left hand[89], a procedure that is already familiar to us from Egypt.

The Ethiopians were famous for their bow and knew how to use it so skillfully that even the Persians, who had the highest reputation as archers, could not equal them. In particular, drawing the Ethiopian longbow was considered a great achievement. We recall here the Ethiopian king's response to Cambyses's scouts: „The Ethiopian king advises the Persian king that if the Persians can draw a bow of such size as easily, they should enter into a dispute"[90]. We must already emphasize here that proper bending and tension of the bow was

---

[79] Lepsius, Denkmäler, III, 160.

[80] J. H. Breasted, a. a. O. p. 214. M. Duncker, Geschichte des Altertums, Leipzig 1874, Bd. I4, p. 146. F. Studniczka, Jahrbuch, Bd. XXII (1907), p. 149. Perrot et Chipiez, Histoire de Tart dans l'antiquité, Paris 1882, Bd. I, p. 703.

[81] H. Brugsch-Bey, Geschichte Ägyptens, Leipzig 1877, p. 9-10. Perrot et Chipiez, a. a. O. Bd. I, p. 20-21. A. Wiedemann, Ägyptische Geschichte, Gotha 1884, p. 14.

[82] W. Max Müller, a. a. O. p. 2 f. i 6.

[83] Herodot VII, 69; Diodor III, 8, 4; See Strabon XVII, 2, 3. (C 822 ed. Meineke).

[84] H. Nissen, Griechische und römische Metrologie, J. v. Müllers Handbuch, I, p. 666.

[85] Lepsius, Denkmäler, V, 20, 21, 40, 50, 71, 74 and next.

[86] A. Schaumberg, a. a. O. p. 24.

[87] See Pollllx, Onomasticon I, 138: Αἰϑίοπες ἐχρώντο ... λίϑῳ ὀξεῖ ἀντί σιδήρου.

[88] Lepsius, Denkmäler, I, 40, 46, 49, 50 usw.

[89] F. v. Luschan, a. a. O. in Zeitschrift für Ethnologie, Bd. XXIII, Verhandlungen p. 671.

[90] Herodot III, 21, 22.

considered evidence of overall good workmanship. We will touch on this issue from time to time when discussing the role of the Greek bow in agonism.

As to why the drawing of the Ethiopian bow was considered a great achievement, more detailed information is given by Diodorus' message: Αἰθίοπες ... τοξεύουσι τῷ ποδὶ προσβαίνοντες, 'die. The Ethiopians shoot arrows with their feet." This procedure would remain obscure to us if Xenophon had not transmitted a similar method of archery among the Kardus: Anab. IV, 2.28 (Καρδοῦχοι) εἶχον δέ τόξα ἐγγύς τριπήχη. εἶλκον δέ τάς νευράς ὁπότε τοξεύοιεν πρὸς τὸ κάτο) τοῦ τόξου τῷ ἀριστερῷ ποδί προσβαίνοντες. It is not clear from this that both the Ethiopians and the Cardushians stepped on the bow to string it, i.e., to string it, but it does appear that they placed the lower end of the bow on the ground and kicked it with their left foot as they fired the arrow. It is interesting, therefore, that the Kardushes and Ethiopians not only, like other archers, put their left foot forward, but also placed one end of the bow on the ground[91] to give it support. This procedure was unknown to the Persians because they carried much shorter bows than the Ethiopians.

Finally, we would like to note that this is a very long bow, but rather stiff. A short draw of the bow was enough, and the length of the arrows had to adapt to the short draw length. In this way we can explain Herodotus's message that the Ethiopians have short arrows (σμικρούς). We do not know whether poisoned arrows, the use of which we have few occasional statements by ancient writers[92], were always or only exceptionally used by the Ethiopians.

3. Arabs

We have very rare information about the bows and arrows of the Arabs in ancient literature. In Herodotus we read only[93]: ῾Αράβιοι ... τόξα δε παλίντονα εἶχαν προς δεξιά, μακρά. Pollux writes against this[94]: ἱστέον δέ ἅτι καί φοίνικας σπάθγ Αράβων τινές αντί κέρως ἐχρώντο und weiter καί εχριον τάς ακίδας ἱφ φαρμακωθεί Αραβες. However short this message is, we consider it very important. According to Pollux's statement, the Arabs used two types of bows, the straight[95] and the composite bow. It is natural that the simple African bow was older. It was only when Arabs came into contact with other Asians that the compound bow became popular among them. The latter was the παλίντονον

---

[91] See Strabon XVI, 4, 10 (C 772 ed. Meineke). See Arrian ῾Ινδική, i6, 6 (by Indian archers).

[92] Agatharchides, De mari Erythraeo I, 19, bei C. Müller, Geogr. Gracc. Minor. Bd, I, p. 118-119: χρώνται δέ επί των κινδύνων των πολεμικών Αίθ'ίοπες τοῖς μέν τόξοις μεγάλοι;, βραχέαι δέ τοίς αίστοῖς. επί δέ της άκρας τοῦ καλάμου κερκίδος αντί τοῦ σιδήρου παραμήκης τώ τύπφ λίθος άνεστήρικται, νεύοοις έσφιγμένος, ὁῦς μέν. ὑπερβολή., φαρμάκοις δέ θανάσιμοις βεβαμμένος. See auch Cl. Claudian, De cons. Stilich. I, 351-353 (ed. J. Koch).

[93] Herodot VII, 69.

[94] Pollux, Onomasticon I, 138; see Strabon XVI, 4, 24 (781-882 ed. Meineke).

[95] See A. Schaumberg, a a. O. 31 f.

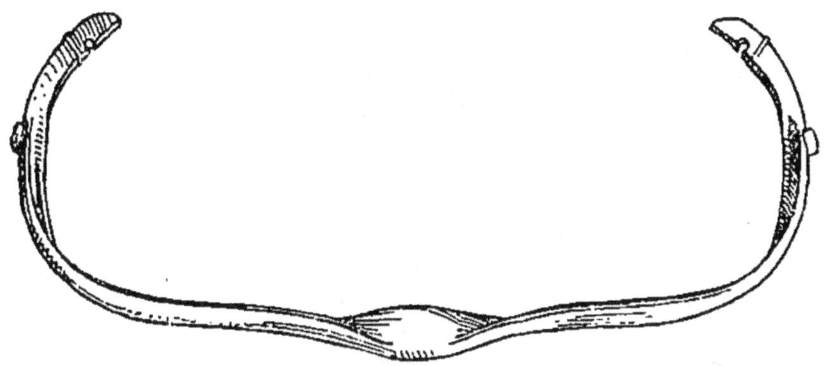

Fig. 11

W. Boeheim, Handbuch der Waffenkunde, Fig. 474

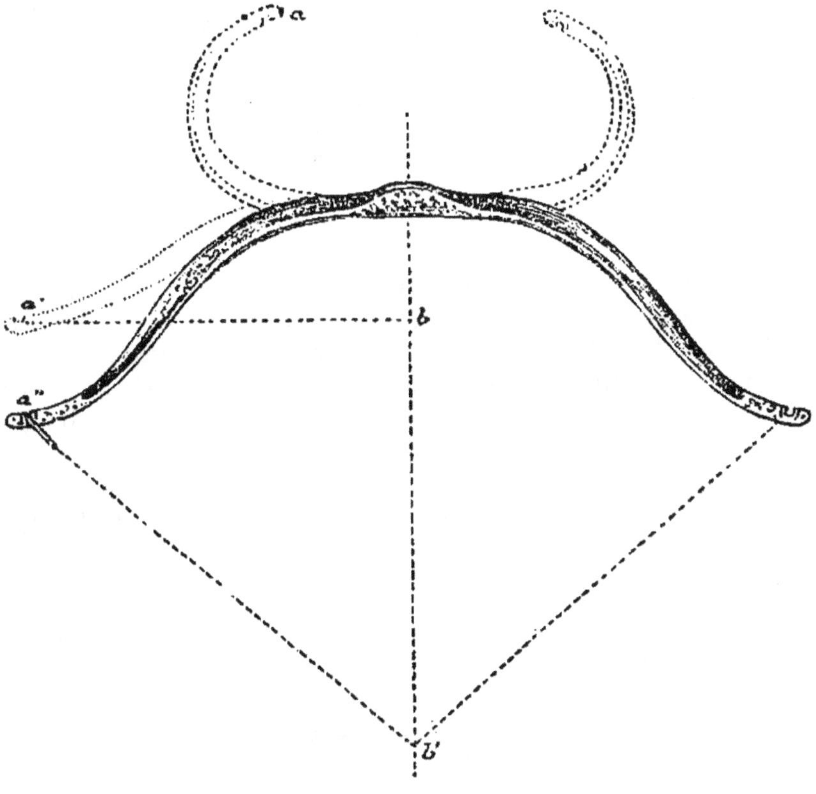

Fig. 12

W. Boeheim, a. a. O. Fig. 475

bow; there is already extensive literature on this name[96], but almost all these explanations are inadequate from a factual point of view, and it is quite strange that commentators always try to explain otherwise such a clear explanation of Hesychius – pulled back (down) or turned inside out. According to Hesychius, τόξον παλίντονον is a bow that can also be drawn backwards, but which at the same time has the property of returning to its previous position when the string is removed.

Whereas in straight bows the string is attached in such a way that the natural curve (κάμπολον τ.) of the curved wood is bent more and more inward until the string is attached. In the case of bows called παλίντονον, the tendon is not attached to the usual side, but on the outside or, more clearly, on the opposite side of the natural curve. We base this claim on the medieval Arabic bow[97]. It is highly probable that the ancient Arabian bow remained unchanged until the Middle Ages, except for very minor modifications. Such Arabic bows from the Middle Ages are in the Vienna Court Museum and were described by W. Böheim[98].

Fig. 11 shows such an unstrung Arabic bow according to Böheim. If it were to be strung in the ordinary way, the ends would have to be inclined even more towards the center, which in itself does not seem impossible, but the way in which the notches for attaching the string to the ends of the bow are made show that the bow must have been strung differently. How this was usually done is shown in Fig. 12, which shows a Turkish bow from the same period. "If the string is attached, the bow must be pulled firmly down to a," with its tensile force already acting. If the string is additionally twisted to accelerate the flight of the arrow, the bow bends even more to „a", and its relative strength is exploited for a moment to its maximum[99]". Does this method of attaching the bowstring not correspond to the meaning of the word παλίντονον that Hesychius gave us? We do not deny that it took a lot of effort to stretch this τόξον παλιντονον. But when this bow was drawn, it imparted much greater power and speed to the arrows and thus enabled a more reliable encounter with the target.

Herodotus also tells us that the Arabs carried a bow on their right shoulder (ειχον προς δεξιά) – strange news since no other people of antiquity used this method of carrying a bow, but it is even stranger because, according to other

---

[96] C. Wex, Über τόξα παλίντονα, in Zeitschrift für die Altertumswissenschaft, Nr. 145 (1839), Sp. 1161 (wo auch die ältere Literatur). H. Stephanus, Thesaurus linguae graecae, Bd. VI, p. 95. Ameis, Anhang zur Odyssee, p. 11. Ebeling, Lexicon Homericum, Bd. II, p. 125. Daremberg et Saglio, Dictionnaire, p. v. arcus u. v. dgl.

[97] Medieval bows, their nomenclature, production, and significance are discussed in detail by Hammer-Purgstall, Über Bogen und Pfeil, den Gebrauch und die Verfertigung derselben bei den Arabern und Türken, im 4. Bande der Denkschriften der philosophisch-historischen Klasse der Kaiserlichen Akademie der Wissenschaften, Wien 1853.

[98] W. Boeheim, Handbuch der Waffenkunde, Leipzig 1890, p. 395-398, fig. 474.

[99] W. Boeheim, a. a. O. p. 396-397, fig. 475. See bows bei H. v. Mayr und p. Fischer, Genre-Bilder aus dem Orient, Stuttgart 1846-1850. Lief III, Taf. XVIII, 6.

sources, the Arabs only since Muhammad began to wear a bow on his right shoulder[100].

Arab arrows were made of palm wood and roughly resembled Egyptian ones; colorfully feathered, they had sharp stone arrowheads, which were sometimes poisoned[101].

Livy testifies that the Arabs sometimes shot their arrows while sitting on camels[102]: „his (camels) insidebant Arabs sagittarii, gladios habentes tenus", etc.

4. Babylonians

The classical writers have left us no information about the old Babylonian bow, nor did they. Unfortunately, Babylonian monuments are very poor in this respect. However, it is certain that the god Assur used a bow, which seems to indicate that the bow was used from the earliest times[103]. Ancient images depict this god as half a sun disk with two hands, one of which holds a bow[104]. Surprisingly, it is a very simple bow, perhaps made of reeds, which grew in large quantities in Mesopotamia[105] (Fig. 13). Religion, of course, proved conservative here too, and undoubtedly preserved the oldest bow in Mesopotamia. Later bows are of a different type. Already on the triumphal stele of King Naram-Sin (around 2470-2440) there is a composite bow[106]. Here a victorious ruler appears and pursues the enemy with his troops in the mountains[107]; he has a stretched bow in his left hand, open to the outside – i.e. pointing παλιντονον[108] with an arrow to the right (Fig. 14). This is the same bow that we have on

---

[100] M. Jähns, a. a. O. p. 321: »When one day Eidam Ali ben Ebi Talib Muhammad appeared with a bow under his right armpit, the Prophet cried out to him, „Dressed in this way and wielding a bow in this way, the angel Gabriel appeared to me on the day of the slaughter of Bedra!" And since then, Muslims have been wearing a bow on their right side«.

[101] See Pollux Onomasticon I, 138. Nicander von Coloph Alexipharmaka 444-448 und das Scholion zu dieser Stelle. A. J. Reinach, a. a. O. in L'Anthropologie, Bd. XX, p. 56, Anm. I. Hiob VI, 4.

[102] T. Livius XXXVII, 40, 12: about this type of struggle Strabo XV, 1, 52 (C 709, ed. Meineke); Herodot VII, 86.

[103] The oldest inhabitants of Mesopotamia, the Sumerians, according to Ed. Meyer, Geschichte I2, p. 418; Sumerer und Semiten in Babylonien (Abhandlungen der Königlichen Berliner Akademie, 1906), p. 113 they didn't use a bow at all.

[104] M. Jähns, a. a. O. p. 298; Taf. XXXVI, 13. Perrot et Chipiez, a. a. O. Bd. II, p. 89 ff.

[105] F. Hommel, Geschichte Babyloniens und Assyriens, Berlin 1885, p. 188 und p. 191, Anm. 1.

[106] See also Revue bow. Bd. XXXIV (1899), Taf. I. Springer-Michaelis, Kunstgeschichte, Bd. 1, fig. 128, p. 51. For the time of origin of this stele, see also E. Meyer, Geschichte, Bd. I2, p. 475 ff. J. de Morgan, Mémoires de la Mission scientifique en Perse, Paris 1900, Bd. I, p. 144: »La stele de Naram-Sin, decouverte à Suse le 6 avril 1898, est, sans contredit, l'oeuvre artistique la plus remarquable en même temps que l'une des plus anciennes qui aient jamais été rencontrées en Chaldée et dans les pays voisins. C'est surtout par Pensemblede sa composition que ce basrelief est incomparable, bien que l'execution des détails surpasse tout ce que nous connaissons de la statuaire asiatique«.

[107] According to A. Jeremiasa, Das Alte Testament im Lichte des alten Orients, 2nd ed., Leipzig 1906, p. 290, footnote 2, this stele represents the triumph of the Babylonians over the Elamites.

[108] J. de Morgan, Mission scientifique en Perse, Paris 1896, Bd. IV, Taf. X. »L'arc à double courbure«.

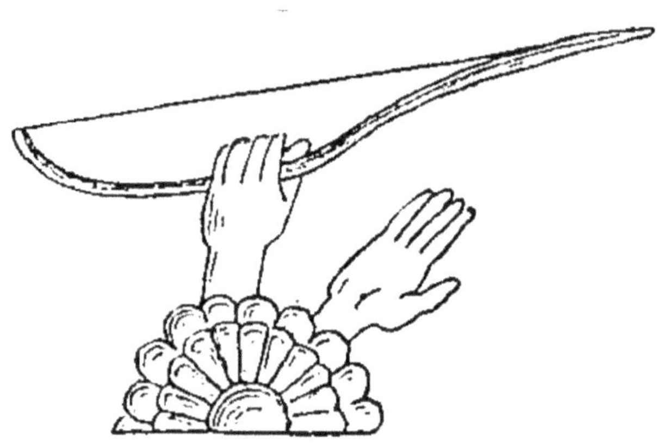

Fig. 13

M. Jähns, Entwicklungsgeschichte, Taf. XXXVI, Fig. 13

a very old Chaldean cylinder made of Erech (c. 3500 BC)[109], where a warrior with a quiver is visible – παλίντovov. He has a bow on his left shoulder, some of them lead captured enemies. It should be noted here that on the Naram-Sina stele, one of the warriors also has a bow, which is different from the king's bow. We can certainly talk about the king's weapon as a composite bow, on the one hand because it is παλίντovov, and on the other hand because it has the characteristic bend of a taut composite bow[110]. On the other hand, the bow of an ordinary warrior appears to be a straight bow[111]. In another monument, which is located at Hourin-Cheikh-Khân and whose photo is published by Morgan[112], we again see a shooter with a bow, which must be considered as compound because, like the Assyrian „angular" bow, it has an angle where it is held[113].

Since there are no finds for this type of bow in Babylonia, we must come to the aid of earlier examples found in Egypt, which are relatively much younger, but from the Old Babylonian and Asian compound bow, in our opinion, do not

---

[109] A. H. Layard, Discoveries in the ruins of Niniveh and Babylon, London 1853, p. 538. G. Rawlinson, The five great Monarchies, London 1879, Bd. III4, p. 3. F. Hommel, a. a. O. p. 206. The inscription reads after it: „To U-bil-dar, the brother of King Erech (consecrates it) the scribe of the tablet, his servant." M. Jähns, a. a. O. p. 320, błędnie odnosi się do tego łucznika jako arabskiego. A. Furtwängler, Die antiken Gemmen, Berlin 1900, Bd. I, Taf. I, n. 3, Text Bd. II, p. 2. Springer-Michaelis, Kunstgeschichte, Bd. I, fig. 132b.

[110] See, e.g., composite bows in W.Reichela, Homerische Waffen, II. Aufl., p. 112, fig. 57 a, b.

[111] J. de Morgan, Mémoires de la Mission, Bd. I, p. 150-151. A. Schaumberg, a. a. O. p. 33, He declares, without giving any reason, that the king has a straight bow like a warrior.

[112] J. de Morgan, Mission scientifique en Perse, Bd. IV, p. 156-158, Taf. X, p. 160, schreibt de Morgan von diesem Denkmal: »Les caractères de l'inscription dénotent une antiquité très reculée, le bas-relief doit être plus ancien encore et remonter aux premiers âges du développement des Sémites en Chaldées.«

[113] G. Rawlinson, a. a. O. Bd. III4, p. 7, followed by M. Jähns, a. a. O. p. 298, Taf. XXXVI, n. 14, gives us images of a monument on which the king is located, in front of which the goddess Nini stands, allegedly he is depicted with a bow in his left hand. A recent inspection of this monument and a drawing published by de Morgan showed that the king definitely did not have a bow, „but two curved sticks, the exact use of which is (as yet) unknown" (Morgan, Mission scientifique en Perse, Bd. IV, p. 160).

Fig. 14

J. de Morgan, Memoires de la Mission scient. en Perse, Bd. I, Fig. 361

differ substantially. We provide here a description of an older bow from the 13th century BC. per F. v. Luschan[114]. As shown by the drawings attached to von Luschan's work (Fig. 15), this bow is damaged at both ends (the right one is completely missing). Its supposed length was about 1.245 m, today it is only 1.025 m long. We must regret the lack of griffins, especially since we are unable to determine what the κορῶναι looked like, which it must certainly have. "At first glance," writes von Luschan, "one notices a deep groove that runs along the entire spine of the bow; However, upon closer inspection, it also becomes clear that the bow as it stands today is composed of two completely different elements. Only the two pieces that surround the gutter on the side are made of wood. At the bottom of the gutter appears the main component of the whole piece, an extremely hard, shiny fibrous fabric of yellowish-white color that is of animal origin. There are also two wooden strips that frame the gutter on the side. For this third layer we hardly think of anything other than the horn, especially the ibex horn, which must have been suitable for this purpose primarily because of its extraordinary hardness, strength and elasticity[115]. According to von Lushan, it is no wonder that this horn has now disappeared,

---

[114] F. v. Luschan, a. a. O. in Zeitschrift für Ethnologie, Bd. XXV (1893), Verhandlungen p. 266 ff.

[115] F. v. Luschan, a. a. O. in Zeitschrift für Ethnologie, Bd. XXV, p. 268. See auch M. Jähns, a. a. O. p. 288 f., Taf. XXXV, n. 6.

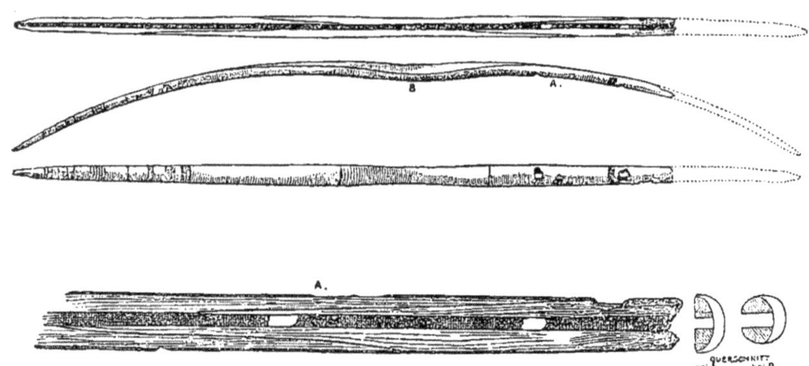

Fig. 15

v. Luschan, Zeitschrift für Ethnologie, Bd. XXV, Verhandlungen, S. 267, Fig. 2-5

because Homer already gives us the best and unambiguous testimony that it could have been damaged by worms (Od. XXI, 393-395).

Much better preserved is the second bow from the 7th century BC[116], which, in addition to the same main materials, i.e. wood, horn, animal tendons glued together with glue, is still completely covered with birch bark, thanks to which its components were invisible, both during the times of its use, as now. Babylonian composite bows were also made in this way, perhaps with only minor local variations.

It is a pity that we are unable to identify the origin of this bow. In any case, its distribution in northwestern Central Asia and Eastern Europe proves that it must have been invented in this area. His invention was probably due to the lack of sufficiently good wood, and we can probably assume that it came from those countries in Asia where there was a constant shortage of wood, or that there was a center of its spread there. We are establishing a second center in the north of Europe and Asia for all other ancient countries where the composite bow was known and used. This would make its spread among the Inuit more understandable, who seem to have had no closer relations with the heartland of northwestern Asia and eastern Europe, much less with the south Asians[117].

It is clear that the lack of wood also played an important role, especially among the Inuit.

We cannot say whether ancient Babylonian bows were in common use, but it is certain that they were the „weapons of the king." For on the stele of

---

[116] H. Balfour, a. a. O. in Journ. of the Auth. Inst. Bd. XXVI, p. 212 ff, tab. IX, 2-3.
[117] D. N. Anuczin, a. a. O. p. 351. F. v. Luschan, a. a. O., in Festschrift für O. Benndorf, p. 194.

26

Nebukadnezzar I[118] the king holds a composite bow in his left hand, two arrows in his right, and a dagger in his belt[119]. It is obvious that the finishing of the bow, like any weapon in general, depended on the owner. As in Egypt, it may have been customary in Babylonia to decorate and strengthen the bow with bronze fittings. Its length was probably about 1 m[120]. As in other countries at the time, it was a common custom in Old Babylonia to wear it on the left shoulder or in the left hand[121].

The arrows, which were probably the same length as the Egyptians, would have had notches at the bottom and, as elsewhere, were feathered. As for arrowheads, stone arrowheads are much rarer than in Egypt, for example, which can be explained by the fact that Mesopotamia was poor in stone[122]. On the other hand, we find brown points very early, although not in sufficient numbers to be able to study the development of the types in more detail. A selection of arrowheads is offered by J. P. Peters[123].

Unfortunately, ancient Babylonian monuments rarely show us the quiver, so that we cannot fully understand its nature. Based on the monuments, it can be seen that it was quite large, oblong, without a cover (?), but always with fringes hanging at the bottom[124].

The rare monuments and the rather inaccurate way of presenting them do not allow drawing further conclusions about the attachment of the bowstring, the methods of stringing and tensioning[125]. Suffice it to say that the Babylonians drew the string to the chest or to the ear[126]. Numerous monuments prove that chariot archery was already known[127].

---

[118] The king is called by this name after Hommel, but in Perrot et Chipiez, for example, he is called Mérodach-idin-akhi, Bd. II, fig. 233.

[119] The Best Image of Stella Nebuchadnezzar I. see Fr. Hommel, a. a. O. p. 457, also M. Jähns, a. a. O. Taf. XXXVI, 15, p. 299.

[120] G. Rawlinson, a. a. O. Bd. III4, p. 8.

[121] Cf. the above-mentioned monuments: the stele of Naram-Sin, the cylinders of Erech, etc.

[122] Fr. Hommel, a. a. O. p. 191.

[123] John Punnet Peters, Nippur or Exploration and Adventures on the Euphrates, New York and London, Vol. II, Appendix A, p. 381, Taf. III, 3, 4, 6. See auch A. H. Layard, Discoveries in the ruins of Niniveh and Babylon, London 1853, p. 503.

[124] Decouvertes en Chaldée par Ernest de Sarzec, publié par les soins de Léon Heuzey, Paris 1889-1896, Taf. V bis 3a, p. 199; also L. Heuzey, Catalogue des Antiquités chaldéenes, Paris 1902, Nr. 21 A. Vg. l. den oben erwähnten Zylinder aus Erech bei Furtwängler, Antike Gemmen, Bd. I, Taf. I, 3. Vgl., also E. Meyer, Sumerer und Semiten, p. 88 f., and M. Pancritius, Der kriegsgeschichtliche Wert der Geierstele, in Memnpn, Bd. II (1908), p. 161.

[125] Two isolated examples of the Mediterranean grip occur on a boundary stone from the time of Nebuchadnezzar I., C. Bezold, Ninive und Babylon, fig. 41, i na cylindrze II tysiąclecia, De Clercq, Catalogue de Collection, Paris 1888, Bd. I, Taf. XXIX, n. 304.

[126] Sarzec, Découvertes, Taf. V bis 3a (Fragment d'une stèle de victoire). See de Clercq., a. a. O. Bd. I, Taf. XXIX, Nr. 305, 309, 311.

[127] de Clercq, a. a. O. Bd. I, Taf. XXIX, Nr. 310.

5. Assyrians

Victorious battles very early led the Assyrians to particularly great development of war accessories. As shown by numerous monuments with various types of battle scenes, infantrymen were divided into archers, javelin throwers and slingers[128]. However, the bow undoubtedly occupied the first place among the offensive weapons of the Assyrians. In times of peace and war he was the faithful companion of every Assyrian, king and ordinary warrior. It becomes the weapon of Assur – God[129]. And when the new land was conquered, it was called „the spoils of the bow."[130] How the Assyrians were able to cope with this is shown by Assyrian inscriptions[131], as well as numerous monuments of Assyrian art that have survived to us – the best testimony, as we want to remind you here, are the lions wounded by arrows from the 7th century BC[132] in the British Museum.

Never and nowhere in ancient times did the bow enjoy such a high reputation as among the Assyrians, where it was a royal weapon in the true sense of the word, for we always see it in the hands of kings. If a war began or a city was to be captured, the first arrow was sent by the king[133]. We see him with a bow and arrows in his hand both when he offers sacrifices to the gods, either for victory or for a successful hunt, and when he receives captured enemies[134]. How the Assyrians were feared as archers, we have the testimony of the prophet Isaiah, V. 27-28:

27 There is not one weak or weary in him,
    no one naps or sleeps,
    no one unbuckles his belt from around his waist
    nor is there a torn strap on the shoes.
28 His arrows are sharp
    and every bow is bent;
    his horses' hooves are like flint,
    the wheels of his chariots rush like a hurricane.

(Bible)

---

[128] G. Rawlinson, a. a. O. Bd. I4, 406-440. Über das Heerwesen im allgemeinen vgl. G. Maspero, a. a. O. Bd. II, p. 626-642. W. Manitius, Das stehende Heer der Assyrerkönige und seine Organisation, in Zeitschrift für Assyriologie, Bd. XXIV (1910), p. 97 ff. Über die Bogenschützen vgl. p. 127-132.

[129] E. Schräder, Keilinschriftliche Bibliothek, Berlin 1896, Bd. II, p. 109, Prisma-Inschrift des Sanherib (705-681 v. Chr.), Z. 65-67.

[130] E. Schräder, Keilinschriftliche Bibliothek, Die Inschrift des zerbrochenen Prismas B des Königs Asarhaddon, C. V, 7, p. 149.

[131] Derselbe, Keilinschriftliche Bibliothek, Bd. I, p. 125, Z. 8 (Jagdinschrift Asurnasir-abal's), Bd. II, p. 135, A-C. Col. V, Z: x-2 (Inschrift Asarhaddon's), Bd. II, p. 107, C. V, Z. 58-59 (Prisma-Inschrift Sanherib's) und 65-67. See auch Fr. Hommel, a. a. O. p. 532.

[132] Perrot et Chipiez, a. a. O. Bd.. II, p. 571, fig. 269, 270 (from the reign of King Ashurbanipal).

[133] A. H. Layard, Monuments of Niniveh, London 1849-1853, Bd. I, Taf. 17, 19, 20.

[134] A. H. Layard, Niniveh and its remains, London 1849, Bd. II, p. 322-323. Derselbe, Monuments of Niniveh, Bd. I, Taf. 12, 23, 82.

Fig. 16

G. Rawlinson, The five great monarchies, Bd. I4,
Fig. p. 450

Fig. 17

G. Rawlinson, a. a. O. Bd. I4, Fig. p. 450

In the magnificent Assyrian reliefs we find two forms of bows, a rounded, straight one[135] and an angular or so-called „angular" bow[136] (Figs. 16, 17). Unfortunately, we have no information about how the latter was performed and what the main purpose of this angle refraction was. But one thing is certain for us, that we cannot talk about any artistic convention here, as H. Balfour[137] believes. If we knew only this one form of the Assyrian bow, perhaps we could speak of a „continuation of artistic error", but since both forms are often found on one and the same relief, Balfour's explanation is unacceptable[138]. Scholars' opinions on the Assyrian bow vary, with some believing it to be simple[139], others, such as F. v. Luschan, believing it was assembled[140]. In our opinion, an „angular" bow was installed because only with this type of bow was such a strong bend possible. Under such a bend, any type of wood would be at risk of completely breaking due to only slightly greater stress[141]. If we see bent bows depicted relatively rarely, this is explained by the fact that most of the illustrations show the bows stretched and in use, and that in this state the bending has disappeared, especially if the method described by the Arabs, i.e. back-drawing, is used. While the thickness of angular bows is the same along their entire length, in curved round bows it increases evenly towards the center, which is probably explained by the fact that in the case of straight bows the handle was most exposed to the risk of breaking during shooting.

---

[135] A. H. Layard, Monuments of Niniveh, Bd. I, Taf. 12; Bd. II, Taf. 35. Perrot et Chipiez, a. a. O. Bd. II, fig. 211, 307. Collection Barracco, Bd. I, Taf. XVII. A. Furtwängler, Antike Gemmen, Bd. I, Taf. I, n. 10.

[136] G. Rawlinson, a. a. O. Bd. I4, p. 450. M. P. E. Botta et M.E. Flandin, Monuments de Ninive, Paris 1849- 1853, Bd. II, Taf. 159. H. Gosse, Assyria, her manners and customs, arts and arms, London 1852, p. 246. M. Jähns, a. a. O. S 299, Taf. XXXVI, 16.

[137] H. Balfour, Journ. of the Anthr. Inst. Bd. XXVI, p. 219 (perpetuation of an artist's error). Longman; Journ. of the Anthr. Inst. Bd. XXIV, p. 55 f. See auch Edinburgh Review, July 1895, p. 37 f.

[138] Perrot et Chipiez, a. a. 0. Bd. II; fig. 205, 307, Taf. XII. A. H. Layard. Monuments of Niniveh, Bd. I, Taf. 5, 15, 18; Bd. II, Taf. 32. G. Maspero, a. a. O. Bd. II, p. 624; Bd. III, p. 407 etc. A. H. Layard, Niniveh and its remains, Bd. II, p. 341. If such an artistic convention were to be adopted among Assyrian artists, it would have to be assumed for Egypt as well, where these curved bows also occur and no one would go that far. Precisely in the fact that we find this form also in Egypt, we have proof that it really existed and that it represents a complex bow. See J. Rosellini, a. a. O. Bd; I, Taf. 46, 48, 49, 50, 52, 56, 67, 84, 86 usw. On the relations of the Middle Kingdom with Asia, por. M. Müller, a. a. O. p. I ff.

[139] D. N Anuczin, a. a. O p. 352. G. Rawlinson, a. a. O. Bd. I4, p. 449.

[140] F. v. Luschan, a. a. O. in Festschrift für O. Benndorf, p. 194. H. Balfour, Journ. of the Anthr. Inst. Bd. XXVI, p. 214 ff.

[141] F. v. Luschan, a. a. O. in Zeitschrift für Ethnologie, Bd. XXV, Verhandlungen p. 269. M. Jähns, a. a. O. p. 299.

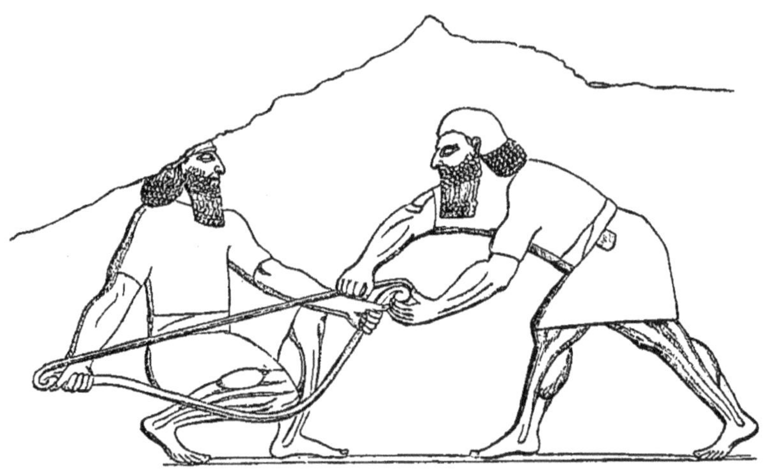

Fig. 18

G. Rawlinson, a. a. O. Bd. I4, Fig. p. 450

If we recall what F. v. Luschan explained about the production of the composite bow, how much effort, work, time and cost this type of bow required, we will not be surprised that despite the invention of the composite bow, the simple bow remained in use for a long time[142]. We cannot give a specific length for the Assyrian bow, but we can assume that it was the same as the Egyptian composite bow, i.e. one meter or a little over. On monuments he is usually depicted waist-high[143]. To attach the string, the ends of simple bows were provided with notches, while in composite bows they were decorated with knobs, which later became more ornate and often resembled the head of a duck or other bird[144]. The heads of these birds, curved outwards, could be made of wood, metal or ivory[145]. We do not know for sure what the bowstrings were made of, but we will not be mistaken if we assume the same substances that were used for this purpose in Egypt.

Fitting the string to the Assyrian bow must have been an extremely difficult task, as it required two people, proving how stiff it was. Of course, anyone could draw a simple bow without any special effort.

This brings us straight to the question of whether the Assyrian bow was παλίντονον or not. In the case of „angled" bows, we must answer this question in the affirmative, because if they were strung in the usual way, they would be unusable, the deflection would become even greater, and they would have no

---

[142] F. v. Luschan, a. a. O. in Festschrift für O. Benndorf, p. 192.

[143] See Delitzsch, Bibel und Babel, III, p. 22. Springer-Michaelis, Kunstgeschichte, Bd. I, fig. 152. Perrot et Chipiez, a. a. O. Bd. II, Taf. XIV, 1; fig. 307 usw.

[144] A. H. Layard, Niniveh and its remains, Bd; II, p. 299. G. Rawlinson, a. a. O. Bd. I4, p. 449.

[145] G. Klemm, a a. O. Bd. VII, p. 334.

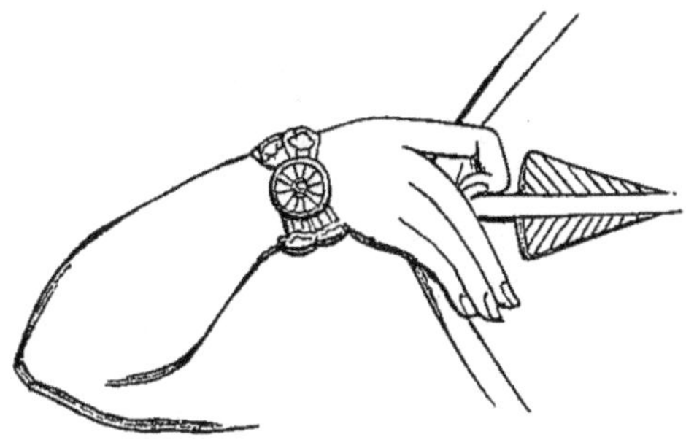

Fig. 19

G. Rawlinson, a. a. O. Bd. I4, Fig. p. 455

tension at all. Thus, the Angular bow could only be drawn like an Arabian bow, i.e. the archer pressed the center of the outer side firmly with his knee, while simultaneously pulling the ends of the bow with both hands to his chest, while the assistant attached the string at the appropriate moment (Fig. 18).

We are unable to determine whether this type of tricking was the only one or whether the Assyrians used other methods. In any case, cocking according to the method described above was extremely difficult and even dangerous in battle, since both warriors were exposed and exposed to the enemy's arrows; It is therefore understandable that the bow was very rarely left undrawn, which immediately explains why undrawn bows are almost completely absent from depictions[146].

As for the drawing of the bow among the Assyrians, the same applies to the Egyptian drawing methods[147]. The fact that the illustrations in the reliefs are sometimes unclear does not need to be emphasized here. The most commonly used method of stringing was with the thumb and forefinger[148] (Fig. 19).

In later times, the Mediterranean grip was also used (Fig. 25), but it is much rarer than, for example, among Egyptian archers[149]. This method is best seen in those archers who turn the inside of the drawing hand towards the viewer[150].

When shooting, foot archers, if they lacked a quiver, carried one or more spare arrows in their left hand,[151] a procedure we have already recorded in Egypt. It is worth noting that the pull extended up to the right shoulder; it was

---

[146] See A. Schaumberg, a. a. O. p. 37.

[147] See z. B. A. H. Layard, Monuments of Niniveh, Bd. II, Taf. 20.

[148] A. H Layard, Monuments of Niniveh, Bd. I, Taf. 13, 14, 17. 20, 27, 28, 31. E. Botta et Flandin, a. a. O. Bd. II, Taf. 93. G. Rawlinson, a. a. O. Bd. I4, p. 297, 398, 435, 437, 438, 445 usw.

[149] A. H. Layard, Monuments of Niniveh, Bd. I, Täf. 10, 18, 19. E. Botta et Flandin, a. a. O. Bd. I, Taf. 61. M. Jähns, a. a. O. p. 300.

[150] G. Rawlinson, a. a. O. Bd. I4, p. 429. H. Gosse, a. a. O. p. 311.

[151] A. H. Layard, Monuments of Niniveh, Bd. I, Taf. 10, 17, 18, 19. Derselbe. Niniveh and its remains, Bd. II, p. 341 f. G. Rawlinson, a. a. O. Bd. I4, p. 432.

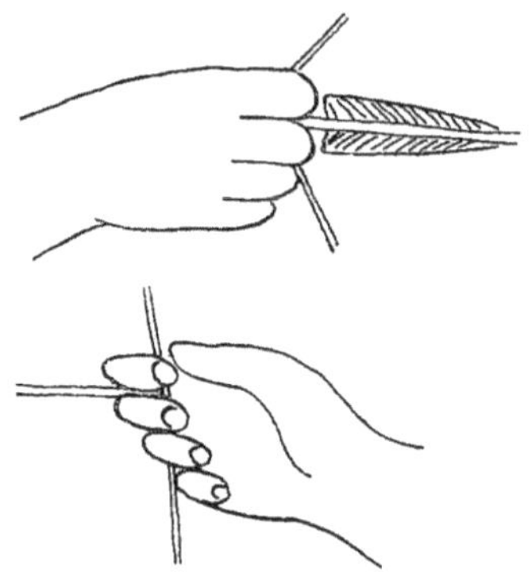

Fig. 20

E. Morse, a. a. O. Fig. 23, 24

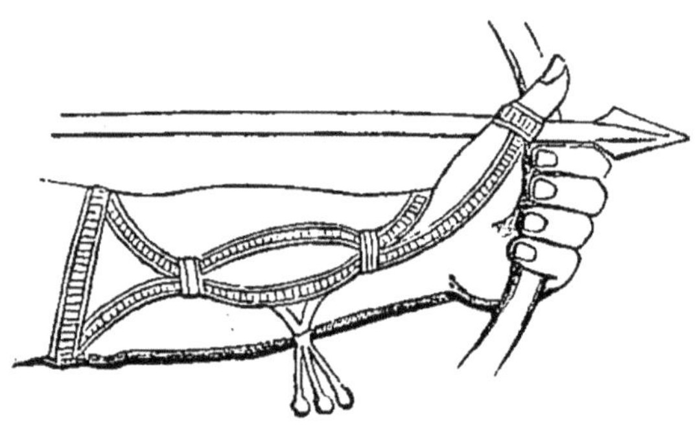

Fig. 21

G. Rawlinson, a. a. O. Bd. I4, Fig. p. 456

this extremely high tension of the bow that forced the Assyrians to use a protective element for the left hand before striking the returning string (Fig. 21)[152].

Assyrian arrows were made of palm wood, as was the case with other peoples discussed earlier[153].

It is obvious that arrows were always provided with a notch at one end of the shaft, but the notch in palm wood would have been too weak, because if the bow was strong, the arrow would have to split. Therefore, in order to protect it from this splitting, it was customary to add a piece of solid wood as a base, and sometimes perhaps a horn, of course with a groove cut in it[154] — an arrangement that we have already mentioned in the case of the Egyptians

---

[152] A. H. Layard, Niniveh and its remains, Bd. II, p. 342. A. Schaumberg, a. a. O. p. 42.

[153] E. Botta et Flandin, a. a. O. Bd. II, Taf. 159. According to A. Schaumberg, a. a. O. p. 58, with the Assyrian arrow drawn out on average three-quarters of the length of the bow. G. Rawlinson, a. a. O. Bd. I4, p. 454-455.

[154] H. Balfour, Journ. of the Anthr. Inst. Bd. XXVI, p. 216-217, Taf. X, fig. 10-17.

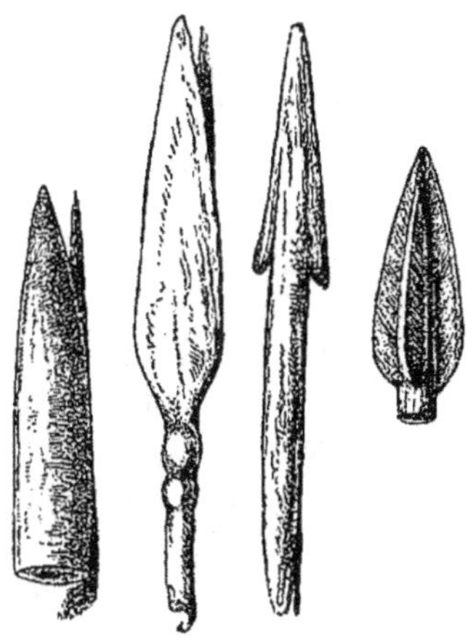

Fig. 22

G. Rawlinson, a. a. O. Bd. I4, Fig. p. 454

(Fig. 8). The flat way of presenting arrows on monuments does not allow us to determine whether the end of the shaft was feathered with two or three flights.

During his second excavations at Nimrud, A. H. Layard found several small iron rods, which he probably mistakenly believed to be arrow shafts. First, we have no literary evidence that such iron arrow shafts existed anywhere, and second, they must have been too heavy and therefore unsuitable for shooting, apart from the fact that shooting such arrows would have been too expensive even for the wealthier Assyrians.[155]

Like all other peoples, the Assyrians always had arrowheads made of a material other than rays. However, while the Egyptians mainly used stone arrowheads, of which a great number have been found; while in Assyria they were few in number, and almost exclusively in the form of pieces of fine, beautifully worked flint.[156] The most common form here is also the leaf. More and more metal points appear, although not yet in such numbers that we can assume that we know all the shapes precisely. We provide several here based on a drawing by G. Rawlinson[157] (Fig. 22).

The points were either pin-ended or provided with a spout for attachment to the radius. Rare or not at all unknown in other countries is the arrowhead in the form of a hollow cone (Fig. 22) with a recess for mounting.

The use of a bow case was similarly uncommon among the Egyptians[158]. Hanging on the back or over the left shoulder, we find such a container among

---

[155] A. H. Layard, Discoveries in the ruins of Niniveh and Babylon, p. 194.

[156] G. Rawlinson, a. a. O. Bd. I4, S, 454 und Anm. 2. A. H. Layard, Discoveries in the ruins of Niniveh and Babylon, p. 194.

[157] See A. Schaumberg, a. a. O. p. 38.

[158] H. Gosse, a. a. O. p. 247 G. Rawlinson, a. a. O. Bd. I4, p. 451. A. H. Layard, Monuments of Niniveh, Bd. 1, Taf. 32.

archers with pointed helmets[159], who sometimes carry a round shield on their backs, a custom which is otherwise never observed[160]. Much more often, the bow was carried in the hand or on the left shoulder[161]. But if A. H. Layard believes[162] that the bow was also carried on the back by passing a taut bow over the head and left hand, this is incorrect, because this way of carrying the bow is seen only among the Assyrians. In depictions of archers, we always see the entire bow on the left side.

It is rare to meet Assyrian archers without a quiver and holding only a few spare arrows in their left hand. Most carried the quiver diagonally on the right side, or often under the left shoulder, so that when shooting, it was easy to pull a new arrow from it with the right hand[163]. With the same basic shape, two types of quivers can be distinguished, those with lids and those without lids[164]. The kings, and perhaps the nobility of the Assyrian army, rarely carried quivers and almost always had servants with them to give them new arrows[165]. Archers who fought from wagons had both their own personal quivers and those attached to the chariot. The bow container was always attached to the outside of the chariot walls[166].

The Assyrians attached great importance to decorating their quivers. The simplest ones were decorated only with metal ribbons along the edges and on the surfaces, and at the same time they were naturally reinforced[167]. The wealthier Assyrians covered them with delicate, mainly star-shaped ornaments[168]. The quivers of Assyrian kings and highest dignitaries could, in addition to the above-mentioned decorations, have colorful patterns and figurative representations of people and animals[169]. The suspension of the quiver was also decorated with colorful strings and tassels. Most archers in Assyria, as in other countries, never had a shield, they were always protected from the enemy while shooting by their comrades, who always stood next to them[170]. Some-

---

[159] Springer-Michaelis, Kunstgeschichte, Bd. 19, fig. 154. A. H. Layard, Monuments of Niniveh, Bd. II, Taf. 23.

[160] A. H. Layard, Monuments of Niniveh, Bd. I, Taf. 33.

[161] Perrot et Chipiez, a. a. O. Bd. II, fig. 233, 303, Taf. XIV. E. Botta et Flandin, a. a. O. Bd. I, Taf. 66.

[162] A. H. Layard, Niniveh and its remains, Bd. II, p. 342. See drawing on p. 338, which directly contradicts Layard's own assertion.

[163] G. Maspero, a. a. O. Bd. II, p. 625. Perrot et Chipiez, a. a. O. Bd. II, fig. 213. E. Botta et Flandin, a. a. O. Bd. I, Taf. 13, 77; Bd. II, Taf. 117, 142 A. H. Layard, Niniveh and its remains, Bd. II, p. 341.

[164] Without lid see A. H. Layard, Monuments of Niniveh, Bd. I, Taf. 11, 17, 19; Bd. II, Taf. 46, 55; with lid Bd. I, Taf. 81; Bd. II, Taf. 34, 38, 45. See A. Schaumberg, a. a. O. p. 38 ff.

[165] A. H. Layard, Niniveh and its remains, Bd. II, p. 341.

[166] A. H. Layard, Monuments of Niniveh, Bd. I, Taf. 14, 31. E. Botta et Flandin, a. a. O. Bd. I, Taf. 65. 76. Sometimes the archers had two crossed quivers on the side parapet of the wagons, apparently in order to have more arrows at hand, Lt. Layard, Monuments of Niniveh, Bd; I, Taf. 13, 31.

[167] H. Gosse, a. a. O. p. 251. G. Rawlinson, a. a. O. Bd. I4, p. 425.

[168] The choice of quivers is given by E. Botta et Flandin, a. a. O. Bd. II, Taf. 159.

[169] A. H. Layard, Niniveh and its remains, Bd. II, p. 299. G. Rawlinson, a. a. O. Bd. I4, p. 452. Also H. Gosse, a. a. O. p. 251.

[170] E. Botta et Flandin, a. a. O. Bd. I, Taf. 49, 60, 77; Bd. II, Taf. 86. A. H. Layard, Monuments of Niniveh, Bd. I, Taf. 17, 18, 19, 20, 62; Bd. II, Taf. 18, 21, 39 usw. Perrot et Chipiez, a. a. O. Bd. II, fig. 105, 467. A. H. Layard, Niniveh and its remains, Bd. II, p. 346.

34

Fig. 23

v. Luschan, Festschrift für O. Benndorf, Taf. X

times the shield bearer protected two archers at the same time[171]. Shooting arrows from a chariot was particularly noble[172], and even those archers who fought from the chariot sometimes had squires with them, whose task was to protect the shooter from enemy arrows[173].

Among the Assyrians we also find mounted archers[174] who, in addition to the bow, also carried a spear[175] – something that cannot be found anywhere else. When they used the bow and when the spear depended on whether they were engaged in melee or ranged combat. One may also ask how it was possible for a rider to shoot arrows and steer his horse at the same time – the monuments also give us the best answer to this question: almost every mounted archer had an assistant who steered his horse while shooting[176].

---

[171] A. H. Layard, Monuments of Niniveh, Bd. I, Taf. 94.

[172] A. H. Layard, Monuments of Niniveh, Bd. I, Taf. 10, 13, 27, 28, 31, 80.

[173] E. Botta et Flandin, a. a. O. Bd. I, Taf. 58, 59 bis. Perrot et Chipiez, a. a. O. Bd. II, fig. 221. A. H. Layard, Niniveh and its remains, Bd. II, p. 345; Monuments of Niniveh, Bd. II, Taf. 19, 24.

[174] A. H. Layard, Monuments of Niniveh, Bd. I, Taf. 26, 48; Bd. II, Taf. 38.

[175] G. Rawlinson, a. a. O. Bd. I4, p. 425. A. H. Layard, Monuments of Niniveh, Bd. I, Taf. 32, 66.

[176] A. H. Layard, Niniveh and its remains, Bd. II, p. 358. A. H. Layard, Monuments of Niniveh, Bd. I, Taf. 26. It's worth noting that sometimes these companions also use shields to shield the horse archer from the arrows of enemy warriors. See e.g. A. H. Layard, Monuments of Niniveh, Bd. I, Taf. 11, 26, 32. M. Jähns. a. a. O. p. 300.

6. Hittites and other peoples of Asia Minor

Excavations in recent years and information from the literature also allow for some reflections on the arc of the peoples of Asia Minor. These, however, can by no means be conclusive, because to this day we do not know at all the bows of many peoples of Asia Minor, while among others monuments have been discovered, but only those that are unsuitable for our purposes. Relatively best known to us are the bows of the Hittites, whose empire with its capital located on the site of today's Boghazkiöi in the 15th century BC. quickly expanded into Asia Minor and northern Syria, and almost as suddenly succumbed to the great migration of peoples from the west at the beginning of the 12th century B.C.[177] The monuments of this people that are significant to us come from the period from around the 15th to the 8th century B.C.[178]

First of all, the wonderful bas-relief of Sendschirli, already published by F. V. Luschan and discussed in detail[179], is taken into account. The depicted warrior, an unbearded, naked man in a long, tight cloak, wears a rather small bow on his left armpit, not even reaching to his waist. This bow is strung, and the ends of its arms are equipped with bird heads, as in Assyrian bows. Similarly to Fig. 23, the bow consists of several materials wrapped at the handle with another material, probably leather, or, as in other composite bows, birch bark. Near the ends, the weapon shows an ornament in the form of a fitting, which should also be considered as a reinforcement for the bow. So we have a method that we have already found in some Egyptian specimens. The bow is shown as strung, so the decision as to whether it should be strung backwards cannot be made with complete certainty, but we do have a comparison with modern Turkestân[180] bows. The παλίντονον bow is also suspected in this weapon. According to Luschan, this Sendschirli relief dates from 730 BC, so it is relatively young.

The relief of King Pseudo-Sesostris from the Karabel Pass in Nymph shows a bow of various shapes[181]. The warrior, turned to the right, wearing a tight cloak and beaked boots, with a pointed cap on his head, carries a covered bow on his right shoulder. The string here forms sharp corners with limbs at either

---

[177] E. Meyer, a. a. O. Bd. I2, p. 618 f. J. H. Breasted, a. a.O. p. 309 und 331. H. Winkler, Mitteilungen der Deutschen Orient-Gesellschaft, Nr. 35, 1908. Perrot et Chipiez, a. a. O. Bd. IV, p. 483 ff. und passim. G. Maspero, a. a. O. Bd. II, p. 351 ff. W. Wright, The empire of the Hittites, II. Aufl. London 1886, p. 79 ff. J. Garstang, The land of the Hittites, London 1910, passim.

[178] E. Meyer, a. a. O. Bd. P, p. 618.

[179] V. Luschau, a. a. O. in Festschrift für O. Benndorf, p. 195 f.

[180] V. Luschan, a. a. O. in Festschrift für O. Benndorf, fig. from p. 191.

[181] Kiepert, Archäologische Zeitung, 1843, p. 33. Curtius und Humann, Archäologische Zeitung, 1875, p. 50. Sayce, Transactions of the Society of Biblical Archeology, Bd. VII (1882), p. 266; Bd. XXXI (1909), p. 331. G. Hirschfeld, Die Felsenreliefs in Kleinasien, in Abhandlungen der preußischen Akademie der Wissenschaften, 1886, p. 10 und 69. Perrot et Chipiez, a. a. O. Bd. IV, p. 748, fig. 361. Revue bow. Bd. VI (1885), p. 302, fig. 5. P. Jensen, in H. Hilprechts, Explorations in the Bible Lands during the 19th Century, Philadelphia 1903, p. 262.

end, and the bow appears to have a sharp angle as to the handle[182]. This archaic representation is much older than that of Sendschirli, probably dating from before 1200 BC.[183] In line with what we have said about the angular bow of the Assyrians, we also see here a compound bow of the same type as in the Sendschirli relief. In our opinion, the difference in representation is due, on the one hand, to the time distance between the two pictorial works, and, on the other hand, the place of origin and external influences also play an important role in the style. The fact that Assyrian influence should be taken into account is evidenced by the Assyrian cuneiform finds at Kaisariye-Mazaka[184] and various documents from Assyria itself, which prove that Assyrian power reached as far as Halys around 1600 B.C.[185] It is also interesting that the Egyptian depictions of bows Hittite bows bring us mainly small, triangular, or angular bows[186].

Other depictions of bows found at Sendschirli,[187] most of which date from the 9th and 8th centuries BC, have been preserved in such a weathered condition that details are difficult to discern. It should be noted, however, that in these bows at the ends of the arms one can see the decorative fittings that we have already mentioned with the Sendschirli warrior. All these arcs, as I said, are complex in nature, but we cannot demonstrate simple arcs with complete certainty. It seems to us beyond any doubt that they were also in use[188]. We believe that the lion hunting relief from Arslantepe near Malatié (Melitene), today in Constantinople[189], contains a straight bow because it tapers strongly towards the end, but this presumption must remain problematic in the case of the primitive mode of presentation[190]. There is also uncertainty in this respect in some representations of the Sendschirli bows[191]. What is interesting about them is the reconstruction of a taut string that is „bent upwards", „probably so that it does not rest on the face and eye[192]".

---

[182] W. Max Müller, a. a. O. p. 328. A. Schaumberg, a. a. O. p. 46.

[183] P. Jensen, a. a. O. p. 261 f.

[184] E. Meyer, a. a. O. Bd. II2, p. 594 f. and p. 595 Anm. die Literaturangabe.

[185] E. Meyer, a. a. O. p. 593, cf. also pp. 618 and 676. When, about a century and a half later, the Hittites gained control of these lands, they found Assyrian culture already well developed. It is to the contact and connection with this culture that the Hittites owe their great cultural flourishing. Of course, other influences, such as those of Egypt, cannot be ruled out.

[186] See Lepsius, Denkmäler, III, 130a, 166. W. Max Müller, a. a. O. p. 328. Messerschmidt, Der alte Orient, IV (1902), p. 20.

[187] Mitteilungen aus den orientalischen Sammlungen, XIII. Ausgrabungen in Sendschirli, 3, p. 207 ff., Taf. 39; vgl. auch Studniczka, Jahrbuch d. deutsch. bow. Inst., Bd. XXII (1907), p. 152, fig. 7.

[188] For example, according to the Egyptian depiction, Lepsius, Denkmäler, III, 166. W. M. Müller, a. a. O. p. 325.

[189] Mitteilungen der Vorderasiatischen Gesellschaft, 1900. 4, Taf. 16A. G. Maspero, a. a. O. Bd. III, fig. p. 37. P. Jensen, a. a. O. p. 779. Annals of Archaeol. and Anthrop. Liverpool 1908, I, Taf. IV, 1. J. Garstang, a. a. O. Taf. XLIV.

[190] The bow on the relief depicting the hunting of the lion from Saktsche-Gösü, now in Berlin, could also be considered straight, cf. K.Humann and O. Puchstein, Reisen in Kleinasien und Nordsyrien, Berlin 1890, p. 377 ff., Taf. 46. Studniczka, Jahrbuch, B.d. XXII (1907), p. 153, fig. 10. Perrot et Chipiez, a. a. O. Bd. IV, fig. 279.

[191] Ausgrabungen in Sendschirli, 3, p. 207, fig. 99; p. 212, fig. 102; p. 215, fig. 108.

[192] Ausgrabungen in Sendschirli, 3, p. 207.

The arrow, the length of which, according to depictions, usually exceeds the length of the bow, is best depicted in Luschan's Sendschirli relief. At the lower end we see a sharp notch, and a comparison of the thickness of the radius at this point with that above the notch clearly shows that the lower end of the rod was made of a different material, probably bone, to prevent splitting. A similar procedure in Assyria and Egypt has already been indicated above. The flight feathers were probably glued and tied, as we believe that this is how the two visible cuts above them should be interpreted[193]. The arrow radius was also reinforced in the center with tape. The two arrows of the Sendschirli archer simply taper forward[194], but other monuments also show arrowheads which should be considered brown, with distinct barbs[195].

We cannot say anything certain about the Hittite stress and tension methods[196]. F. v. Luschan showed in his work Über den antiken Bogen, which has already been mentioned several times, that the Hittites used strong leather collar rings for tensioning[197], from which it can be concluded that they used the Mongolian grip[198].

However, the archer Sendschirli still has a mysterious plate-shaped device in his left hand, next to his fingers. The only assumption remains that it was a device capable of drawing a short arrow even further than it was possible without this object, held with the left (bow) hand[199]. However, we were unable to detect fingers or this device on other Hittite monuments.

The Sendschirli warrior's quiver has a cylindrical shape, flattened at the bottom, without a cover at the top. On both the top and bottom of the quiver you can see a circumferential decorative band with diamond patterns as decoration. The surface between these bands is filled by two intersecting, diagonal bands, at the intersection of which a rosette is attached.

From the upper edge of the quiver, a thick, large fringe hangs on a braided rope. The archers who fired arrows from the cart attached two intersecting quivers to the side sill of the cart[200].

---

[193] A. Schaumberg, a. a. O. p. 48, He points out that „the fletching is terminated at the top by two rings running around the shaft." The plumage is also visible on the relief of the orthostat from Sendschirli, excavations in Sendschirli,Ausgrabungen in Sendschirli, p. 215, fig. 108.

[194] Also without arrowhead on relief Saktsche-Gösü, in: Jahrbuch d. deutsch, bow. Inst., Bd. XXII (1907), p. 153, fig. 10.

[195] See Mitteilungen der Vorderasiatischen Gesellschaft, 1908, 3, p. 16, fig. 23, Orthostatrelief von Euyuk. Relief von Malatie, Heuzey, Les origines orientales, Paris 1891, Taf. X.

[196] The tendon is stretched behind the ear on the reliefs of Malatie, Saktsche-Gösü, Euyuk and Sendschirli.

[197] v. Luschan, a. a. O. in Festschrift für O. Benndorf p. 195 f.

[198] E. Morse, a. a. O. p. 158 f. v. Luschan, a. a. O. in Zeitschrift für Ethnologie, Bd. XXIII, Verhandlungen p. 671. For more information on this method of suspense, see the overview of Trojan finds.

[199] See auch M. Jahns, a. a. O. p. 300. Also, the presumption A. Schaumbergs, a. a. O. p. 49. According to the fact that the latter object is perhaps to represent an arm protector seen in profile, it seems impossible to us because of the form, apart from the fact that at this time it is difficult to think of drawing from the profile.

[200] Cf. e.g.Ausgrabungen in Sendschirli, p. 212, fig. 102. G. Maspero, a. a. O. Bd. III, p. 37. Jahrbuch d. deutsch. bow. Inst., Bd. XXII (1907), p. 152, fig. 6; p. 153, fig. 9. Humann und Puchstein, a. a. O. Taf. 46.

The bow appears to have been the chief weapon of these ἔθνος ἱπποπόλον, the horse-breeding people, Teshub[201] being represented with a bow in his hand, similarly a powerful king was depicted as a conqueror in a mine near Ephesus.

If some important questions about the Hittite bow were to remain unanswered, we are even less or not at all informed about the bows of other peoples of Asia Minor. Herodotus and other writers are our only source, apart from a few excavations.

VII 64: Βάκτρtοί ... τόξα καλάμινα.

VII 64: Σάκαι δέ οι Σκύθαι ... τόξα δέ επιχώρια.

VII 66: 'Άριοι ... δέ τόξοισι Μηδικοισιν ....

VII 66: Πάρθοι, Χοράσμιοι, Σόγδοι, Γανδάριοι, Δαδίκαι τήν αυτήν σκευήν εχοντες τήν και Βάκτριοι έστρατεύοντο ... (τόξα καλάμινα).

VII 67: Κάσπιοι τόξα επιχώρια καλάμινα.

VII 67: Σαράγγαι ... τόξα δέ καί αίχμάς Μηδικάς.

VII 67: Πάκτυες ... τόξα επιχώρια.

VII 68: Ούτιοι, Μόκοι. Παρικάνιοι εσκευασμένοι ήσαν κατάπερ Πάκτυες (τόξα επιχώρια).

VII 77: Μιλόαι ... είχον δέ αυτών τόξα μετεξέτεροι Λυκια.

VII 92: Λυκιοι ... είχον δέ τόξα κρανέϊνα καί όϊστους καλάμινους άπτέρους.

Among the peoples already mentioned by Herodotus who used the bow are probably the Thracians (Herodotus IV 94), the Kosseers (Strabo XI 13, 6 = C 524 ed. Meineke), the Soans who used poisoned arrows (Strabo XI 2, 19 = 0 499), Carduches (Xen. Anab. IV 2, 28), Armenians (Lucian Phars. VIII, 221). The compilation of Herodotus' records, in our opinion, clearly testifies to two types of bows, the simple καλάμινα, and those that Herodotus refers to only as επιχώρια, which can be assumed as composite bows. If a people used native but simple bows, Herodotus emphasized this especially, as in the case of the Capsians or Lycians. It is important to remember that according to Herodotus (VII 73), the Armenians in Xerxes' army were equipped in the same way as the Phrygians[202]. To learn about the bows of this last nation, it is necessary to look at the results of the excavations at Gordion[203]. A clay slab serving as a wall covering with a deer hunting scene was found there. On the left, in a chariot whose image is damaged, stand two dressed men, also partially preserved. One of them draws a composite bow – judging by the arms that are bent outwards. The taut string reaches above the shooter's elbow. The arrow is clearly visible, but further details are not clearly visible. During the same excavations, an undamaged, brown, triangular arrowhead with a spout (length 0.027, spout diameter 0.005) was also found. In the Phrygian tumulus in Bosöjuk, A. Körte

---

[201] Cornell, Expedition to Asia Minor and the Assyro-Babylonian Orient (Travels and studies in the Nearer Est), Bd. I, II. Teil, Hittite inscriptions, New York 1911, p. 41, fig. 41.

[202] Eudoxos bei Steph. B. 'Αρμενία = Eustath. zu Dion. Per. 694 mówi, że Ormianie γένος ἐκ Φρυγίας καί τῇ φωνῇ πολλά φρυγίζουσι .... See Näheres darüber bei P. Kretschmer, Einleitung in die Geschichte der griechischen Sprache, Göttingen 1896, p. 208 ff.

[203] G. und A. Körte, Gordion, Ergebnisse der Ausgrabung im Jahre 1900, Berlin 1904, p. 157 ff., fig. 141.

Fig. 24

Based on Photo by prof. P. Bieńkowski

found a bone arrowhead with barbs and a rather long tongue[204]. These are the few traces of the Phrygian bow that we have left. For completeness, we still mention the statuette from the early Roman period (Fig. 24). It is a mounted shooter whose bow is not visible, but hidden in the quiver. The quiver itself is oblong, rounded at the bottom and slightly curly, and is decorated with four peripheral envelopes. We cannot say whether the quiver was faithful to the Phrygian model[205].

In connection with the Phrygian Arch, Trojan finds should also be discussed, since the removal of the mentioned burial mound at Bosöjuk revealed a culture „completely consistent with the older Trojan culture down to the details"[206]. Finds from the pre-Mycenaean layers are particularly important. As evidence that the bow was already in use, we primarily use arrowheads, a significant number of which came to light during Schliemann's excavations. Thus, in the Berlin collection of Trojan antiquities no. 6920 there is an arrowhead made of

---

[204] A. Körte, Ath. Mitt. Bd. XXIV (1899), p. 21, Taf. IV, 4.

[205] Prof. Peter von Bieńkowski writes about it, who kindly provided the photograph: „Equestrian statuette, photograph taken by me in 1897 in Kasino Villa Borghese in the shop of the Giacomini company, then examined in the spring of 1905 by the art dealer Alessandro Marcocchio (total height 1.19 m; height of the statuette 1.09; plinth thickness 0.10; Length 0.98). Coarse-grained, shiny, white marble. Made of marble restorations on horses: front legs, tip of the muzzle, ears. On the rider: the left forearm, the left foot, the nose, the right hand, the upper part of the sword hilt and the tip of the cap are made of plaster. Both reins broken, except for small remnants. The quiver and sword except for the hilt are intact and the left hand with the bracelet is also original. A young woman sits on a jumping stallion, whose raised front legs are supported by a vertical shield and whose torso is supported by a pillar richly profiled above and below.

[206] G. und A. Körte, a. a. O. p. 6 f. A. Körte, Ath. Mitt. Bd. XXIV (1899), p. 1-45.

40

barbed antlers and a rather long shaft tongue (greatest length 0.103)[207], no. 6921-6929 awl-like, straight arrowheads (?) made of antler or bone (greatest length 0.047-0.110)[208]. Excavations at Troy revealed another type of circular radius hole[209], bone arrowheads; pieces without a radius hole are probably unfinished specimens[210]. In addition, we also have stone arrowheads, although in small quantities[211], and bronze arrowheads, which were also in use in pre-Mycenaean times[212]. It is also worth mentioning a fragment of a two-piece casting mold for arrowheads with a strong central rib and a shaft tongue[213].

We have proved among some peoples the use of protective devices against the blow of the returning string, and we believe that this protective device was also known in Troy, since we still have two protective plates from there: (a) an elliptical shard of a clay vessel with two holes at each end; maximum length 0.065, maximum width 0.045[214];

b) an oblong, rectangular plate carved into a boar's tooth, with two holes on each of the shorter sides; greatest length 0.034, greatest width 0.014[215].

Thanks to the Trojan excavations, we finally have two rings for drawing the bow[216], which, according to contemporary analogies, were intended to protect the thumb during drawing[217]. In the „Mongolian method", the thumb is placed on the string from the inside and tensioned only with the index finger placed around the thumbnail[218] (Fig. 25), where the index finger is used to support the thumb and at the same time to hold the arrow. Such a ring serves to protect the thumb from the string. One bronze ring from Troy is oval and has a hook in the shape of a bird's head[219]. The second ring is generally quite similar to the first, but has a rather modern appearance, so it may be of Turkish origin[220]. Although we are unable to provide any other explanation for the use of the first ring, which is certainly ancient, we would like to emphasize that similar equip-

---

[207] H. Schliemann, Troja, Leipzig 1884, p. 127, Nr. 44. H. Schmidt, H. Schliemanns Sammlung trojanischer Altertümer, p. 270 (undatierbar). A. Götze in W. Dörpfelds, Troja und Ilion, Athen 1902, Bd. I, p. 371, refers to those arrowheads belonging to the II-V layers.

[208] H. Schmidt, a. a. O. p. 270 (also undated).

[209] H. Schmidt, a. a. O. p. 270, Nr. 6905-6909, five arrowheads made of antlers and bones with a hole for the shaft. One of them (No. 6905) is also pierced transversely to fix the arrow radius, the largest length 0,034-0,046.

[210] H. Schmidt, a. a. O. p. 270, Nr. 6910-6914, but poor rounding and smoothing.

[211] H. Schmidt, a. a. O. p. 270, Nr. 6904 (made of quartzite), II-V layer.

[212] We give the development of the types of Trojan arrowheads made of stone and bronze in connection with purely Greek arrowheads.

[213] H. Schmidt, a. a. O. p. 268, Nr. 6773. H. Schliemann. Ilios, p. 484, Nr. 604.

[214] H. Schmidt, a. a. O. p. 270, Nr. 6902 (from the Trojan layers II-V). A. Götze, a. a. O. Bd. I, p. 371, fig. 309. A. Schaumberg, a. a. O. p. 57.

[215] H. Schmidt, a. a. O. p. 270, Nr. 6903 (II.-V. Schicht). A. Götze, a. a. O. Bd. I, p. 371, fig. 310. A. Schaumberg, a. a. O. p. 58.

[216] A. Götze, a. a. O. Bd. I, p. 419.

[217] v. Luschan, a. a. O. in Zeitschrift für Ethnologie, Bd. XXIII (1891), Verhandlungen p. 672 f.

[218] Likewise Zeitschrift für Ethnologie, Bd. XXIII (1891), Verhandlungen p. 671 f. See also E. Morse, a. a. O. p. 158 f.; M. Jähns, a. a. O. p. 293.

[219] A. Götze, a. a. O. Bd. I, fig. 450 (marked as unreproducible). H. Schmidt, a. a. O. Nr. 6539, 6540 (originating from layers VII-IX).

[220] A. Götze, a. a. O. Bd. I, p. 419.

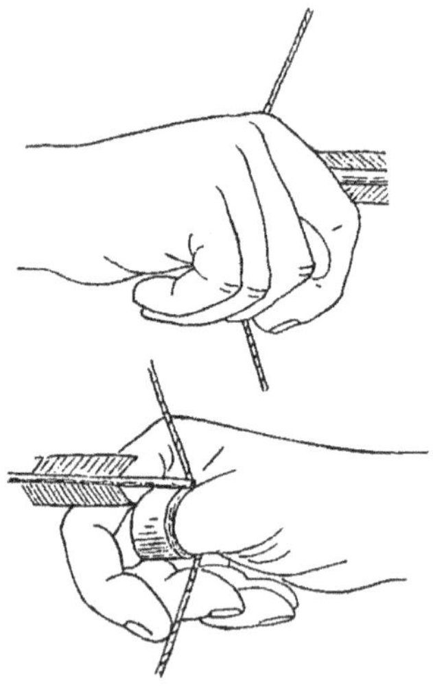

Fig. 25

M. Jähns, a. a. O. Taf. XXXV, Fig. 12

ment is not seen on any ancient monument, nor is there any explanation of such a ring among ancient writers as a protection for the thumb. Contrary to the opinion of A. Götze, who claims that the rings are mentioned for the Mediterranean tension, we note that in the case of the Mediterranean tension, the ring could not be used at all, because in this method the thumb, for which the ring was supposed to provide protection, remains inactive.

7. Medes and Persians

The Medes and Persians, along with the Scythians, were considered by the Greeks to be outstanding archers[221]. It is almost impossible to separate these two nations, which are so closely related, because in ancient times they fought together against the Greeks and were therefore mentioned together and often confused[222]. Their fame as archers is proverbial[223]. According to Pferser's description of weapons[224], Herodotus says that the Medes are armed in exactly

---

[221] According to Herodotus I, 103, Kyaxares τοξοφόροι introduced to his army.

[222] Herodot. I, 102, 130, also VII/ 62. Aisch. Pers. V, 761-775. Strabon XV, 2, 3. Xenophon. Kyrup. I, 2, I. This confusion is common among Greek writers who dealt with the Persian wars; is written τά Περσικά oder τά Μηδικά oder ὁ Πέρσης i ὁ Μήδος. Więcej na ten temat see G. Rawlison, a. a. O. Bd. II4, p. 306 f. und Bd. III4, p. 164 f. Perrot et Chipiez, a. a. O. Bd, V, p. 411, 773 usw. Ed. Mayer, Gesch. d. A. III, 27.

[223] Herodot III, 35; IX, 49. Xenoph. Anab. III, 3, 15; 4, 17; Kyrup. I, 2, 8; 2, 9; 2, 10; III, 3, 50; 3, 57. Aisch. Pers. V, 26-27, 87 usw. Hor. Od. II, 16, 6; Od. I, 29, 4.

[224] Herodot VII, 61: αιχμάς δέ βραχέας είχον, τόξα δέ μεγάλα, οίστοός δε καλα μινοος...

the same way as the Persians[225], namely with a spear and a bow. Even after the monuments, we cannot treat weapons, and especially bows, separately for each of these peoples, because no representation has reached us that could with certainty be described as coming from the Medes[226]. As Persian scriptures testify, the bow was an essential part of the weaponry of every warrior[227], and every Persian had to be skilled in archery[228]. And that is why every boy was familiar with the bow from the age of five[229].

It is true that the Persian bow was large, according to information given by Herodotus[230] and Xenophon[231], but in sculptures[232] we find two types of bows, longer than waist-length, those on the left shoulder with the quiver[233], and shorter ones, which are kept in a tight bow container suspended on a strap[234], or worn on the left shoulder[235].

This also results in two types of bows, a larger, straight one and a significantly smaller one, most often carried in a container[236]. M. Jahns believes that the Persians used a bow that was made only of animal sinews[237] and indeed, in the famous battle mosaic of Alexander of Pompeii we clearly find such a bow[238]. However, it is not possible to determine whether this type of bow was common; this is not mentioned anywhere else and was of little practical use[239].

---

[225] Herodot VII, 62: Μηδοι δέ τήν αόιήν ταύτην έσταλμένοι έστρατεύοντο. Cavalry units had the same armament, Herodot VII, 84; 86.

[226] Only twice do we read of the Median bows in Herodotus, without further determination. VII, 66: Ἄριοι δέ τόξοισι μέν έσκευασμένοι ήσαν Μηδικοῖσι. VII, 67: Σαράγγαι (ειχον) τόξα δέ καί αιχμάς Μηδικάς.

[227] See M. Dieulafoy, L'art antique de la Perse, Paris 1885, Bd. V, p. 140. Each archer should have two bows, four bowstrings, and 160 arrows.

[228] Herodotus VII, 86, reports that even in modern times the Sagartians used only short knives and long spears. It would be desirable to know whether Herodotus' message is accurate and whether the bow was indeed not used by this people. In our opinion, Herodotus' message should be taken literally; It is the use of the spear that excludes the bow.

[229] Herodot I, 136: παιδεύοοσι τους παῖδας τρία μουνα, ίππευειν καί τοξεύειν καί άληθ'ίζεσθ'αι Nach Strabon XV, 3, 18 (C. 733 ed. Meineke) άπό δέ πέντε έτών εως τετάρτου καί εικοστού παιδεύονται τοξεύειν καί ακοντίζει καί ίππάζεσθαι καί άληθ'εύειν.

[230] Herodot VII, 61. See Anm. 3.

[231] Xenoph. Anab. III,. 4, 17. Μεγάλα δέ καί τά τόξα τά Περσικά.

[232] G. Rawlinson, a. a. O. Bd. III4, p. 175. M. Jähns, a. a. O. p. 303. G. Klemm, a. a. O. Bd. VII, p. 334.

[233] See Perrot et Chipiez, a. a. O. Bd. V, Taf. XII, fig. 485, 488, 498 usw.

[234] Perrot et Chipiez, a. a. O. Bd. V, fig. 436, 472.

[235] Flandin et Coste, Voyage en Perse, Taf. 164. See Kondakoff, Tolstoi et Reinach, Antiqu. de la Russie mérid. p. 306.

[236] See G. Rawlinson, a. a. O. Bd. III4, p. 175. M. Jähns, a. a. O. p. 303. J. de Morgan, Memoires de la Mission, Bd. I, p. 160, Taf. XIII. In the bronze relief we see seven people, all depicted with composite bows. Bd. II, p. 23, Taf. II.

[237] M. Jähns, a. a. O. p. 303.

[238] F. Winter, Das Alexander-Mosaik aus Pompeji, Straßburg 1909 (Wiener Vorlegeblätter, Serie IV, Tafel VIII).

[239] If the bow had been made of animal tendons, perhaps this would explain the strange use of weapons in a closed case. Moisture could not do much damage to the straight or composite bow, but a bow made of animal tendons had to be very carefully protected from any kind of moisture. It should be especially noted that this way of carrying the bow is not to be found among any other people, not even among the Assyrem, the closest neighbors of the Persians, whose bow container occupied only a little more than half of the bow.

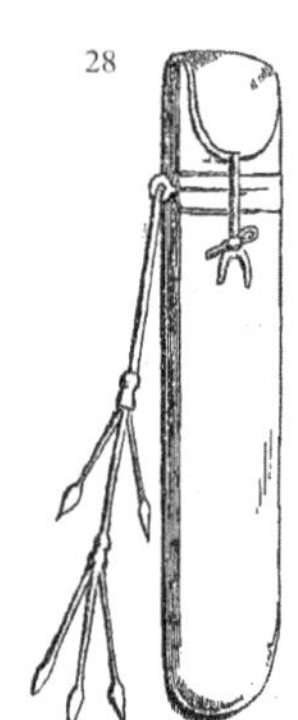

Fig. 26

Flandin et Coste, Voyage en Perse, Bd. III, Taf. 164

Fig. 27

Flandin et Coste, a. a. O. Bd. I, Taf. 12

Fig. 28

G. Rawlinson, a. a. O. Bd. II4, Fig. p. 314

We often see bows in the hands of Persian kings on coins, but it is impossible to say with certainty what type of bow they are; based on the shape opening towards the target, composite models can be considered[240].

The bow was carried freely over the left shoulder[241] or in the left hand[242]. The latter probably happened less often, much more often, as already mentioned, it was worn in a wide container on the left shoulder (Fig. 26) or hung on the left side of the belt[243]. It was a specifically Persian custom to use it because it was Fig. 27. shows that it is worn in such a way that the head is stuck into a covered bow. For archers who carried their bows on belts, the bow case also served as a quiver for arrows. Much more often, however, especially in other ways of carrying bows, the quiver of arrows was an independent, round sheath, probably made of leather, with or without a cover (Fig. 28), which was suspended with a belt[244]. As with all other peoples of antiquity, the Persian quiver was richly decorated with furnaces and colors, and even the simplest ones were used to attach at least a multi-stranded plague (karbach)[245].

---

[240] See Ern. Babelon, Monnaies grecques, Paris 1910, Bd. II, p. 43 ff., Taf. LXXXVI, LXXXVII.

[241] Flandin et Coste, Voyage en Perse, Taf. 18.

[242] G. Maspero, a. a. O. Bd. III, p. 681. G. Rawlinson, a. a. O. Bd. III4, p. 210.

[243] Flandin et Coste, a. a. O. Taf. 95-97.

[244] G. Rawlinson, a. a. O. Bd. III4, p. 174, 210. G. Maspero, a. a. O. Bd. III, p. 677. Por. also Stolze, Persepolis, die achäm und sassanid. Denkmäler und Inschriften, Berlin 1882, Bd. I, Taf. 44, 45; Bd. II, 79-81. See Schaumberg, a. a. O. p. 51.

[245] G. Rawlinson, a. a. O. Bd. III4, p. 174.

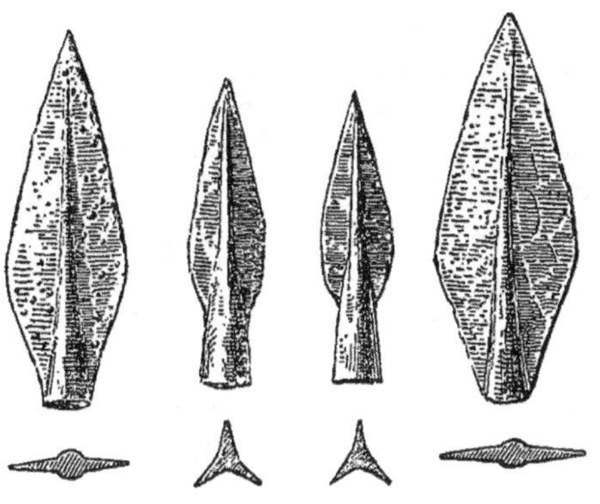

Fig. 29

J. de Morgan, a. a. O. Fig. 264-267

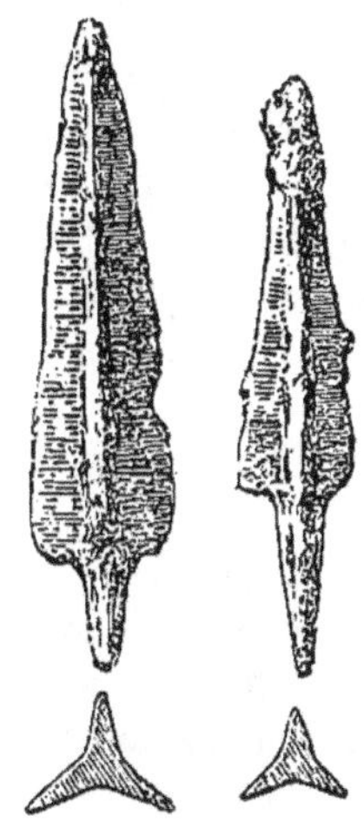

Fig. 30. J. de Morgan, a. a. O. Fig. 268-269

Persian arrows, like the arrows of almost all peoples, were made of reed[246], and their length was about two to two and a half feet. Feathered above the incised base, they ended with specially prepared tips. However, we only know a few examples of stone arrowheads, but this is probably not due to the rarity of their use, but rather to the limited advancement of excavations so far. De Morgan brings some[247] and even if they do not come from the center of the Persian Empire but from the Tâlyches Valley, we can still claim that they are

---

²⁴⁶ Herodot VII, 61: οίστους είχον καλαμίνους.

²⁴⁷ J. de Morgan, Mission en Perse, Bd. IV, p. 73-77; Memoires de la Mission, Bd. II, fig. 82-83, 186-187, 189-191, 198.

45

examples of Persian arrowheads. No new form can be observed here, they resemble Egyptian and Assyrian ones[248]. The same can be said about bronzes, which until now were most often found on Persian soil; some simply imitate stone ones, i.e. showing a leaf with a pin to be inserted into the stem, others have two barbs, and finally they are two- or three-sided, usually provided with a spout (fig. 29). Very rarely and only late do we encounter iron triangular tips with a pin insert, because this type was not able to spread generally, of course, due to the difficulty and cost of production (Fig. 30)[249].

All the peoples mentioned in the previous sections, except the Hittites and Trojans, used the Mediterranean grip in drawing the bow in addition to very simple methods (thumb and index finger), while Persian archers preferred the „Mongolian” grip[250]. However, in ancient Persia, the index finger remained rigidly extended, unlike the modern „Mongolian” method of use, while the third and fourth fingers supported the thumb as it was drawn[251]. This method of tension necessarily required a protective apparatus for the thumb to protect it from too much pressure from the string. As is known, archers who use Mongolian stringing methods use a special ring for this purpose, but no protective device of this type is visible on Persian monuments. Xenophon's information[252] that the Persians used gloves clearly emphasizes that they were gloves with fingers; but even as a matter of protecting the hands from the cold, it seems probable that these gloves were used not only against the cold, but also to protect against the bowstring. For the same purpose, an object was used, which was attached to the hand with a belt (Fig. 31) and resembles a device already known to us from the relief from Sendschirli[253].

Persian archers, like all others, have no shield, but as with the Assyrians, each archer had a shield bearer to protect him from the enemy while shooting[254]. We said earlier that there were two ways of carrying the bow, and also two kinds of foot archers: those who had only the bow, and those who used both the spear and the bow – a combination not found among any other people[255]. The best example of this combination of spear and bow among the Per-

---

[248] G. Rawlinson, a. a. O. Bd. III4, p. 175, Anm. 6.

[249] For more information, see J. de Morgan, Mémoires de la Mission, Bd. I, p. 151. Morgan reports that a large number of arrowheads have been found at Susa, most of bronze and only a few of stone. At the same time, he mentions that bone arrowheads were used in antiquity, but does not give an illustration of them.

[250] E. Morse, a. a. O. p. 158-159. v. Luschan, a. a. O. in Zeitschrift für Ethnologie, Bd. XXIII, Verhandlungen p. 671.

[251] E. Morse, a. a. O. p. 192.

[252] Kyrup. VIII, 8, 17: Περί ἄκραις ταίς χερσί χειρῖδας δασείας καί δακτυλήθρας εχουσιν κτλ.

[253] See fig. 23.

[254] This is how the message of Herodotus (IX, 61) should be conveyed: Φράξαντες γάρ τά γέρρα οἱ Πέρσαι ἀπίεσαν των τοξευμάτων πολλά ἀφειδέως. Also important to us is Herodotus's further statement that the Greeks could not advance because the Persians were firing their arrows so massively. It was only when it came to hand-to-hand combat, and the Persians could not use bows, that they had to succumb, and Herodotus (IX, 62) clearly states that they were defeated because they were ἄνοπλοι.

[255] On rotogravure printing, Antiquites du Bosphore Cimmérien, Taf. XVI, 5, we see a Persian archer fighting a hoplite. He attacks the Greek with a spear in his left hand, while parrying his opponent's blows with a bow in his right. Whether this procedure was often common, we cannot say. Flandin et Coste, a. a. O. Taf. 98-99, 103-104 (Speertrag ende Bogenschützen). See auch Perrot et Chipiez, a. a. O. Bd. V, fig. 498.

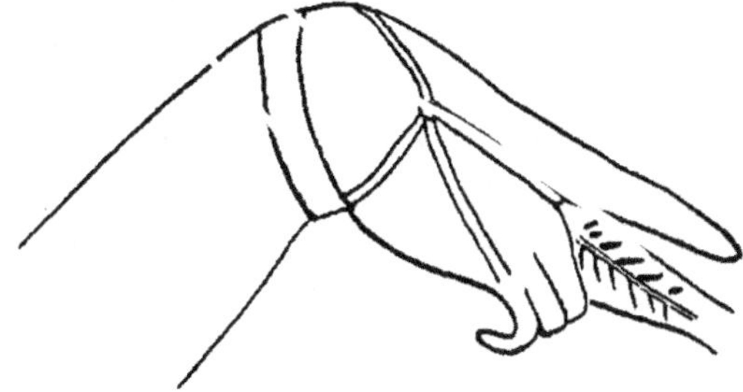

Fig. 31. Monumenti dell' Instituto, III, Taf. 51

sians is provided by the famous archers on the friezes of Susa or Persepolis[256]. The bow and spear could be used simultaneously by a select royal guard, but the rest of the archers remained limited to the bow.

The real core and the part of the Persian army that the Greeks feared the most was the cavalry[257], which aroused great admiration in Greece because it was used to shooting arrows not only forwards but also backwards[258]. Even when they were forced to leave their positions, it could not be defeated because it prevented the enemy from pursuing arrows[259]. It is, however, very strange that at the Battle of Marathon the Persian cavalry did not perform sufficiently, although according to Herodotus[260] it was thanks to them that they landed on this plain which seemed to offer the most favorable terrain. Only the Persian cavalry could effectively fight the heavily armed Greek hoplites; because the great mass of archers could only be used in long-distance combat. If there was a breast-to-breast clash, they would obviously have to surrender, because they consisted only of „defenseless" soldiers – ανοπλοι[261]. As we know, chariot fighting was common among the Assyrians, and it seems strange that, unlike the Assyrians, the Persians rarely used it[262]. Kings always appear on a chariot, but only to gain a better view of the battle[263] or, if necessary, escape danger more quickly[264]. In any case, it is worth noting that both Darius and Xerxes used almost no chariot warriors in their armies during their wars

[256] Perrot et Chipiez, a. a. O. Bd. V, Taf. X and fig. 496.

[257] H. Delbrück, a. a. O. Bd. I. p. 37.

[258] Xenoph. Anab. III, 3, 10: οἱ δέ βάρβαροι ἱππεις και φεύγοντες ἅμα ἐτίτρωσκον εις τούπισθεν τοξεύοντες.

[259] G. Rawlinson, a. a. O. Bd. III, p. 184.

[260] VI, 102: ἥν γάρ ὁ Μαραθών ἐπιτηδεότατον χωρίον τῆς ᾿Αττικῆς ἐνιππεῦσαι καί ἀγχοτάτω τῆς ᾿Ερετρίης, ἐς τοῦτό σφι κατηγέετο ῾Ιππίης ὁ Πεισιστράτου ... It may be doubted, however, whether this plain was really as suitable for cavalry as Corn. Nep. Milt. 5 speaks of the Arborum tractus. For more information on the topography of the Marathon Plain, see H. G. Lölling, Topographische Studien (Zur Topographie von Marathon), Ath. Mitt. Bd. I (1876), p. 67, Taf. IV.

[261] There is also great uncertainty about the size of the Persian troops at the Battle of Marathon. See R. v. Pöhlmann, Grundriß der griechischen Geschichte, IV. Aufl., München 1909, p. 104, Anm. 3, und über Ausrüstung der Griechen und Perser H. Delbrück, Die Perserkriege und die Burgundenkriege, 1887, p. 1 ff.; 8 ff.

[262] Perrot et Chipiez, a. a. O. Bd. V, fig. 474, 496.

[263] Herodot VII, 40; 100. Xenoph. Anab. I, 2, 16.

[264] Arrian, Exp. Alex. II, 11, 4.

with the Greeks. However, this can ultimately be explained by the fact that chariots were not used in wars fought in distant lands due to transportation difficulties[265].

As in Assyria, in Persia the bow was a royal weapon that always accompanied both the king and every free Persian[266]. Cyrus himself made special efforts to ensure that warriors constantly practiced using these weapons[267]. According to custom, he also appeared at court with a bow in his hand. The king either carried it himself[268] or had a special carrier who always accompanied him[269].

Under Persian rule, the bow remained a real weapon of war in the East. All the peoples who marched with the Persians against the Greeks were armed mainly with spears and placed their trust in them, δοαρικλύτοις ἀνδράσι τοίόοσμνον Ἄρη...[270].

8. Canaanites and Jews

When examining the Palestinian arc, we rely on Egyptian and much later Israeli sources, which, however, give us only a very incomplete picture. Excavations in Palestine have added little to our knowledge, revealing only a few examples of arrowheads. In any case, these excavation finds indicate that the bow was used in the area as early as the Neolithic period. For example, B.W.M. Flinders Petrie, during his excavations at Part el Hesy, found stone arrowheads in the shape of a finely crafted, pointed blade with a shank tongue[271], and similar finds have also been reported elsewhere[272]. The fact that not only stone but also bone points were used is confirmed by the find from Part ej-Judeideh, which we owe to the research of the English[273] (Fig. 32). A bone spearhead has almost the same shape as a stone spearhead, with the only difference being that its shaft is more prominent. When bronze and iron became popular, arrowheads began to be made from these metals. However, it is worth noting that their shape has also changed slightly; here, too, the dominant type is a leaf-shaped point, sharpened towards the front and equipped with a shaft feather (Fig. 33 a, b). Specimens from the Sandahannah part are interesting, with the edges of the lower part curved inwards. Arrowhead Fig. 33 d from the Za-

---

[265] G. Rawlinson, a. a. O. Bd. III1, p. 179. Xenoph. Anab. I, 8, 10, of Cyrus he claimed to have had about 20 chariots, αρματα δρεπανηφόρα, on the other hand his brother Artaxerxes was said to have had 200. Arrian, Exp. Alex. III, 11, 7, says that Darius had only 50 chariots.
[266] Arrian, Exp. Alex. II, 11, 4. Herodot, III. 35. M. Jähns, a. a. O. p. 303.
[267] Xenoph. Kyrup. I, 2, 4.
[268] Perrot et Chipiez, a. a. O. Bd. V, fig. 469.
[269] See Schaumberg, a. a. O. p. 52 f.
[270] Aisch. Pers. V. 85-86.
[271] W. M. Flinders Petrie, Tell el Hesy, London 1891, p. 49, Taf. X. See F. T. Bliss, A Mound of many Cities, London 1894, p. 124, fig. 255. H. Vincent, Canaan, Paris 1907, p. 391, fig. 272.
[272] H. Vincent, a. a. O. p. 390.
[273] F. T. Bliss and Stew. Macalister, Excavations in Palestine, London 1902. p. 147, Taf. 76, Nr. 23.

Fig. 32

Bliss and Macalister, Excavations, Taf. 76, Nr 23

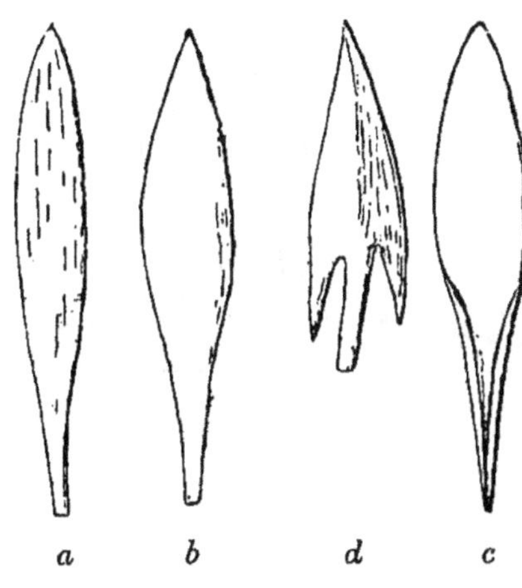

Fig. 33

(a, b, c, d) Bliss and Macalister, a. a. O. Täf. 79, Nr 1-2, 11-12

karîya part belongs, according to the finder, to a much later period[274]. Iron arrowheads[275] also come from the last pre-Israeli period. Excavations at Part es
Sâfi also uncovered a device that most likely provided protection against the
impact of the returning string (Fig. 34). It is a plate, slightly convex, with holes
at the top and bottom through which the string passes. The decoration is made
of incised lines at both ends.

Excavations have given us little information about the bow itself. We will
have to judge him by the Egyptian representations. In Beni-Hassan's[276] photo
we depicted immigrants from Asia. Among them, the archer holds in his left
hand a bow reaching above the waist and having a quite strong notch in the

---

[274] F. J. Bliss and Stew. Macalister, a. a. O. p. 149.

[275] F. J. Bliss and Stew. Macalister, a. a. O. p. 150, Taf. 81, Nr. 15-16. „No iron has been found in the
early pre-Israelite layers. Teil es Sâfi extended from the surface, through the Jewish layer, to the upper part
of the late Israelite layer".

[276] Lepsius, Denkmäler, II, 131-133; see also Rosellini, Mon, Stör. Taf. XXVIII-XXIX. Newberry,
Beni-Hasan, Bd. I, Taf. XXX-XXXI. G. Maspero, a. a. O. Bd. I, p. 468-469. About these Asians, see also
Ed. Meyer, Abhandlungen der Berliner Akademie, 1906, p. 21, i W. Max Müller, a. a. Ö. p. 35 ff.

Fig. 34

Bliss and Macalister, a. a. O. Taf. 77, Nr. 3

middle. The bow is drawn and the string touches the central element of the weapon. Since the bow tapers from the center towards the tips and the arms of the bow are not open towards the target, it is probably a straight bow. On Egyptian monuments we have another representation of the Palestinian bow (Fig. 35). Becoming uniformly thinner towards the ends from the middle sec-

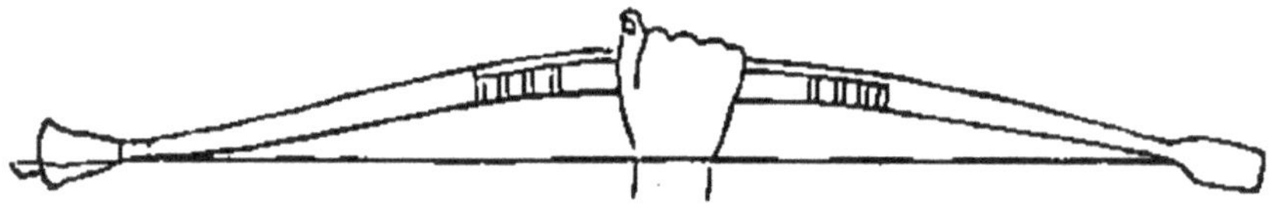

Fig. 35

W. Max Müller, Asien und Europa, Fig. p. 304

tion, it shows four lines on each side of the handle which, as on other bows, probably represent the wrapping of strings. More striking are the ends of the bow's arms, which end in a plate. The left plate is separated from the actual arm by lines that may indicate that it was specially attached to the bow arm. We would therefore have to have a kind of hook here – κορώνη – on the plates for attaching the string. As for the material of the bow, one could think of ibex horns, which are extremely common in Syria[277], [278].

We believe that W. M. Müller rightly suspects that the weapon described is the famous Palestinian „Haru bow". We believe it was a horn bow of the same type found in Egypt. In the latter representation, the handle is not separated from the arms of the bow; however, the lines above seem to indicate that it could be considered to be made of a different material. W. M. Müller continues: "We consider this 'bow of Haru' to be the same as the 'bow of brass,' 2 Sam. 22, 36. This weapon was by no means entirely made of metal, as already claimed, but was reinforced with metal fittings. The bows reinforced with fittings were, as far as we can judge, composite bows, since fittings cannot be imagined in a horn bow. If the bow was indeed reinforced with metal

---

[277] W. Max Müller, a. a. O. p. 304.
[278] Lepsius, Denkmäler, II, 133; vgl. A. Schaumberg, a. a. O. p. 29 f.

50

fittings, this reinforcement was also expressed in the way it was presented, as we also observed in Egypt. The Haru bow and the copper bow are two different weapons, probably separated since their invention. The former were highly sought after as war spoils[279].

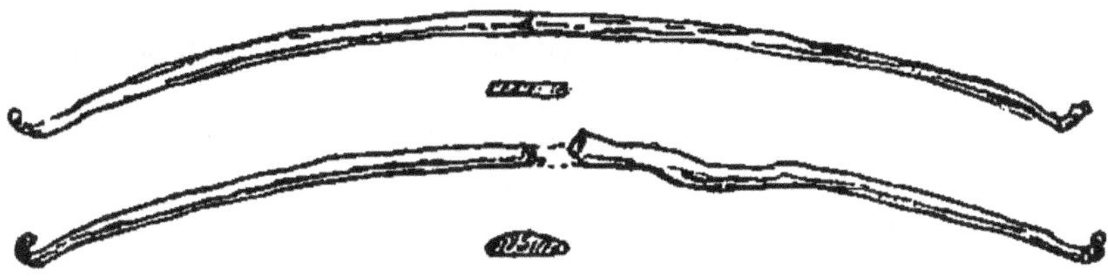

Fig. 36

J. de Morgan, Mission en Perse, Bd. I, Fig. 107

De Morgan's excavations at Susa uncovered two bronze bows[280] (fig. 36). The finder believed that these were not used items, but only votive offerings. But we cannot agree with this opinion, because even if there are no mentions of the brass bow among the Persians, there is evidence of its existence among the Jews, Job XX, 24: καὶ οὐ σωθή ἐκ χεφός σιδήρου, τρώσαι αὐτόν τ ὅξ ον χάλκειον[281]. Today it is impossible to determine how widespread the use of this fourth type of bow was. We do not know whether the Bow of Har can be attributed only to the Canaanites and the Bronze Bow only to the Jews in Palestine, but we should not forget that for many decades the Canaanites lived side by side with the immigrants, sometimes in dispute, sometimes in peace, and that it was David who destroyed the last the stronghold of the Canaanites, the stronghold of the Jebusites in Zion, and thus laid the foundations of Jerusalem. Judging from this, it would be possible that in Palestine the Haru bow, as well as bronze bows and straight bows, which have not been confirmed but which were almost certainly used by a lower warrior, were used side by side in both war and peacetime[282].

Jews used the bow in war[283] and during hunting[284], some tribes were even famous for their skillful use of the bow[285]. It is also interesting that the archers drawing the bow used both hands, „equipped with a bow, skilled with both

---

[279] See W. Max Müller, a. a. O. p. 151 i 304.

[280] J. de Morgan, Mission en Perse, Bd. I, p. 170, fig. 107.

[281] See auch 2 Sam. XX, 35: Διδάσκων χεϊράς μου, εἰς πόλεμον καί κατάξας τόξον χαλκόδν ἐν βραχίονί μου. Mamy powtórkę w Psal. XVII (XVIII), 35: Διδάσκων χείράς μου, εις πόλεμον, καί εθου τόξον χαλκουν τους βραχίονας μου. See auch Pindar, Nem. III, 38-39 (ed. Christ): καί ποτέ χαλκότοξον 'Αμαζόνων μετ' άλκάν επετο θοι.

[282] Rieht. I, 27; 2 Sam. V, 7 ff.

[283] Gen. XLVIII, 22.

[284] Jes. VII, 24; Gen. XXI, 16.

[285] I Par. VIII, 40; II Par. XIV, 8.

hands, on stones and with bows and arrows[286]." However, it has not yet been possible to determine how the bow was to be drawn, what common drawing methods were, or how the bow was carried. The quiver was known and used. According to Egyptian representations, it was oblong, rounded at the bottom, usually decorated, sometimes with a lid[287], sometimes without a lid[288]. Gorytos also seems to be attested among Jews[289].

As a sign of anger, the Jewish poets put the bow into the hands of their God[290].

9. Scythians

We now come to the bows of this people, whose skill in archery was known everywhere among the ancients[291], so that the name Scythian was considered by the Greeks almost synonymous with archer[292]. Since ancient times, the Greeks have written much[293] about the nation itself and its homeland, but many questions still remain unanswered[294]; e.g. how far the borders of their country stretched, there were different opinions on this subject in ancient times[295]. The ancients also never knew whether these people constituted a united nation or consisted of different tribes. According to Pliny[296] it was a „multitudo populorum innumera", encompassing 20 tribes, all of which were said to have belonged to the Scythians. All these tribes constantly migrated between Europe and Asia, which does not surprise us, since the constant change of their residence was already in the nature of these steppe peoples; Pliny also recognizes this when he writes[297]: „nec in alia parte maior auctorum inconstantia, credo propter innumeras vagasque gentes[298]." The people living on the banks of Pontus were actually called Scolotes[299], but the Persians called them Sakai[300].

---

[286] I Par. XII, 2.

[287] Lepsius, Denkmäler II, 132, 133.

[288] W. Max Müller, a. a. O. p. 304.

[289] Habak. III, 9.

[290] Psal. VII, 13; Job VI, 4.

[291] Even the Persian king Cyaxares entrusted his children to the Scythians for their education. Herodot I, 73 Κυαξάρης παῖδάς σφι παρέδωκε την γλώσσαν τε ἐκμαθ'έειν καί την τέχνην τών τόξων.

[292] Asklepiodotos I, 3 (ed. Rüstow-Köchly p. 134).

[293] B. Latyschev, Scythica et Caucasica e'veteribus scriptoribus graecis et latinis collegit et cum versione Rossica edidit. 2 Bände, St. Petersburg 1904.

[294] K. Neumann, Die Hellenen im Skythenlande, Berlin 1855. J. G. Cuno, Forschungen im Gebiete der alten Völkerkunde, I, Die Skythen, Berlin 1871. E. Bonnell, Beiträge zur Altertumskunde Rußlands, 2 Bände, St. Petersburg 1882-1897.

[295] After Pomponius Mela, De chorepgraphia, III, 36, The Scythians lived where there was always snow and unbearable frost.

[296] N. H. VI, 17.

[297] N. H. VI, 17; see też Herodot IV, 2, 46, 114, 121, 127.

[298] More information on the Scythian question, in addition to the works cited, see P. Cesare A. De Cara, Gli Hethei-Pelasgi, Roma 1894, Bd. I, p. 468-498.

[299] Herodot IV, 6.

[300] Herodot VII, 64.

52

Pliny gives a legend[301] that the bow and arrow were invented by Cos, the son of Jupiter (according to others, it was Perses, the son of Perseus); Herodotus[302] tells a Scythian folk tale according to which Heracles spent the night wrapped in a lion's skin with the Geryones cattle in a desolate land attacked by winter weather, and while sleeping he lost his horses, which had been let out to graze. He searched the area in vain, but could no longer find the horses, which had disappeared due to the action of the gods. But he found a hermaphrodite, half-woman, half-snake, Echidna, with whom he stayed to recover the horses she had saved. Echidna bore the hero three sons and asked him whether she should send her sons to him when they grow up or keep them in Scythia. Then Heracles replied that she should order them to draw the bow as he had shown, and that the one of her sons who could do it should be left in the country and the other two should be sent away. The hero then gave her one of his two bows and a belt. The two older sons, Agathyrs and Gelonus, were unable to cope with the task set before them, only the youngest, Scythes, could and therefore remained in the countryside, while the older ones were driven away from their mother[303].

We can therefore assume that the Scythians learned to use the bow only later, which is contradicted by another story that has come down to us from Theocritus[304], according to which Heracles used to draw the bow according to the Scythian method, and the scholiast states here that Heracles used a Scythian bow. A certain Scythian, Teutares, taught him how to use a bow according to the Scythian method[305]. All these reports are only testimony to how much respect the Scythians had for the bow, and that it was in fact a Scythian national weapon[306].

Let us now try to get to know the Scythian bow in more detail, based on the many existing descriptions by ancient writers and monuments[307].

Ammianus Marcellinus gives us almost the best and most accurate account of the occasional descriptions of the Black Sea coast, according to which the Scythian or Artic bow consisted not of one curved element, as among other peoples, but of two horns, each in the shape of a waning moon, which were

---

[301] Plinius, N. H. VII, 57, »arcum et sagittam Scythen Jovis filium, alii sagittas Persen Persei filium invenisse dicunt«.

[302] Herodot IV, 8-10.

[303] See E. Bonneil, a. a. O. Bd. I, p. 179 f. and annotation 2.

[304] Id. XIII, 56 Μαιωτιστί λαβών ευκαμπέα τόξα ...

[305] Schol. ad Theor. Id. XIII, 56 Μαιωτιστί, ήτοι Σκοθῖστί. ..... ἐχρήτο δέ 'Ηρακλής τοίς Σκυθικοῖς τόξοις διδαχθείς παρά τίνος Σκύθου Τευτάρου ..... (ed. H. Fritsche). See Schol. ad Apoll. Argon. IV, 321 (ed. A. Keil). See Lycophr. Alexandra, 56, und Schol. ad Lycophr., 56 ... Τεύταρος Σκύθης βουκόλος 'Αμφιτρύωνος ἐδίδαξε τον 'Ηρακλέα τοξεύειν παρασχών αότώ καί τά τόξα αύτού (ed. E. Scheer). Apollod. II, 4, 9.

[306] See Herodot I, 214; IV, 131. Xenoph. Anab. III, 4, 15. Aisch. Choeph. 160-163 (ed. Wecklein). Plato, Leges, VII, 795 A.

[307] See K. Neumann, Die Hellenen im Skythenlande, p. 290 f. J. G. Cuno, Forschungen, I, p. 193. Daremberg et Saglio, Dictionnaire, p. v. arcus (Saglio). Kondakoff, Tolstoi et Reinach, Antiquites de la Russie méridionale, p. 210.

connected by a straight rod[308]. The shape of the northern coast of the Black Sea leads Ammian to speak of an arc here. This coastline really resembles an arc, because in this way the two bends in the middle are divided by the Crimean Peninsula like a straight rod. The chord of this arc forms the Asian coast of the same sea. To make sure that we do not make a mistake in interpreting the message of Ammianus and comparing the north coast with the actual arc and the south coast with the chord, we have the following testimony from Dionysius Periegeta: According to its (Pontus's) curvature, it is round. A shape comparable to a bow, namely the chord would be the right (southern) side of Pontus, which runs in a straight line, except for the carambis which projects from it to the north. The left side, curved twice, resembles the corners of an arch[309]. All these accounts are very clear and do not allow for any other interpretation than that the bow consisted of two horns, connected by a crossbar, most likely a wooden bridge, which served as both a handle and a support for the arrow tip.

However, we have other information about the Scythian bow that cannot be reconciled with the shape of the northern coast of Pontus and in which, surprisingly, there is no mention of horns[310]. So, for example, B. Lycophron compares

---

[308] Ammianus Marcell. XXII, 8, 37 ... . cum arcus omnium gentium flexis curvantur hastilibus, Scythici soli vel Parthici, circumductis utrimque introrsus pandis et patulis cornibus, effigiem lunae decrescentis ostendunt, medietatem recta et rotunda regula dividente. A. Schaumberg, a. a. O. p. 104, is of the opinion that Ammianus' message is useless.

[309] Dionysii Perieg. v. 156-162 (Geog. gr. minor. Bd. II, p. III, ed. C. Müllerus).

Ἐκ του δ᾽άν καί Πόντον ιδοις διθάλασσον Ιόντα,
τόρνω ἐειδόμενον περιηγέος ἄμματι τόξου
ἀλλ᾽ ε᾽ίη νευρής σημήια δεξιά Πόντου,
ἰθύ διαγραφδέντα, μόνη όέ τοί ἔστι Κάραμβις,
γραμμής εκτός ἐοῦσα καί ἐς βορέην δοόωσα
σήμα δ᾽ εχει κεράων σκαιός πόρος, οστ᾽ επί δισσήν
είλεῖτάι στροφάλιγγα, βιοῦ κεράεσσιν ἐοικώς.

See also Eustathius ad Dionys. Perieg. v. 157 ff. ed. C. Müllerus, Geogr. graec. minor. II, p. 245.

„Ότι τον Εύξεινον, ου λόξας εφίθασεν είπών τάς κελεύθους, τόξω ἀπεικάζει τεταμένω Σκυθτκω. Σκυθικά δέ τόξα τά έκ κεράτων συγκείμενα ....

Τά δέ του Πόντου βόρεια τά τοῖς εκ τής Προποντίδος είσπλέουσι σκαιά, ήγουν άριστερά, σχήμα εχειν φησί των του τόξου δύο κεράτων, διά τό καί αυτά ομοίως τοῖς του τόξου κέρασιν επί δισσήν κυρτοῦσθαι στροφάλιγγα εκατέρωθεν, τοῦ Μετώπου του κριού ..... ἄμμα δέ τόξου τόν σύνδεσμόν τοῦ Σκυθικοῦ τόξου περιγές δέ τό περιηγμένον ήτοι καμπύλον, τοιοῦτο δέ τό ἐντεταμένον τόξον, ίνα λέγη ἐοικέναι τό του Εύξείνου πέλαγος τόξω ού σκολιω, αλλά στρογγύλφ γενομένω διά τήν τάσιν της νευράς. Περιάγει γάρ ή τάσις τά κέρατα εις καμπήν, καί ούτως από σκολιοῦ γίνεται περιφερές κατά τάς άψῖδας τό τόξον. „Οτε δέ καί εις βολήν ἐπιταθη, τότε κυκλοτερές τό τόξον γίνεται ... Weiter vgl. Strabo, II, 5, 22 (C. 125 ed. Meineke): είκάζουσι δέ τινες τό όχημα τής περιμέτρου ταύτης ἐντεταμένω Σκυδικω τόξω, τήν μέν νευράν ἐξομοιοῦντες τοις δεξιοις καλουμένοις μέρεσι τοῦ Πόντου (ταῦτα δ᾽ἐστίν δ παράπλους δ από τοῦ στόματος μέχρι τοῦ μυχου τοῦ κατά Διοσκουριάδα πλήν γάρ τής Καράμβιος ή γε άλλη πάσα ήών μικράς εχει είσοχάς τε και ἐξοχάς ώστ᾽ ευθεία ἐοικέναι), την δέ λοιπήν τω κέρατι του τόξου διττήν εχοντι τήν επιστροφήν, τήν μέν άνω περιφερεστέραν τήν δέ κάτω εύθυτέραν ούτω δέ κάκείνην ἀπεργάζεσθαι δύο κόλπους, ών ό ἐσπέριος πολύ θατέρου περιφερέστερός ἐστιν. Zob. Plinius, N. H. IV, 24 ... vastum mare Pontus Euxinus, qui quondam Axenus, longe refugientes occupat terras magnoque litorum fiexu retro curvatus in comua ab iis utrimque porrigitur, ut sit plane arcus Scythici forma. See dazu: Pomponius Mela, Chorogr. I, 19 (ed. C. Frick). Valerius Flaccus, Argon. IV, 728 (ed. P. Langen). M. Manilius, Astronom. IV, 755 (ed. Fr. Jacob). Terentius Maurus, de litteris, syllabis et metris, v. 15-19 (ed. C. Lachmannus). Sallustius apud Servium ad Aen. III, 533 (ed. G. Thilo et H. Hagen).

[310] See A. Schaumberg, a. a. O. 103 f. Both groups of messages fit into one and the same shape, the sigma bow. Of course, this is only possible if we put aside some of the ancient messages.

54

it to a snake[311]. πω ...[312], in Euripides has the form αγράμματον[313], which describes the name ΘΗΣΕΥΣ as follows:

> ἐγὼ πέφυκα γραμμάτων μὲν .οὐκ ἴδρις,
> μορφὰς δὲ λέξω καὶ σαφῆ τεκμήρια.
> κύκλος τις ὡς τόρνοιτιν ἐκμετρούμενος·
> οὗτος δ’ ἔχει σημεῖον ἐν μέσῳ σαφές.
> τὸ δεύτερον δὲ πρῶτα μὲν γραμμαὶ δύο,
> ταύτας διείργει δ’ ἐν μέσαις ἄλλη μία.
> τρίτον δε βόστρυχός τις ὣς εἰλιγμένος, ...

Agathon also has αγράμματον a farmer describing the name of Theseus[314]:

> γραφῆς ὁ πρῶτος ἦν μεσόμφαλος κύκλος·
> ὀρθοί τε κανόνες ἐζυγωμένοι δύο,
> Σκυθικῷ τε τόξῳ (τὸ) τρίτον ἦν προσεμφερές . . . .

In Theodectes, the farmer also describes the same name, but compares Sigma to a lock of hair, curled like the tendrils of a vine: τρίτον δ’ ἑλικτφ. βοστρόχφ προσεμφερές ... κτλ[315].

The question arises how the sigma sign was written in Greece; whether it was a symbol in the sense in which we use it today, i.e. Σ, or was it similar to the Latin C. The answer can easily be found in the inscriptions[316], which clearly state that it can only be the symbol Σ, but never the Latin C, what it certainly does not correspond to the comparison with a curl or a snake. Illustrations of Scythian bows will show that we are correct in assuming the sign Σ. However, the matter is not yet resolved, as this sigma does not in any way correspond to the nature of the bow described by the previously cited authors, as it cannot correspond to the northern bank of Pontus with two vaults connected by a crossbar. It is therefore obvious that in the case of these authors on the one hand and tragedians on the other, we are dealing with two completely different descriptions. We must therefore examine monuments with depictions of Scythian bows to shed light on this issue.

On the golden tablet[317] from Kul-Oba (Fig. 37) we see two Scythians, with their backs turned to each other and shooting at the same time. Each of them holds a bow whose shape refers to the sigma sign. The Scythians have the same bow, or rather the same type of weapon, on the well-known[318] electron

---

[311] Lycophr. Alex., v. 917-918.

[312] In δράκων there is certainly an indication of a multiple curve.

[313] Athen. X, p. 454b, c (X, 80, ed. G. Kaibel).

[314] Athen. X, p. 454 d.

[315] Athen. X, p, 454 d, e.

[316] On the sigma of the inscription, cf. W.Larfeld, Griechische Epigraphik (J. V. Müllers Handbuch. I), p. 352 et seq., and a table on the history of the development of local Greek alphabets from about 650 B.C.E. Inscriptions show that from the 7th century onwards only the sign Σ.

[317] See Antiquites du Bosphore Cimmerien, Taf. XX, 6.

[318] Antiquites du Bosphore Cimmerien, Taf. XXXIII, 1. See further sights with the Scythian sigma bow: Kondakoff, Tolstoi, Reinach, Antiquites, fig. 13, 109, 143, 151, 178, 179, 192, 198, 264. Monum. ined. dell’ Inst. II, Taf. 50; V, Taf. 11; VIII, Taf. 44.

Fig. 37

Kondakoff, Tolstoi, Reinach, Antiquites de la Russie mer. Fig. 150

vase (Fig. 38), also found at Kul-Oba, so we should have no reservations about the existence of such shaped bows[319].

This form, so often repeated in purely Greek art, is somewhat obscure in the case of an bow consisting of horns connected by a simple bridge. In the case of a horn bow, we should be able to recognize individual elements, but above all the crossbar connecting the horns. On the other hand, we see a sigmoid bow described precisely as weakly curved, but having a rather angular shape; the horn or wood would certainly not allow such formation without damage. So what type of arc was it? There is no doubt that we are dealing with an artificially complex bow. Only the Sigma bow assembled in this way could withstand such bends and be open towards the target during shooting[320]. And it is no wonder that this shape of the bow was so common among the Scythians, considering how much the Scythians had in common with Asian peoples, especially Assyrians and Persians, both in times of peace and war.

---

[319] This sigma bow has retained its shape both stretched and unstretched. See e.g. Furtwängler-Reichhold, Griech. Vas. Taf. 112, i Hartwig, Die griechi schen Meisterschalen, Stuttgart-Berlin, 1893, Taf. 14. Nr. 1.

[320] A. Schaumberg, op. cit., p. 105, concluded that the Scythian sigma bow was made of wood because it was said to have too little reflectivity. Immediately afterwards, however, he talks about the extremely long range of the Olbian Anaxagoras and assumes that this master shot was obtained from a composite bow, which, however, was not τόξον Σκυθικόν. He denies the horn bow (which we will discuss later), but since it is, as far as we know, technically impossible to produce a wooden bow in the form of a sigma, the wood would have to break at the slightest stress (cf. what we have said about the angular bow), we must ask what other composite bow he has in mind. On the information of Herodotus Σάκαι δε οἱ Σκύθ'αι ... (ειχον) τόξα επιχώρια (VII, 64) it is not possible to construct a thesis, Herodotus only emphasizes that they were domestic, customary bows, but not that they were wooden bows. Where they really are wooden bows, it always says either καλάμινα (VII, 64 Βάκτριοῖ, 65 Ἰνδοι), κρανέϊνα (VII, 92 Λύκιοι), or επιχώρια καλάμινα (VII, 67 Κάσπιοι), also mentions a type of wood. By the way, it is very common to see marks at appropriate intervals on depictions of the Scythian sigma bow, which indicate that at these points the bow was somehow bound due to strength. A composite bow from the time of Ramses II, found in Egypt, still has lace grooves. (F. v. Luschan, a. a. O. in Zeitschrift'für Ethnologie, Bd. XXV, Verhandlungen p. 268.) Furtwängler-Reichhold, Griech. Vas. Taf. 90; Wiener Vorlegeblätter, Ser. I, Taf. XII; Ser. II, Taf. I und II; Ser. III, Taf. IV; Ser. D, Taf. III; Wiener Vorlegeblätter, 1889, Taf. IV, Nr. 3b; Archäologische Zeitung, 1884, Taf. IV u. v. a.

Fig. 38

Kondakoff, Tolstoi, Reinach, a. a. O. Fig. 262

Let us now return to the descriptions of the Scythian bow, which compare it with the northern bank of the Pontus Euxinus and thus confirm the composition of the bow with two corners connected by a crossbar. Luschan, who from the beginning denied the possibility of such an bow, wrote[321]: „For example, the theorem of Ammian XXII, 8, 37, which I happened to know, that the bow of the Parthians and Scythians had two flexible arms (in the Ammian language „cornibus") that were connected in in the middle with a straight bridge, it doesn't worry or surprise me, because I already knew this fact from the photos[322].

So how did Luschan explain this simple bridge, and what does he make of all the unambiguous messages from the ancients that we cannot and should not completely ignore? In our opinion, they are only understandable if the horn bow actually existed.

We want to omit for the moment the numerous depictions of this type of bow in Greek vase painting, as they are not always accurate in detail, and will first present two depictions, somewhat more recent, from Sassanid times, but the horns and the cross element connecting them are particularly accurate. Fig. 39 shows us a galloping king[323] who shoots a boar with his arrow. We can clearly see the elements of the bow, the horn arm, the handle and the eye of the bow string to which the string is tied. The arm is curved in the shape of a crescent, undoubtedly made of horn, on the upper end of which is attached an ear in the form of a slender staff decorated with tassels. We also see the entire bow on another silver bowl, which also depicts the king riding forward but shooting arrows backwards. It is a bow with „large dimensions, but at the

---

[321] v. Luschan, a. a. O. in Festschrift für O. Benndorf, p. 192.

[322] „In general, the shape of the handle is naturally subject to much greater fluctuations in place and time than any other part of the bow. In the Assyrian bow, the hilt was almost perpendicular, kinked, which seems technically possible only with a particularly strong bow design, but it was not entirely devoid of advantages" (Anm. v. Luschans).

[323] Auch Monum. dell' Inst. III, Taf. 51.

Fig. 39

Kondakoff, Tolstoi, Reinach, a. a. O. Fig. 379

Fig. 40

Kondakoff, Tolstoi, Reinach, a. a. O. Fig. 373

same time obviously having considerable flexibility." The force of tension can be seen in the shape of a chord, which forms a very sharp angle when held in the hand[324] (Fig. 40).

---

[324] See Kondakoff, Tolstoi, Reinach, a. a. O. p. 417. See also depictions of the bows on Trajan's Column, Cichorius, Die Reliefs der Traianssäule, Taf. II and III, where this composition is reproduced unambiguously.

58

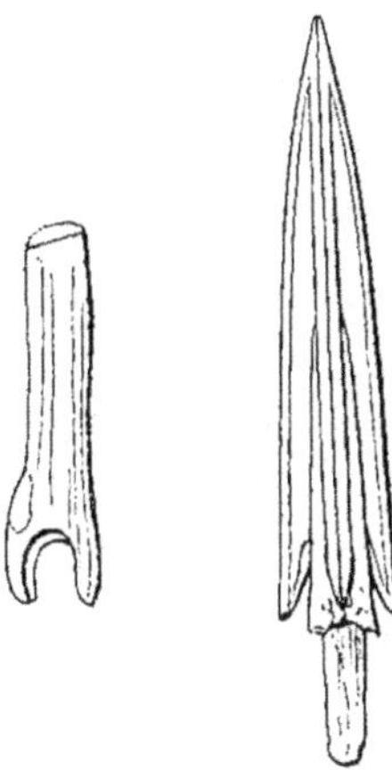

Fig. 41

Antiquités du Bosphore Cimmérien, Taf. XXVII, Nr. 20

Fig. 42

Antiquités du Bosphore Cimmérien, Taf. XXVII, Nr. 11

We will have the opportunity to return to the way of working with horns, handle and ears. At this point it is only necessary to note that the Scythian bow, pontus and sigmoid form were παλίντονον, as Aeschylus said in Choephors B.C. 160-161 and confirms: Σκυθικά τ'ἐν/ χεροῖν παλίντον' ἐν ἐ'ργῳ βέλη ... κτλ.

We are unable to provide anything specific about the actual methods of drawing the bow used by the Scythians, because the discussed depictions on Greek monuments cannot under any circumstances be considered reliable evidence.

It is common knowledge that Scythian archers were considered by the Greeks to be role models in archery. Their skill in using these weapons was so developed that when holding a bow, they used not only their left hand, like all other peoples, but also their right hand, as Plato clearly mentioned them[325].

When drawing, the Scythians, unlike the Cretans, did not pull the string to their chest, but to their shoulders[326].

Scythian arrows, like the arrows of other peoples, always had fletches and a strong insert at the lower end of the shaft, probably made of wood. Of course, there was always a notch there, allowing it to sit better on the string (Fig. 41).

---

[325] Plato, Leges. VII, p. 795A (ed. G. Stallbaum): των Σκύθών νόμος οὺκ ἐν αριστερά μέν τόξον ἀπάγων, ἐν δεξιᾶ δὲ οιστόν προσαγόμενος μόνον, ἀλλ' ομοίως, ἑκατέραις επ' αμιροτερα χρωμενος.

[326] Schol. Il. VIII, 325: ὁ μέντοι Νεοτελης Σκυθἴκήν είναι τήν τοξείαν εφασκεν, τοῦ τόξου προς τον ώμον ἑλκομένου (ed. G. Dindorfius, Lipsiae, 1875, Bd. I, p. 285); Schol. II, VIII, 328: Νεοτελης ... τών Σκυθών οὺκ επί τον μαστόν ἀλλ' επί τον ώμον ἑλκόντων (ed. G. Dindorfius, Bd. III, p. 361).

Arrowheads[327] were made of bone, stone and bronze, and in later times also of iron. Stone and bone arrowheads[328] are similar in all respects to the arrowheads of other peoples, while the bronze ones, which have been preserved in large numbers in graves, have, one might even say, typical shapes[329]. They are always triangular, with spines and always have a beak (Fig. 42). Of course, there are also very simple types of points with only one barb[330].

It is strange that Herodotus, who is almost always so precise, reports nothing about the poisoned arrows of the Scythians. The poison of the Scythian arrow was well known to the Greeks, as suggested by the name σκυθικόν or τοξικόν[331]. According to Pseudo-Aristotle, it was prepared from rotten vipers and human blood[332]. The Scythians caught snakes, let them rot, and then mixed this evil matter with human blood, which was buried in dung in a vessel for several days[333]. Arrow poison was in common use among both the Scythians and their neighbors, the Sarmatians[334].

Quivers were made of strong leather and always had a lid. Their equipment, of course, depended on the owner. The simpler ones were probably left in their natural color or trimmed with leather of a different color. The quivers of wealthier people were certainly decorated with metal decorations.

In Roman times, the Scythians lost their fame as archers, and their place was taken by the Parthians. It is not our business to investigate whether the Scythians and Parthians formed a nation or not[335], we are only interested here in the Parthian arc, which, as said above, was similar to the Scythians. We have already mentioned the bows of Trajan's Column and we immediately

---

[327] See Herodot, IV, 81.

[328] See E. A, Gardner, Ornaments and armour from Kertsch, in Journ. of Hellenic Studies, Bd. V (1884), p. 67, Taf. XLVI, n. 5.

[329] On this and on the spread of this type outside Scythia, cf. P. Meinecke, Die skythischen Altertümer im mittleren Europa, in Zeitschrift für Ethnologie, Bd. XXVIII. (1896), p. 6, 8-9, 20-21.

[330] See the pictures and news about the arrowheads: Compte Rendu de la Commission archéol. de St. Petersbourg 1876, p. 115, Atlas Taf. II, Nr. 21. Recueil d'antiquites de la Scythie, St. Petersbourg 1886, p. 4, Atlas Taf. I, n. 11 22. A. Ouvaroff, Recherches sur les antiquites de la Russie mérid. St. Petersbourg 1885, p. 40. Revue bow.; Bd. I (1904), p. 11. Aischylos, Septem ap. Theb. v. 714-718 describes steel as being of Scythian origin (similar to how V. 801-802 refers to iron). Is the poet saying that other tribes were still using stone and bronze weapons at the same time? In any case, Pausanias I, 21:5-6, for example, tells of the bone arrowheads of the Sarmatians.

[331] Schol. ad Nicandri Alexipharmaca, v. 207 (ed. O. Schneider): τοξικον δέ καλείται τό τοιουτον φάρμακον οτακο ομοίως τοῖς τοξεύμασιν άναιρείν παραχρήμα βρωθέν ή ποθέν, η έπεί οί Πάρθοι καί Σκύθαι τοξεύοντες τουτω παραχρίουσι τάς τών βελών ακίδας ... λέγεται υπό τινων Σκυθικόν; See auch Schol. ad Nicandri Alexiph. v. 207 (ed. E. Abel et R. Vári). A. J. Reinach, a. a. O. L'Anthropologie, Bd. XX, 54 f.

[332] Pseudo-Aristoteles, De mirabilibus, p. 153 (ed. J. Beckmann): Φασί τό Σκυθτκόν φάρμακον, ῷ άποβάπτοοσι τούς όϊστούς, σοντίθεσθαι εξ έχιδνης τηροῦσι δέ ώς έοικεν οί Σκύθαι τάς ήδη ζωοτοκούσας καί λάβοντες αύτάς τήκουσι ημέρας τινάς όταν δέ ικανώς αύτοίς δοκή σεσήφθαι παν, το του άνθρώπου αίμα εις χοτρίδιον έκχέοντες, εις τους κοπρίους κατορύττοοσι πωμάσαντες οταν δέ καί τούτο σαπνμ τό όφιστάμενον επάνω τού αίματος, ό δη, έστι ύδατώδες, μιγνύοοσι τφ τής έχίδνης ίχώρι καί ούτω ποιούσι θανάσιμον.

[333] Plinius, N. H. XI, 53: Scythae sagittas tingunt viperina sanie et humano sanguine ...; vgl. auch XI, 115. See Aellan, de natura anim. IX, 15: λέγονται δέ οί Σκοθαι προς τώ τοξικφ, ω τούς οίστούς έπιχριουσι, καί άνθρώπειόν ίχώρα άναμιγνύναι φαρμάττοντες, έπιπολάζοντά πως αιματ, οπερ ίσασιν άπόκριμα αύτοις. See auch.V, 16 (ed. R. Herscher); Lucian, Nigrinus, 37 (ed. J. Sommerbrodt). Lucan, III, 266-267 (ed. C. Hosius) See auch K. Neumann, a. a. O. p. 292 f.

[334] Ovidius, Trist. V 7, 15-16; Ex Ponto I, 2, 15; IV, 7, 36.

[335] See G. Rawlinson, The sixth great oriental monarchy, London 1873, p. 15 ff. und 118 f.

60

recognized them as horn bows. The same type of weapon is depicted by an archer on the Parthian monument[336]. Even though we only see the top half of the bow in the bas-relief, we can still see the horn bow with the string. Images of Parthian coins provide the best evidence that the Parthian bow was consistent with the description of Ammianus[337]. The Romans especially feared and hated the Parthian archer cavalry[338] who, although forced to flee, fired back and forth at the pursuing enemy – καί τούτο κράτιστα ποιύοσι μετά Σκύθας ...[339]

10. The bow in the Cretan-Mycenaean culture

In ancient times, the Cretans were very famous archers. Their craftsmanship was already known to Homer. Although the Salamis Teukros in Il. XIII, 314 is praised as the best archer among the Achaeans, who Il. VIII, 297-304 never missed his target, but was finally defeated by the Cretan Meriones, Il. XXIII, 850-883. Information received from Greek and Roman writers[340] and monuments from Crete[341] provide us with sufficient information about the fame of Cretan archers, as well as the spread of the bow. Evidence shows that Crete was considered the cradle of the art of archery, and according to Diodorus, Apollo himself, the inventor of the bow, taught archery to the Cretans[342].

The bow found on Cretan-Mycenaean monuments appears to be a simple bow. We see such a simple bow on an ancient Cretan soapstone bas-relief depicting an archer (fig. 43) shooting[343]. This bow is identical to those found on

---

[336] G. Rawlinson, The sixth greath oriental monarchy, p. 394, fig. p. 395; also fig. p. 415.

[337] Warwick-Wroth, Catalogue of the coins of Parthia, London 1903. Tab. I 1, 5, 13, 15; Tab. II 1-2; Tab. III 3-4; Tab. IV 3-8; Tab. V 3-7 usw.

[338] Horat. Od. I, 19, 11; II, 13, 16. Tacit. Ann. VI, 35. Vergil. Georg. III, 31. Appian Parth. 144 ff. See M. Dieulafoy, L'art antique de la Perse, Bd. V, p. 52.

[339] Plut. Crass. 24.

[340] Diodor V 74, 5; Xenoph. Anab. I 2, 9; III 3' 7; V 2, 12; Hellen. IV 2, 16; Paus. I 23, 4; IV 8, 3; Plat. Leges VIII 834 A-D; Plut. Gracch. 16; Cleom. 21; Tit. Liv. XXIV 30, 12; XXXV 29, 2; XXXVII 39, 10; XXXVII 40, 8; XXXVII 41, 9; XXXVIII 21, 2; Caes. Bell. Gail. II 7; Appian. Bell. civ. 49, 71; Arrian, Anab. III 12, 2; Polyb. V 36, 4; 65, 7; 82, 4; Ovid, Met. VII 778. Plat. Leges I 625 E says the Cretan Kleinias that the nature of the country (Crete) compels his countrymen to use the bow, των οή τόξων κάί τοξέυμάτων ή κουφότης άρμόττειν δοκεῖ. απολογείται διά 'την τών τόξων χρήσιν καί γάρ όνειδος ήν ώς τό, τοξότα, λωβητήρ, ob γάρ άγχέμαχοι, άλλα πόρρωθε βάλλουσι οι τοξόται. αίτιάται τόν τον τόπον ..., because Crete is mountainous, there is a lot of hunting, etc.

[341] Ausonia III (Roma 1909), p. 290; see Sepulchral reliefs: in the Museum of Candia,Mon. antichi VI, p. 198 fig. 38; von Elyros, Museo italiano, Bd. III, 748 n. 205; auch Jahreshefte, Bd. VI, fig. 2-3, p. 1-8. Catalogue of the Greek Coins of Crete, London 1886, Taf. II 6,- 7; VII 1-3, 5; VIII 5-7, 15. Svoronos, Numismatique de la Crete ancierne, Macon 1890, Taf. VII 24-27; XI 15-28; XVI 15-20; XXIV 1-7; XXXII 25; 'Εφημ. άρχαιολ. 1889,πιν. 12, 24 u. V. a.

[342] V. 74, 5, εόρετήν δέ καί του τόξου γενόμενον διδάξαι τους εγχωρίους τά περί τήν τοξείαν, άφ' ής αιτίας μάλιστα παρά τοις Κρησίν εζηλώσθαι τήν τοξικήν καί τό τόξον Κρητικόν ό νομασθηναι. And V 65, 3, where Diodorus writes that the Curetians introduced an arc to Crete. See also L. Grasberger, Erziehung und Unterricht in der klassischen Antike, Würzburg 1881, Bd. III, p. 153. See Pind. Pyth. V. 41; Simonid. apud Athen. XIII 573 E. Apollo is very often depicted with a bow on Cretan coins: J. N. Svoronos, Numismatique de la Crète ancienne, Taf, XI 5, 8-20, 22-29; Taf. XVI 15-20. Über den Kult Apollos in Kreta vgl. W. Aly, Der kretische Apollonkult, Leipzig 1908.

[343] A. J. Evans, in Annual British School, Bd. VII (1900/01), p. 44, fig. 13. M. J. Lagrange, La Crète ancienne, Paris 1908, fig. 85. See noch A.J. Evans in Annual British School, Bd. VIII, p. 21, fig. 10. Eine

Fig. 43

Annual of the British school at Athens, Bd. VII, S. 44, fig. 13

Egyptian monuments. All other illustrations clearly show only the same simple construction. We remember, for example, the bow appearing on the Egyptian palette, in which we recognized straight bows[344]. A straight bow of exactly the same type occurs on a carnelian from Crete[345] (fig. 44). As there, the bow here is exceptionally large and only slightly curved towards the ends. A female figure, apparently a goddess related to the Greek Artemis, strings it on to shoot an arrow[346]. It is worth noting at this point that this type of bow was placed in the hands of Artemis throughout antiquity.

On monuments of the historical era, Apollo is always depicted with a simple bow, which is noteworthy because on Cretan coins, also from the historical period, Heracles wears a completely different bow, namely a compound one, but not one composed of two horns, but one of a much more artificial nature,

---

Terrakotta aus Präsos (abgebildet Journ. Amer. Archeol. Bd. V, fig. 25, p. 392. is supported by E. Forster, Annual British School, Bd. VIII, p. 281, misinterpreted as an archer. He is a kneeling warrior with a helmet on his head, a shield in his left hand, and a sword in his right.

[344] A. J. Reinach, who used to see straight arcs on pallets, now changed his mind, believing that they were composite; leek. Le disque de Phaistos, in Revue bow. Bd. XV (1910), p. 36, Anm. 2.

[345] See A. Furtwängler, Antike Gemmen, Bd. I, Taf. II, n. 24. Perrot et Chipiez, a. a. O. Bd. VI, p. 843, fig. 426, n. 11. A. Furtwängler und G. Loeschcke, Mykenische Vasen, p. 77, Taf. E, 36. Tsountas and Manatt, The mycenaean age, London 1897, p. 298, fig. 153.

[346] The goddess does not wear a quiver on her back, Furtwängler-Loeschcke, Mykenische Vasen, p. 77, but a kind of fringed handkerchief, one end of which is visible to the back, while the other in front, falling between the legs, touches the ground. See L. A. Milani, Studi e materiali, Firenze (1899-1901), Bd. I, p. 193.

62

Fig. 44

Milani, Studi e Materiali, Bd. I, S. 193, fig. 24

made of various materials. The shape of the weapon indicates that it is a composite bow; which is very similar to the Greek sigma[347]. The fact that Heracles wields a different type of weapon characterizes him specifically as a god who emigrated to Crete and generally to Greece from elsewhere. In Greek monuments other than those from Crete, Heracles, unlike Apollo, wields almost exclusively a composite bow, which indicates his Asian origin[348], since, as we have seen, almost all Asian peoples use this type of bow.

Other sculptures also prove that the simple type of bow dominated in the Cretan-Mycenaean era. The archer carries a simple weapon on a well-known dagger blade from the fourth Mycenaean grave on the shaft[349], and the archers also wield straight bows on a silver chalice from the same grave on the shaft[350].

---

[347] J. N. Svoronos, Numismatique de la Crète anc. Taf. XXIII, 6, 13, 17-18; Taf. XXIV, 1-3, 6-7, 12-15, 23; Taf. XXVII, 1-10; Taf XXVIII, 7.

[348] See v. Wilamowitz, Euripides, Herakles, Bd. I2, p. 19 ff. L. A. Milani, Studi e materiali, Bd. I, p. 22.

[349] Perrot et Chipiez, a. a. O. Bd. VI, Taf XVIII. Tsountas and Manatt, a. a. O. p. 200 f., fig. 89. W. Reichel, Homerische Waffen, fig. 1. Springer- Michaelis, Kunstgeschichte, Bd. I9, Taf. V, 2 b.

[350] Tsountas and Manatt, a. a. O. p. 213, fig. 95. Perrot et Chipiez, a. a. O. Bd. VI, p. 774, fig. 365. W. Reichel, a. a. O. p. 13, fig. 17. Τσούντας, in Ἐφημ ἀρχαιολ. 1891, Taf. II, n. 2. Luigi Pernier, Un singolare monumento della scrittura pittografa Cretese, in Rendiconti d. R. Accad. d. Lincei, 1908, p. 642-651. Derselbe, II disco di Phaestos, Ausonia III. (Roma 1909), p. 255-302, Taf. IX-XIII. Al. Della Seta, II disco di Phaistos, Rendiconti d. R. Accad. d. Lincei, 1909, p. 297-367, mit 4 Taf. Ed. Meyer, Der Diskus von Phästos und die Philister auf Kreta, in Sitzungsberichte der Königlichen Preußischen Akademie der Wissenschaften, 1909, p. 1022-1029. A. J. Reinach, Le disque de Phaistos, in Revue bow. Bd. XV (1910), p. 1-65.

Fig. 46

Monumenti antichi, Bd. VII, Fig. 38a

We also have a monument depicting a completely different bow. This is an arc on the disk from Phästos[351] (Fig. 45). It consists of two corners connected in the middle by a rod[352] and is equipped with a string. Was this a bow often used in Crete, or does the depiction on the disk date back to a foreign model? The material for this bow – horns – was undoubtedly available to the Cretans, as there were many animals in Crete, as can be seen in numerous images on gems and stones[353]. But the fact that in all other arcs of the Cretan-Mycenaean era, as well as in the Cretan period until the last historical period, we can only recognize simple systems, forces us to recognize in this case a model alien to the Cretans[354]. As is well known, scientists' opinions on the origin of the disk vary greatly. A. J. Evans found ibex horns, or rather pasenga, depicted on

A. Mosso, The dawn of mediterr. civilisation, p. 22 ff., fig. 5 und 6. A. J. Evans, Scripta Minoa, Oxford 1909, Bd. I, p. 22-38, 273-293.

[351] Luigi Pernier, Un singolare monumento della scrittura pittografa Cretese, in Rendiconti d. R. Accad. d. Lincei, 1908, p. 642-651. Derselbe, Il disco di Phaestos, Ausonia III. (Roma 1909), p. 255-302, Taf. IX-XIII. Al. Della Seta, Il disco di Phaistos, Rendiconti d. R. Accad. d. Lincei, 1909, p. 297-367, mit 4 Taf. Ed. Meyer, Der Diskus von Phästos und die Philister auf Kreta, in Sitzungsberichte der Königlichen Preußischen Akademie der Wissenschaften, 1909, p. 1022-1029. A. J. Reinach, Le disque de Phaistos, in Revue bow. Bd. XV (1910), p. 1-65. A. Mosso, The dawn of mediterr. civilisation, p. 22 ff., fig. 5 und 6. A. J. Evans, Scripta Minoa, Oxford 1909, Bd. I, p. 22-38, 273-293.

[352] L. Pernier, Ausonia III, p. 290: »un arco concavo-convesso di tipo. scitico«. A. J. Reinach, a. a. O. in Revue bow. Bd. XV (1910), p. 35: »il est exactement composé comme celui du Lycien Pandaros«.

[353] See Annual British School, Bd. IX, Taf. III.

[354] A. J. Reinach, a. a. O. in Revue bow. Bd. XV (1910), p. 35-36.

64

Fig. 47

Ausonia, Bd. III, Fig. p. 283

many tablets unearthed in Knossos[355] and believes that these signs may indicate the use of a horn bow. As an example, he gives a long-known bronze tablet from Crete, which in our opinion shows only a simple bow[356]. We see two hunters, one of whom is carrying on his shoulders a killed Cretan paseng (a bezoar goat „αγρίμι"), the other is holding a bow in his left hand and at the same time the horn of the killed animal, which makes the difference between the horn and the material from which the bow is made stand out, become even clearer. Even on monuments from the historical period in Crete, we only have simple bows (except for coins with Heracles). Without a doubt, a simple bow is depicted on a stela from Elyros[357] and on another, very similar one[358] (Fig. 46), whose origin is uncertain (Knossos?)[359].

Additionally, you should pay attention to another symbol appearing on the disk – a closed, gloved hand (Fig. 47). Gloves may have been used by boxers in Crete, and indeed they were[360], but the ones depicted on the disc can be interpreted differently, namely as protection against the bowstring when drawing. It is impossible to say whether this use was common in Crete, but it was certainly attested among Asiatic peoples[361], and was always common with composite bows, which were so difficult to draw that the string easily injured the hand.

---

[355] A. J. Evans, Annual British School, Bd. X, p. 58-59, fig. 21b, c.

[356] See A. Milchhoefer, Bronzi arcaici di Creta, in Annali dell Istituto, 1880, p. 213 ff, Tav. d' agg. T. Also A. Milchhoefer, Anfänge der Kunst in Griechenland, Leipzig 1883, p. 168-169, fig. 65.

[357] T. Halbherr, Iscrizioni cretesi, in Museo italiano, Bd. III, p. 747-748.

[358] L. Mariani, Antichità Cretesi, Monumenti antichi, Bd. VI, p. 194-195, fig. 38. Both shown in O. Benndorf, Stele im Museum von Kandia, Jahreshefte d. öst. bow. Inst., Bd. VI, p. 2-3, fig. 2-3.

[359] See also L. Savignoni, Esplorazione archeologica, Monumenti antichi, Bd. χι, p. 301-302, fig. 9; vgl. Taf. XXVI, n. 3.

[360] See R. Burrows, Discoveries in Creta, London 1907, Taf. I. A. Mosso, Escursioni nel Mediterraneo e gli scavi di Creta, Milano 1907, fig. 89, 149.

[361] v. Luschan, a. a. O. in Festschrift für O. Benndorf, p. 195 f. See A. J. Reinach, a. a. O. in Revue bow. Bd. XV (1910), p. 5, Anm. 1.

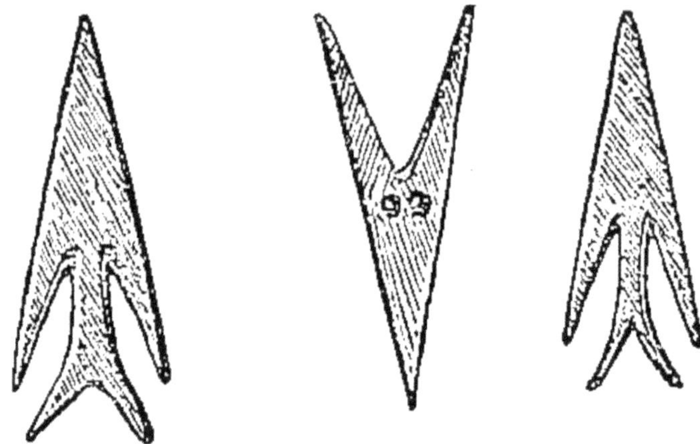

Fig. 48

A. J. Evans, The prehistoric tombs at Knossos, fig. 28

Unfortunately, the previously known Cretan-Mycenaean monuments do not allow for a more detailed examination of the tensioning methods. In ancient times, the tension was weak because the string only reached the elbow. In later historical times, the tension was extremely strong, but it is significant that the bow is not drawn to the ear, as in Egypt, but to the chest[362].

Drawing a Cretan-Mycenaean bow did not require much force, because the straight wood offered little resistance to the archer drawing the string. Perhaps some coins from Kydonia[363] can serve as visual evidence of this process. The archer rests one end of the bow on his right thigh, while holding the flexible wood with his left hand and trying to attach the string to the other end of the bow with his right hand[364]. You may also notice a slight deviation from the method just described. It was customary to hold the bow between the thighs while maintaining the same manipulation with the hands[365].

There are no depictions of arrows on the oldest monuments of Cretan-Mycenaean culture. They were certainly no different from those of other peoples, and were always provided with a notch at the lowest end and plumage just above[366].

---

[362] See Schol. ad. II. VIII, 328.

[363] J. N. Svoronos, Numismatique de la Crète, Bd. I, 5, 99.

[364] J. N. Svoronos, Numismatique de la Crète, Taf. IX, n. 2, n. 8.

[365] Derselbe, Numismatique de la Crète, Taf. IX, n. 3-5, 15-16, 18.

[366] A. J. Evans found two bone remains of lower arrow shafts at Knossos, but they are apparently only votive arrows. He wrote: „The two bone relics are very interesting. They depict the notched end and darts of the arrow, a notched decoration of the shaft with a red inlay. Both specimens are smooth below, with rivet holes that indicate the former existence of a central metal plate. The lower ends of these objects are sawn off and have probably been applied to a metal shaft, attached to a metal plate between two pieces of bone, or forming a single piece. Such an arrow could not have served any practical use, and therefore the relic can be considered votive in nature." Annual British School, Bd. IX, p. 61-62, fig. 405 see also Bd. X, p. 3.

Arrowheads are known in quite large numbers[367]. Stone points mostly resemble those discovered by Schliemann in Mycenae[368]. The brown ones show two types, one with a small handle to attach to the radius, the other without it. It was attached to the shaft of an arrow with a notch forming a barb[369] (Fig. 48). It is quite strange that the tubular arrowheads that were so common later in the Cretan-Mycenaean area are not yet known[370].

Quivers have not been known to us since ancient times. Only later Cretan monuments show us those described in detail by O. Benndorf in his description of the stele in the Kandia Museum. The quiver „is tied twice and ends with a funnel at the top because of the arrow feathers. The lid is formed by a leather flap that is pulled tight and fits over the end of the funnel, covering and overlapping the upper transverse rim. This is almost only indicated by the three-dimensional internal contour, which I initially considered to be a crack and was certainly also colored, while the only thing that can be said about the strip is that it was painted[371].

It is impossible to determine whether the exact same quiver was used in earlier times, nor can it be determined when quivers were even known. It's strange that we can't find them anywhere on Cretan-Mycenaean monuments.

Archers in the Cretan-Mycenaean era did not use shields like the Egyptians, instead shooting exposed.

Some depictions show that shooting arrows from chariots was already known at that time, such as the famous gold ring from the fourth shaft grave in Mycenae[372]. It is impossible to decide whether this type of fighting was common or only slightly widespread.

---

[367] Arrowheads are also often found on later Cretan coins. See J. N. Svoronos, Numismatique de la Crète, Taf. I, 21-23; Taf. IV, 16 18, 20; Taf. V, 22; Taf. VI, 6; Taf. XII, 9-10; Taf. XVIII, 7-9; Taf. XXI, 1-3. See Annual British School, Bd. XI, p. 1-2.

[368] A. J. Evans, Annual British School, Bd. VII, p. 44.

[369] A. J. Evans, Annual British School, Bd. X, p. 61. L. Savignoni, Monumenti antichi, Bd. XIV, p. 536-573, fig. 21. A. J. Evans, The prehistoric tombs of Knossos, London 1906, p. 32, fig. 28. Tsountas and Manatt, a. a. O. p. 206, fig. 92, 93.

[370] W. Reichel, a. a. O. p. 115, Anm. 1.

[371] O. Benndorf, Jahreshefte d. öst. bow. Inst., Bd. VI, p. 2-3, Anm. 6, 7.

[372] See A. Furtwängler, Antike Gemmen, Bd. I, Taf. II, n. 8. W. Reichel, a. a. O. p. 92, fig. 35. Perrot et Chipiez, a. a. O. Bd. VI, p. 839, fig. 420.

II. Greek bows

Among the Egyptians, Assyrians, Persians, Scythians, etc., we considered the bow to be the most important offensive weapon in the entire history of these peoples[373]. And today the bow is still used as a weapon of war not only in all those areas of Africa, Asia and Eastern Europe where modern civilization has not spread firearms, but it is also used in hunting where modern firearms are known due to its noiselessness. In Greece, the bow had little importance in historical times, but here, according to mythical accounts, it is considered the oldest weapon and appeared in the hands of many gods and heroes[374]. It is the feared weapon of Apollo[375] and his sister Artemis[376]. The heroes invoke him, the god of long-distance shooting, before shooting, for example: Odysseus[377], Pandaros before shooting Menelaus[378], Meriones before a shooting competition[379]; he gives gifts to warriors loyal to him[380], punishes and kills those who dared to compete with him in archery[381] or who did not ask him for help before shooting[382]. Strong men who die suddenly[383], as well as those who are elderly[384], are subject to his shots. Taking revenge, he killed Greeks with arrows for insulting his priest Chryses[385], as well as the sons of Niobe[386]. If someone could not commit violence against another, he used to wish his oppo-

---

[373] See M. Duncker, a. a. O. Bd. I4, p. 146.

[374] We hear of skilled archers in pre-Homeric times. Just as Philoctetes inherited the bow from Heracles, so Ulysses received it from Eurytus of the Oechalians, who considered himself such a skilled archer that he even challenged Apollo to a duel (Od. VIII, 226-228). It is also important that it is the bow that knocks down Troy. Paris kills with an arrow from a bow the greatest of the Homeric heroes who fought at Troy. It can also be said that the bow plays a decisive role in the Odyssey, since τόξοο αεθλον gives rise to the killing of Penelope's suitors. See about it M. Jähns, a. a. O. p. 307, i L. Grasberger, a. a. O. Bd. III, p. 152; O. Schräder, Sprachvergleichung und Urgeschichte, Bd, II, p. 105; vgl. noch Il. XI, 85; XV, 313; XVI, 359 u. v. a.

[375] See jego określenia odnoszące się do łuku, takie jak: ἀργυρότοξος Il, II, 766; V, 449; Od. VII, 64; XVII, 251. ἑκάεργος Il. I, 147; XXI, 478; Od. VIII, 323. ἑκατηβόλος Il. XVII, 333; Od. VIII, 339. ἑκηβόλος Il. I, 2i; XVI, 513. κλοτότοξος Il. IV, 101, 119; Od. XXI, 267.

[376] ἰοχέαιρα Il. V, 53 5 Od. XI, 198. τοξοφόρος ll. XXI, 483 χρυσηλάκατος Il. XVI, 183; Od. IV, 122.

[377] Od. XXII, 7.

[378] Il. IV, 119-120.

[379] Il. XXIII, 872.

[380] Pandaros, Il. II, 827; Teukros, Il. XV, 441; Iphitos, Od. XXI, 38.

[381] He kills Eurytus because he dared to challenge him to a duel with a bow. Od. VIII, 224-228. See noch Apoll. II, 4, 9-11; VI, 6, 2, 3. Paus. IV, 27, 4.

[382] Teukros, Il. XXIII, 863 f.

[383] Il. XXIV, 759; Od. III, 280; VII, 64.

[384] Od. XV, 409 fr.

[385] Il. I, 43.

[386] Il. XXIV, 599-620.

nent death by Apollo's arrows[387]. Similarly, his sister Artemis is a master of the bow who, like Apollo, either rewards with a bow or kills with arrows[388]. Achilles wishes Briseis[389] Artemis's arrows, as does Penelope[390].

When, after the first festival of the Olympians, the gods showed their favor with gifts to Heracles, the greatest hero, Apollo gave him his bow and taught him the art of shooting[391]. Later, Heracles himself rivals Apollo[392], and even turns his bow against Hera and Hades[393], whom he wounds with arrows. Idas of Messenia raises his bow against Apollo when the god steals Marpessa from him[394]. Without the bow of Philoctetes, Troy could not be conquered[395].

However, the Greeks in historical times almost never used the bow as their main weapon of war. It was similar in the Homeric-heroic era, according to Wilamowitz[396], because even in Homer the bow is not one of the necessary main weapons of a warrior[397]; sometimes he is even ridiculed[398]. The skillful use of the bow is by no means attributed to Paris and Pandaros; rather, there was a belief that heroes should stand face to face, chest to chest, and that only a coward would hide from his opponent and try to kill him from a distance[399] Il. XI, 385-387:

τοξότα, λωβητήρ, κέραι ἀγλαέ, παρθενοπῖπα,
εἰ μὲν δὴ ἀντίβιον σὸν τεύχεσι πειρηθείης,
οὐκ ἄν τοι χραίσμῃσι βιὸς καὶ ταρφέες ἰοί.

But this disregard for the bow is not universal: the Locrians march on Troy with great confidence in their bows, Il. XIII, 716-717[400]:

ἀλλ' ἄρα τόξοισιν καὶ εὐστρόφῳ οἰὸς ἀώτῳ
Ἴλιον εἰς ἅμ' ἕποντο πεποιθότες . . . .

---

[387] Od. XVII, 251, 494.

[388] Artemis teaches archery to the hunter Scamandrios. 11. V, 49 f. The goddess killed with the arrows appears Il. VI, 428; XXIV, 606; Od. XV, 4, 10, 478.

[389] Il. XIX, 59.

[390] Od. XX, 6 f., 80.

[391] Diodor, IV, 14, 3. See J. H. Krause, Die Gymnastik und Agonistik der Hellenen, Leipzig 1841, Bd. I, p. 600.

[392] Od. VIII, 234.

[393] Il. V, 392-397.

[394] Il. IX, 558 f.

[395] Philoctetes received a bow and arrows from Heracles. See Roscher about it Mythologisches Lexikon, Bd. III, p. 2311 f.

[396] v. Wilamowitz, Euripides, Herakles, I2, p. 44.

[397] O. Schrader, Sprachvergleichung und Urgeschichte, Bd. II, p. 105. O. Lippelt, Die griechischen Leichtbewaffneten bis auf Alexander den Großen, Weida in Th. 1910, p. 19.

[398] A. Lang, Homer and his age, New York and Bombay 1906, p. 105. M. Jähns, a. a. O. p. 307. Ameis-Hentze, Ilias, Anmerkung. Il. XI, 385. A. Schaumberg, a. a. O. p. 82.

[399] See L. Grasberger, a. a. O. Bd, III, p. 150. J. H. Krause, a. a. O. Bd. I, p. 599. A. J. Reinach, a. a. O., in. L'Anthropologie, Bd. XX (1909), p. 70. A. Lang, a. a. O. p. 137.

[400] Hesiod. Ἀσπίς Ἡρακλέους V. 25, bezeichnet die Lokrer als Schwerbewaffnete ἀγχέμαχοι see Paus. I, 23, 4, he writes: »Λοκρούς γάρ τούς Ὀπουντίους οπλιτεύοντας ἤδη κατά τά Μηδικά ἴσμεν (vgl. Herodot. VII, 203), οδς Ὅμηρος ἐποίησεν ὡς φερόμενοι τόξα καί σφενδόνας ἐς Ἴλον ελθοιεν.«

Heracles, the Greek national hero, resides underground armed with a bow, Od. XI, 607:

γυμνὸν τόξον ἔχων καὶ ἐπὶ νευρῆφιν ὀιστόν.

W. Ridgeway wrongly claims[401] that none of the Achaeans used bows in battle; for when Hector wanted to announce the duel between Menelaus and Paris, the Achaeans met him with bows[402], Il. III, 79:

τώ δ' ἐπετοξάζοντο κάρη κομόωντες Αχαιοί ....

Odysseus mentions Achaean archery twice: Od. VIII, 217-218:

. . . . εἰ καὶ μάλα πολλοὶ ἑταῖροι
ἄγχι παρασταῖεν καὶ τοξαζοίατο φωτῶν.

and immediately after 219-220:

οἷος δή με Φιλοκτήτης ἀπεκαίνυτο τόξῳ
δήμῳ ἔνι Τρώων, ὅτε τοξαζοίμεθ' 'Αχαιοί.

The Greeks who sailed against Troy in seven ships under the command of Philoctetes were all archers, Il, 716 et seq.[403] There is no need to explicitly mention such archers as Philoctetes himself, Teucros, Diomedes, Meriones and Odysseus[404].

In historical times, the bow, replaced by the spear and sword among other Greeks, almost completely faded into the background. He was particularly despised by the Athenians, for whom τοξότης sounded even more contemptuous because police soldiers, mainly Scythian slaves, had the same name[405]. The spear became a specific Greek weapon[406], „the wars for freedom appeared to people as a victory of the Hellenic spear over Asian arrows" – writes V. Wilamowitz[407]. While in heroic legend and Homeric poems gods and some heroes still appear as τοξόται, the authors of the tragedy emphasize the disregard for this type of weapon in the heroic period. Aias expresses itself in this sense about the archer Teucus V. 1120:

ὁ τοξότης ἔοικεν οὐ σμικρὸν φρονεῖν.

<hr>

[401] W. Ridgeway; The early age of Greece, Cambridge 1901, Bd. I, p. 301.

[402] See A. Lang, a. a. O. p. 136.

[403] See A. J. Reinach, a. a. O., in L'Anthropologie, Bd. XX, p. 70 f. Il. II, 716-720: οἳ δ' ἄρα Μηθώνην καί Θαυμακίην ἐνέμοντο / καί Μελίβοιαν εχον καί 'Ολιξώνα τρηχείαν, / των δέ Φιλοκτήτης ἦρχε, τόξων ευ ε'ιδώς / επτά νέων ἐρέται δ' ἐν ἑκάστη πεντήκοντά / ἐμβέβασαν, τόξων εὐ εἰδότες ἴφι μάχεσθαι.

[404] Il. X, 260: Odysseus wields a bow and quiver; Il. XIII, 650: Μηριόνης δ' ἀπιόντος ἵει χαλκήρε' διστόν .... κτλ. The archers on the Trojan side were: Pandaros, Il. II, 827; IV, 105 ff; V, 171 f.; Paris, Il. III, 17; XI, 370, 505, 581 usw.; Helenos, Il. XIII, 582-583; Dolon, X, 533 ff., see also Od. XVIII, 262 (Τρώας ... ροτηρας διατών); Il. II, 848 (Παίονες ἀγκυλότοξοι) i X, 428.

[405] G. F. Schümann, Griechische Altertümer, Berlin 1897, IV. Aufl., Bd. I, p. 370, und A. Böckh, Die Staatshaushaltung der Athener, Berlin 1886, III. Aufl., p. 262 ff. St. Waszyński, De servis Atheniensium publicis, Berolini 1898, p. 25 ff.

[406] H. Delbrück, Geschichte der Kriegskunst, Berlin 1900, Bd. I, p. 37.

[407] V. Wilamowitz, a.a. O. I2, p. 139 f. Aischyl. Persai, 86-87 ἐπάγει δόυρικλύτοις ἀνδράσι τοξόδαμνον ῏Αρη. See też V. 150-152, 242-243 (ed. Wecklein); Herodot V, 97.

70

Euripides expressed this disregard much more strongly in Heracles, where Lycus says about the hero 159-162[408]:

ὃς οὔποτ' ἀσπίδ' ἔσχε πρὸς λαιᾷ χειρὶ
οὐδ' ἦλθε λόγχης ἐγγύς, ἀλλὰ τόξ' ἔχων
κάκιστον ὅπλον, τῇ φυγῇ πρόχειρος ἦν.
ἀνδρὸς δ' ἔλεγχος οὐχὶ τόξ' εὐψυχίας.

It is true that this weapon is defended by Amphitryon, who a few lines later in the same drama speaks of the bow, V. 195-201:

ὅσοι δὲ τόξοις χεῖρ' ἔχουσιν εὔστοχον,
ἓν μὲν τὸ λῷστον, μυρίους οἰστοὺς ἀφείς,
ἄλλοις τὸ σῶμα ῥύεται μὴ κατθανεῖν,
ἑκὰς δ' ἀφεστὼς πολεμίους ἀμύνεται
τυφλοῖς ὁρῶντας οὐτάσας τοξεύμασι,
τὸ σῶμα τ' οὐ δίδωσι τοῖς ἐναντίοις,
ἐν εὐφυλάκτῳ δ' ἐστί· . . . . κτλ.

It is certain, however, that the bow in general lost much of its reputation at that time[409]. Of course, it never completely disappeared. During the Persian Wars[410] and throughout antiquity it was in constant use among lighter troops[411].

It is also natural that it remained especially common among the Greeks living on the eastern periphery of the Greek world, on the shores of the Black Sea and in western Asia Minor[412], as well as among the Greeks in Magna Graecia and Sicily[413], who have always had strong ties with archery. As ancient military tactics[414] developed, the bow came back into use with increasing frequency, but it was apparently only used by mercenaries[415]. So, for example, at the beginning of the Peloponnesian War, Pericius in his speech mentions the Athenian army and also mentions 1,600 archers[416]. There is no room here to question whether this number is correct or not[417], but in any case it is a positive

---

[408] See von Wilamowitz's remarks on this passage a. a. O. II2, p. 43 and 44, as well as the rather peculiar statement of Philostratus, Heroic. II, 3, p. 676 (ed. Kays er): τό μέν γάρ τοξεύειν δειλῶν ἡγεῖται, τό δέ παλαίειν ἀργῶν.

[409] v. Wilamowitz, a. a. O. II2, p. 52 Of the defense of Amphitryon it is said that „it is not necessary to prove how feeble is the sophistical argument in all its parts".

[410] At Plataea 300 Athenian archers fought very bravely, cf. Herodotus IX, 22; Simonides wrote an epigram in their honor, Anthol. Palat. VI, 2. See O. Lippelt, a. a. O. p. 36 ff.

[411] O. Lipp.elt, a. a. O. passim.

[412] G. v. Kieseritzky und C. Watzinger, Griechische Grabreliefs aus Südrußland, Berlin 1909, Nr. 574, 575, 597, 600, 606 usw. E. Babelon, Monnaies grecques, Taf. VII, 3, 4; Taf. CLXXIV, 5, 10, 27, 32, 33. Daremberg et Saglio, Dictionnaire, fig. 477.

[413] Thuk. VI, 20, 4; 67, 2; 69, .2; Herodot VII, 158; T. Liv. XXVII, 38, u. v. a.

[414] On the cooperation of hoplites with light armed men, cf. H. Delbrück, a. a. O. Bd I, p. 28 f.; 123 ff. Xenoph. Kyrup. VI, 3, 25; Xenoph. Hellenik. II, 4, 33. After the experience of the Battle of Herodotus VI, 112), Athens returned to the use of archers, so that they also fought at Salamis. See St. Waszyński, a. a. O. p. 30, Anmerkung 23.

[415] Rüstow-Köchly, Geschichte des griechischen Kriegswesens, Aarau 1852, p. 128 ff. L. Grasberger, a. a. O. Bd. III, p. 155.

[416] Thuk. II, 13. 8: ἑ'ξακοσίοος δε καί χιλους τοξότας. H. Delbrück, a. a. O. Bd. I, p. 15.

[417] See H. Delbrück, a. a. O. Bd. III, p. 15 ff.

indication of the existence of this type of weapon[418]. Numerous art monuments provide us with further clear testimony. In some schools, special teachers taught young people archery. An inscription published by Hirschfeld gives more details about one such school on the island of Teos[419]. The inscription, a resolution of the Teos city council, reads, among other things: οπλομάχον δέ καί τόν διδάξοντα τοξεόειν καί άκοντίζειν μισ θο όθωσαν, δ τε παιδονδμος και δ γυμνασίαρχος έπ' άναφορά: τη προς τόν δήμ ον. We will return to this and similar messages later.

1. Homeric bow

Our discussion of the oldest Greek bow must naturally begin with Homer[420].

There are two heroes whose arcs Homer tells us about in more detail, Pandarus and Odysseus. We read about the latter's weapon that it was παλίντονον (Od. XX, 11; 59), μεγα (Od. XXI, 74), έόξοον (Od. XXI, 92) and that Odysseus looked at it carefully to see if the worms they didn't eat the horn while he was away, Od. XXI, 393-395:

> . . . . ὁ δ᾽ ἤδη τόξον ἐνώμα
> πάντῇ ἀναστρωφῶν, πειρώμενος ἔνϑα καὶ ἔνϑα,
> μὴ κέρα ἶπες ἔδοιεν ἀποιχομένοιο ἄνακτος.

The bow of the second hero, Pandaros, II, is described in more detail. IV, 105-111:

> αὐτίκ᾽ ἐσύλα πόξον ἐύξοον ἰξάλου αἰγὸς
> ἀγρίου, ὅν ῥά ποτ᾽ αὐτὸς ὑπὸ στέρνοιο τυχήσας
> πέτρης ἐκβαίνοντα, δεδεγμένος ἐν προδοκῇσιν,
> βεβλήκει πρὸς στῆϑος, ὁ δ᾽ ὕπτιος ἔμπεσε πέτρῃ
> τοῦ κέρα ἐκ κεφαλῆς ἐκκαιδεκάδωρα πεφύκει
> καὶ τὰ μὲν ἀσκήσας κεραοξόος ἤραρε τέκτων,
> πᾶν δ᾽ εὖ λειήνας χρυσέην ἐπέϑηκε κορώνην.

This description shows that the horn was the most important part of both bows. First, however, it is necessary to decide which animal Homer calls αἶξ άγριος; does he mean ibex or pasenga? Based on current knowledge about the distribution of the Alpine ibex, it can be assumed that it was completely un-

---

[418] For more evidence, por. Atist. Ἀθην. πολ. (St. d. Athen.), 24, 3; Aisch. Pers. 460. (Salamis); Herodot IX, 22, 60 (Platäa); Thuk. II, 23, 2; III, 98, I; 107, I; IV, 28, 4; 129, 4; V, 52, 2; 84, I; VI, 22, I; 43, I; VII, 42/1; Plut. Them. 14; IG I, 54, 79; II, 1, 316; see 465, 467, 469, 470 i 471. A. Böckh, a. a. O. p. 326 ff., 331 ff.

[419] Hermes, IX, p. 501 ff. See also the inscription from Sestos, Hermes, VII, p. 116, line 64, where mention is made of the use of javelin throwing and archery: θέσεις άκοντισμοδ καί τοξείας and IG II, 2360.

[420] Nicht ohne Bedeutung ist Aristophanes' Aussage, Homer sei die beste Quelle für das Studium der Waffen, Ranae 1032-1036; see also Horaz. Epist. ad Pisones 73-74.

known in Greece[421]. On the other hand, the paseng, or wild goat (capra aegagrus), was certainly widespread on the Greek islands as well as in western Asia Minor[422], and scholars agree that only this animal can be included in Homer's work[423]. We read e.g.: Od. XVII, 294-295:

τὸν (Ἄργον) δὲ πάροιθεν ἀγίνεσκον νέοι ἄνδρες
αἶγας ἐπ' ἀγροτέρας ἠδὲ πρόκας ἠδὲ λαγωούς,

The young men led Odysseus' dog, Argos, to αίγας, which cannot in any way mean an ibex, because it only lives in the high mountains, not in Ithaca. And even if the epithets ὀρεσκωος (Od. IX, 155) and ἴξαλος (Il. IV, 105)[424] can be attributed to both the paseng and the ibex, since both are known to be good at climbing and jumping in high mountains, the trait may still be ιονθάς (bearded). Pasengi live like ibexes in the mountains, led by an old male who watches over them on a protruding rock while the herd grazes peacefully. Killing such a leader is one of the most difficult feats and when Homer emphasizes the happy encounter (τυχήσας) when he says that Pandaros struck a wild goat (ὑπὸ στέρνοιο) from below as it came down from a cliff (hunter, but in his location ἐν προδοκῆσιν was expected) , we believe this is a selected example of pasenga[425] guide. It is clearly emphasized that the force of the thrown arrow was so great that the paseng fell backwards onto the rock – ὁ δ' οπτιος εμπεσε πέτρη.

The horns of the captured paseng were used by the bow maker to make Pandaros' weapons[426] by joining them together (ηραρε). However, the Homeric description is still insufficient, since it lacks a more precise indication of how these pasenga horns were connected to each other. We must therefore first lead our investigation in this direction. There is now no doubt that the horns themselves had almost no elasticity, or rather that if they had been more curved, they would have broken on the inside, but would also have torn on the outside. But even if this extreme case did not occur, the horn itself could never completely return to its previous position. The necessary flexibility of the bow, which was παλίντονον, should therefore be provided not only in the corners, but also in the binding material. And one should be surprised that this Homeric description caused so many different opinions about the type and type of the

---

[421] O. Keller, Tiere des klassischen Altertums, Innsbruck 1887, p. 37. St. Fellner, Der homerische Bogen, Zeitschrift für österreichische Gymnasien, Bd. XLVI (1895), p. 199. O. Keller, Die antike Tierwelt, Leipzig 1909, Bd. I, p. 299. R. Johannes, De studio venandi apud Graecos et Romanos, Gottingae 1907, p. 5.

[422] O. Keller, Tiere des klassischen Altertums, p. 38: "Paseng (capra aegagrus) is an intermediate genus between the goat and the ibex, distinguished from the latter primarily by its irregularly serrated horns, compressed into a perky shape". See O. Keller, Die antike Tierwelt, p. 296 f. St. Fellner, a. a. O. p. 201. See Schliemann, Ilios, fig. 1883 a whorl with a very primitive depiction of Paseng.

[423] O. Keller, Tiere des klassischen Altertums, p. 40. St. Fellner, a. a. O. p. 201. v. Luschan, a. a. O. in Festschrift für Benndorf, p. 190. Ameis Hentze, zu Il. IV, 105, R. Johannes, De studio venandi, p. 21.

[424] See St. Fellner, a. a. O. p. 200. O. Keller, Tiere des klassischen Altertums, p. 40 f.

[425] See also Od. IX, 152-158 The hunt of Odysseus and his companions for αίγας ορεσκώους.

[426] Pollux, Onom. I, 137: τόξον καί (τά) του τόξου (μέρη), κέρας καί νευρά καί δ'ιστός. See Simmias, Anth. Palat. VI, 113 (ed. Dübner, Bd. I). Philostr. Imag. I, 10: τό μεν γάρ κεράς αίγός ιξάλου τζονητσ.ί φασι, χρήται ... ο τοξότης ἐς τά οίκεία. Oppianus, Halieut. Il, 54-55: εκ δέ κεράων / τόξά κυκλοτερή.

bow, especially since it is philologically quite clear and does not result in anything objectively impossible.

F. v. Luschan, omitting the Homeric description, explains the Pandaros bow as a composite bow („double bow"), which he considers to be the only one possible and Homeric in general. In his opinion, from a technical and ethnographic point of view, it is impossible to make a useful bow from these two corners of the pasenga. But then he writes: „Of course, you can put two such horns on one handle and, with great effort and using various tools, secure them in a really durable way – but no earthly being would ever be able to draw such a bow[427]."

However, from what follows it will become clear that there were people after all; who could not only draw such a horn bow, but also draw it. We do not know what exactly Luschan claims, but it should be noted that a warrior wielding this bow would have to draw it with a force of 500-1000 kg (Il. IV, 131 et seq.).

In subsequent interpretations, Luschans was followed by W. Reichel[428] and M. Jähns[429]. The former tried to adapt Homer's text to the double bow, translating Il, IV, 110-111 as follows: "After the horn-carver had worked them (the horns), he put them together (forming the bow), and when he had carefully finished the whole. After smoothing it, he placed a golden κορώνη on it. It is clear that Reichel's translation of the Homer passage in question is tenable, but in no way requires acceptance of Luschan's „double bow."

M. Jähns also believes that Luschan is right when he perceives the double bow as Homeric; the current interpretation of the Homeric description seems to him to be incorrect. M. Büchner[430] went even further. „The bow of Pandaros, which plays a role in Homer, deserves to be taken seriously and paid attention to." Recently, A. Schaumberg[431] has also been working on the Pandaros bow; in his opinion, the bow consisted of several flat layers of pasenga horns. As a modern analogy, he gives oriental bows, which consist of several layers of horn moldings[432]. It is obvious that all these modern bows which are cited as analogies to the bow of Pandaros cannot be reconciled with Homer's text at all.

Some translators of the Homeric fragment, incorrectly translating κορώνη, believed that the horns were connected by a metal joint[433]. But this is out of the

---

[427] F. v. Luschan, a. a. O. in Festschrift für Benndorf, p. 190; por. też Berliner philologische Wochenschrift, 1899, p. 411 f.; Jahrbuch d. deutsch. bow. Inst., Bd. XII (1899), Anzeiger, p. 12 f.; Zeitschrift für Ethnologie, Bd. XXXI (1899), Verhandlungen p. 228 ff.

[428] W. Reichel, a. a. O. p. 112 ff.

[429] M. Jähns, a. a. O. p. 286 f.

[430] M. Büchner, Das Bogenschießen der Ägineten, in Zeitschrift für Ethnologie, Bd. XL (1908), p. 856.

[431] A. Schaumberg, a. a. O. p. 71 ff.

[432] These bows are from Boeheim, Zeitschrift für historische Waffenkunde, Bd. I, p. 191 f. Schaumberg goes on to mention (p. 77) an Asian bow from the Munich ethnographic collection, „which apparently consists of several layers covered with tendon. Even its central element seems to be made of mass." It is not necessary to show how little this corresponds to the Homeric text.

[433] Rüstow-Köchly, Geschichte des griechischen Kriegswesens, p. 21. J. B. Friedreich, Die Realien in der Ilias und Odyssee, Erlangen 1851, p. 360. H. Draysen, Heerwesen und Kriegsführung der Griechen, Freiburg

74

question, because copper, bronze and iron are not suitable as binding materials and, moreover, they lack the necessary flexibility. One could only think of steel, but Homer was still unaware of the hardened steel needed for the bow[434].

It was Fellner who drew attention to the fact that Homer calls the bow maker τέκτων[435]. In this name, we believe, the answer to the question about the connecting material can be found; it was undoubtedly wood[436]. Homer always calls only the person who worked metal, regardless of the type of material being processed, χαλκεύς[437]. If Homer had named the bow maker χαλκεύς – the setting material plays a very important role in this type of folding bow – one might think of a metal setting. But Homer calls the bow maker κεραοξόος τέκτων. It follows that τέκτων, even if this name characterizes a craftsman who works with skill and a certain craftsmanship, in our case can only describe a class of workers who do not deal with metal. However, in a narrower sense, the word describes a carpenter[438]. In the second word of the employee's name – κεραοξόος – special emphasis is placed on his professional activity[439]. He makes bows by smoothing and scraping the corners, and then, as a skilled carpenter – τέκτων – connects them[440] to create a durable and useful bow. But Homer's text also gives other evidence in favor of the horn bow and the opposite double composite bow. When Odysseus picked up his favorite bow again after twenty years, he looked at it carefully to see if the worms had eaten its horns. XXI, 393-395. If Homer's bow was a „double bow", it would have to be completely covered with birch bark or animal fibers, and then Odysseus would not be able to see the bow in this way, because he would not see its elements at all[441]. But in Homer we find another argument against metal fittings and in favor of a wooden connection, because we read Od. XXI, 176-180 that after unsuccessful attempts by the suitors to draw the bow, Antinous ordered the shepherd Melahthios:

ἄγρει δή, πῦρ κῆον ἐνὶ μεγάροισι, Μελανθεῦ,
πὰρ δὲ τίθει δίφρον τε μέγαν καὶ κῶας ἐπ' αὐτοῦ
ἐκ δὲ στέατος ἔνεικε μέγαν τροχὸν ἔνδον ἐόντος,
ὄφρα νέοι θάλποντες, ἐπιχρίοντες ἀλοιφῇ,
τόξου πειρώμεσθα καὶ ἐκτελέωμεν ἄεθλον.

---

i. B. 1889, p. 19. Guhl und Koner, Leben der Griechen und Römer, Berlin 1893, VI. Aufl., p. 402. J. U. Faesi, VII. Aufl. ad Odyss. XXI, 179.

[434] St. Fellner, a. a. O. p. 202ff. H. Blümner, Technologie und Terminologie der Gewerbe und Künste, Leipzig 1887, p. 212 f. H. Helbig, Homer. Epos aus den Denkmälern erl. Leipzig 1887, II. Aufl., p. 105 O. Schrader, Real-Lexikon der indogermanischen Altertumskunde, Straßburg 1901, p. 795 f. P. Cauer, Grundfragen der Homer-Kritik, Leipzig 1909, II. Aufl., p. 257 f.

[435] St. Fellner, a. a. O. p. 202 ff.

[436] Diels, Jahrbuch d. deutsch. Inst., Bd. XIV (1889), Anzeiger, p. 12. Derselbe, Berliner philologische Wochenschrift, 1899, p. 411 f.

[437] H. Blümner, a. a. O. Bd. IV, p. 42 und 299. A. Riedenauer, Handwerk und Handwerker in den homerischen Zeiten, Erlangen 1873, p. 99 f.

[438] A. Riedenauer, a. a. O. p. 86 ff.

[439] Nonnius Panop. Dionys. III, 76. Simmias, Anth. Palat. VI, 113 (ed. Dübner, Bd. I). Oppianus, Halieut. II, 509-512. Pollux, Onom. VII, 156, calls the bow maker τοξοποιός.

[440] H. Blümner, a. a. O. Bd. II, p. 358.

[441] See what V. Luschan himself reports about ἴπες. See also W. Reichel, a. a. O. p. 114.

Softening the horn with fire was a process known in ancient times[442], and since it is a horn bow, it is understandable that suitors used it. However, tallow cannot make horn or metal fittings softer and more flexible, but it can certainly act on the binding wood. Fellner, who correctly interpreted the word τέκτων, went too far by adopting a complete wooden bow with the horns at the ends only decorative[443]; so that the Homeric bow would simply be a simple wooden bow. It is obvious that this is a wrong approach and that the horns attached in this way do not have a beneficial effect on the flexibility of the weapon, its strength and resistance. And even if we cannot object to the technical possibility of such an bow, we must nevertheless note that this type of bow is not known anywhere, and that it cannot in any case be reconciled with the text of Homer.

It is said that the bow maker freed the horns from the bulges, smoothed them – τά μέν άσκήσας – then connected them with a wooden handle – κεραοξόος ηραρε τέκτων – and after polishing everything, i.e. both the horns and the central part – πανδ 'εύ λειήνας – to one he attached golden κορώνη to the end. Bow production is developing, so to speak, before our eyes.

There is even evidence of bows built in this way, according to Luschan[444] using „the horns of some Central African antelopes as well as Tibetan pantolopes." We are now also in the fortunate position of having discovered the remains of horn bows, made in the same manner as Homer describes, from a private grave at Abydos, which was located next to the tomb of Den Setui (1st Dynasty) (Fig. 2).

This find gives us answers to all controversial questions and solves all the mysteries of the Pandaros bow[445], and although it is regrettable that these bows have not been preserved in a completely good condition, they are quite sufficient to demonstrate that bows of this type actually existed in ancient times, described by Homer. Egyptian horn bows were made from oryx horns, while in Homeric Greece paseng horns were used.

This also confirms the assumption that the manufacturer's marking as τέκτων is a reference to the material from which the central part of the handle is made. It was a piece of wood tapering on both sides (handle), to which smooth, protuberant corners were attached. In Fig. 2 we see such a central element in the middle between the two corners. There remains one question that needs to be answered. Would it be possible that if the bow was drawn tighter, the horns would split at the ends or the binding wood to which the horns were attached would split. W. M. Flinders Petrie therefore correctly assumes that the bows were wrapped with string in the places most exposed to stress to prevent loosen-

---

[442] Paus. V 12, 2; see also H. Blümner, a. a. O. Bd. II, p. 358 See further Od. XXI, 245-246.

[443] St. Fellner, a. a. O. p. 205 ff.

[444] v. Luschan, a. a. O. in Festschrift für O. Benndorf, p. 191.

[445] Also, the opinion of Schwatlos, Homerisches und Mykenisches I (Der Kriegsbogen und sein Zubehör) in Wochenschrift für klassische Philologie, 1911, Nr. 47, 49 i 51, The fact that the Homeric poems do not have a two-part arc is therefore obsolete. We don't understand how you can make an bow out of a tubular horn. It is clear that Homer is only talking about a bow in which both horns were used.

ing. We believe that this assumption is also confirmed by Greek vase paintings, in which we sometimes find several lines on both sides of the bow next to the handle, which were supposed to indicate such a bond at the connection points[446].

When Pandaros's bow was ready, the bowmaker attached a golden κορώνη to it. It was a metal hook that was attached to the upper end of the bow. When someone wanted to shoot, the loose end of the string was attached to this κορώνη, which was made of gold, according to the value of the weapon[447]. This κορώνη was either a very simple hook[448] as in Homer, or had the shape of a bird's head[449] like the bows that later vase photos show us. However, it was not a metal fitting that was supposed to connect both corners[450]. The piece of jointing wood that also served as the handle of the bow and on which the arrow rested was called πῆχυς[451].

Il. XI 375, ὁ δὲ τόξου πῆχυν ἄνελκεν ...[452]

This πῆχυς is the same as the „rule" of Ammianus; which we talked about earlier when examining the Scythian bow.

The size of the Homeric bow still remains to be discussed. Those scholars who have recognized the composite bow – the „double bow" – as the Homeric bow believe that the horn plates were εκκαιδεκάδωρα[453]; but Homer does not say that they are horn plates, but only that the paseng had such large horns, which in our opinion only means that the killed animal was a magnificent specimen, but not that the bow maker made a bow from its horns[454]. It is certain that the length of the ancient Greek bow was about one meter[455].

---

[446] See Gerhard, A. V. Taf. 4, 78, 124, 190-191, 221-222.

[447] Eusth. ad Il. IV, 110 = (451 .8) εις ήν δηλαδή ένίεται ή νευρά. See Ebeling, Lex. Homeric, Bd. I, p. 868. W. Reichel, a. a. O. p. 114f. The word κδρώνη appears six times in Homer, Od. I, 441; VII, 90; xxi, 46, 138, 165; Il. IV, III, but only in the Iliad in the sense of a „hook" on the bow for fastening the bowstring, otherwise as a ring on the outside of the door; this should also be understood in the IP. XXI, 138, 165, where it is said: αὐτοῦδ' ὠκυ βέλος καλή προσέκλινε κορώνη; Denn Od. XXI, 136 it is clearly stated that Telemachus laid his bow on the ground τοξον θήκε χαμάξε so he could not rest the arrow on the κορώνη of the bow, but only on the door. See W. Reichel about this in detail, a. a. O. p. 115. Wenn A. Schaumberg, a. a. O. p. 69, If he writes that κορώνη is the upper corner of the bow, this is completely wrong as far as the Homeric text is concerned, since Homer clearly emphasizes the later addition of κορώνη. If, however, the bow did not have a metal hook, then the word κορουνη can only mean notches, which were sometimes made at the upper end for a stronger fixation of the bowstring, but never at the end of the entire upper bow, which is already excluded by Eustace's explanation of the word.

[448] Unfortunately, the material from which κορώνη is made is not marked with any color other than the bow on the vase paintings. See Gerhard, A. V, 28, 29, 61, 78, 144.

[449] See Robert, Sarkophagreliefs, III, p. 186, Nr. 1542 (Athen. Nationalmuseum).

[450] See the works mentioned above, p. 76, footnote 1, which speak of metal fittings.

[451] Eust, ad Od. XXI, 419 (1915, 35) pisze τςηχος, ή τοό τόξου λαβή. Ebeling, Lex. Hom. Bd. II, p. 125. E. Buchholz, a. a. O. Bd. II, Abt. I, p. 354.

[452] See also Il, XI, 58, 2-3.

[453] W. Reichel, a. a. O. p. 114, with a small error; instead of 0.984 it should be 1.184. See also A. Schaumberg, a. a. O. p. 75.

[454] Netölicka, Naturhistorisches aus Homer, Programm des k. k. Gymnasiums in Brünn 1855, explains the expression έκκοαδεκάδωρα in such a way that Piseng's horns have 14-16 transverse, round beads. Similarly, Ameis ad Il. IV, 105. This doesn't seem to be true, as bulges don't grow regularly at the corners. See St. Fellner, a. a. O. p. 201. E Buchholz, a. a. O. Bd. II, Abt. I, p. 354, Anm. 2.

[455] W. Reichel, a. a. O. p. 114.

The bowstring was made of cowhide[456], sometimes twisted several times, probably also braided and strengthened in this way[457]. The string was always firmly attached to one, lower end of the bow; it was usually attached to the upper end when someone wanted to shoot. The reason for not leaving the string permanently tied at both ends is primarily to maintain its full flexibility[458]. The free end of the string was attached to the bow either with an artificial knot[459] or with an eyelet. It seems not only likely, but necessary, that every shooter goes to war equipped with several spare strings.

To conclude these observations about the horn bow, we would like to answer the question of where this type of bow was probably invented. We found the horn bow in Egypt, in Palestine (the Haru bow) and in Scythia. Through Homer he seems to be attested to the Iliad. Since the pasenga horn was probably used everywhere in Asia Minor to make the horn bow, we can assume that the area of distribution of the horn bow was where the Pasengi lived, on the one hand in the Lydian-Phrygian-Mysian mountains, and in Lycia, that is, on the other in southern Asia Minor[460]. From Asia Minor, the bow may have come to Greece either through the Scythians or directly. It should be emphasized that the Egyptian horn bow was made of oryx horns, Haru's bow was made of Syrian ibex horns, and the Asia Minor bow was made of Paseng horns, so each country, or rather each nation, using the horns of this animal used what was available in its area. This is not to say that the horn bow was invented separately in each of these countries, but rather we believe that the horn bow was invented in one center and only spread from there. It seems most likely that this center is located in Asia Minor, perhaps in Lycia. It is impossible to name the inventors, but we will not be mistaken if we trace the invention of this type of bow back to the prehistoric population; through the relationships individuals had at the time.

2. The bow in artistic representations

Research to date has identified three types of bows. First we found a simple wooden bow, then a complex composite bow, and finally we believe we have proven that the Homeric description of the bow is based on fact, i.e. that the horn bow not only really existed, but was probably in common use in Homeric times. All three types of bows can be easily identified on Greek monuments, and when discussing individual forms of bows we will have the opportunity to

---

[456] Il. IV, 122 (νεύρα βόεса). See Eust. ad Il. IV, 122 (452, 31); ad Il. III, 336 (421, 20); ad Od. XVIII, 358 f. (1851, 33); ad Od. XXI, 419 (1915, 34). Roßhaar, Ovid. Ep. ex P. I, 2, 21; Verg. Aen. IX, 622. Kamelsehne, Arist. Hist. anim. V, 2 (Bd. I, p. 540 ed. Acad. R. Boruss.).

[457] See Mon. dell' Inst. V, Taf. 28.

[458] Herodot, II, 173.

[459] See Gerhard, A. V. 130, 264. Furtwängler-Reichhold, Griech. Vas. 21, 91.

[460] O. Keller, Tiere des klassischeil Altertums, p. 38-42.

pay attention to their technical side. However, it should be noted in advance that there are numerous representations of bows in ancient art, which not only do not allow for any distinction based on form, but rather raise doubts as to whether such bows were possible at all, whether they are not merely a product of the artist's imagination or whether they can be attribute them to his substantive ignorance. It therefore became necessary to limit our research only to unmistakable representations of bows.

a) Bows depicted on monuments in a geometric style

Unlike later monuments, those in the geometric style show an bow relatively rarely, and even where it appears, a more or less certain decision for one type or another is almost impossible. Nevertheless, certain distinguishing features can be found in the monuments, which allow us to divide all the useful material into three groups[461].

I. An bow in the form of a simple, one might say „Mycenaean" wooden bow, uniform along its entire length, curved in a semicircle, reaching slightly below the waist. The chord bond is not visible at either end:

Fragment of a vase from Argive Heraion[462] with three figures, of which only the lower part of the body has survived. The archer stands in the center, holding the bow in his hand bent at a sharp angle, ready to draw.

Fragment of a vase also from the Argive Heraion, depicting an archer releasing an arrow[463].

Fragment of a geometric vase from the Acropolis. The man preserved in fragments shoots left at the warrior[464].

II. An bow that is pulled in tightly in the center of the outer side, creating two bulges and at the same time two clearly defined arms. As with the previous group, the chord bond is not visible:

Fragment of a large crater in the Louvre. Among several warriors with swords and lances is an archer. He holds a double-curved bow in his left hand and an arrow in his right. The second warrior holds an object resembling

---

[461] See also A. Schaumberg, a. a. O. p. 92 f.

[462] J. C. Hoppin, The Vases and vases fragments, in Ch. Waldstein, The Argive Heraeum, Boston and New York 1905, Bd. II, Taf 57, Nr. 10.

[463] J. C. Hoppin, a. a. O. Bd. II, Taf. 57, Nr. 13. See also p. 113, where Hoppin points out the resemblance of these bows to images from the Mycenaean silver bowl and the dagger blade from the tomb of the fourth shaft.

[464] B. Graef, Die antiken Vasen von der Akropolis zu Athen, Berlin 1909, Bd. I, Heft I, Taf. 10, Nr, 291. See more similar bows on geometric bronze brooch by Thisbe, Jahrbuch d. deutsch. Inst., Bd. IX (1894), Anzeiger, p. 116, fig. 1; on a shard at Delphi, Perdrizet in Fouilles de Delphes, Bd. V, p. 138, Big. 538; the same bow is also found on an engraved bronze vase in geometric style from Georgia, Transcaucasia, Revue bow. Bd. XL (1902), p. 74, fig. 7.

Fig. 49

Archäologische Zeitung, 1885, Taf. VIII, Nr 1

a bow, which according to Helbig in the side view can be interpreted as a round shield rather than a bow[465].

Fragment of a vase, also in the Louvre. The front part of the ship with three warriors. One of them shoots arrows at the other. The arrow pierced the enemy's neck. The archer grabs the bow in the extended position[466].

Oinochoe in Copenhagen with a pirate fight and two archers, one of whom is on land, the other on the ship. The bow of a warrior standing on land (Fig. 49) has a straight line at the front, while in the part facing the archer there are two semicircles. Apparently we are dealing with an oversight on the artist's part. Even more incorrectly, the bow of the warrior standing on the ship is drawn incorrectly. It has two bulges, both on the side facing the warrior and on the side facing out, giving the bow the shape of an extended Arabic number 8[467] (Fig. 50). The third archer is depicted on the same vessel with a fragmentary bow in his hand. Like the one recently described, the bow probably also had two bulges on each side. Despite graphical errors, these bow forms should be assigned to the same group as the bows mentioned earlier because they have two curvatures.

---

[465] Perrot et Chipiez, a. a. O. Bd. VII, p. 182, fig. 67. E. Pottier, Vas. ant. du Louvre, Bd. I, p. 23, Taf. XX, A 519. W. Helbig, Jahreshefte d. öst. bow. Inst., Bd. XII (1909), p. 52, fig. 38 and p. 56.

[466] Cartault, Monuments Grecs, Bd. II (1882), p. 47, fig. 2. See E. Pottier, a. a. O. p. 24. A 528.

[467] Archäologische Zeitung. Bd. XLIII (1885). Taf. VIII, 1 und 1c. Perrot et Chipiez, a. a. O. Bd. VII, p. 179, fig. 62 and 63. Jahreshefte d. öst. bow. Inst., Bd. XII (1909), p. 55, fig. 40.

80

Fig. 50

Archäologische Zeitung, 1885, Taf. VIII, Nr 1

III. A bow with the ends bent towards the target, the string is strongly rounded so that it can be considered taut, at the ends of the bow the string runs parallel to the ends. The bow itself only reaches to the waist.

Late geometric bowl from Eleusis. Archers on both sides, between the holds. On one side, a gunner on a ship shooting arrows at a bird sitting at the end of the ship. The bow is slightly curved and its upper end is clearly bent towards the target[468]. On the other side of the ship, two archers appear to be shooting arrows at each other. Two men lie on the ground between them. The bow and the string are curved[469].

Bowl in the National Museum of Athens inventory no. 194. On the belly, between the handles, you can see seven running men, each holding a bow in his left hand[470].

These three groups correspond to the three species of bows that we have encountered so far. The first group corresponds to a simple wooden bow. Group II, whose bows have two bulges, can easily be associated with the horn bow. As for the third group, first of all it should be emphasized that it occurs only on vessels of the late geometric style. We would like to recognize it as a composite „double bow". If this assumption is correct, it would be important

---

[468] Ἐφημ. ἀρχαιολ. 1898, πίν. V, Nr. 1.

[469] Ἐφημ. ἀρχαιολ. 1898, πίν. V, Nr. 1a.

[470] See Collignon-Couve, Catalogue des vas. peints du musée national d'Athènes, Textband, p. 61 f., Nr. 241.

81

because it would show the appearance of the double bow in Greek land at the end of the Geometric Age.

ß) Bows depicted on sculptures in the archaic style

Monuments of the Archaic style already show a greater variety of arched shapes, including some that could hardly exist in reality. When working on the shapes of bows of the Geometric era, we have always dealt with representations of the same style, now we are dealing with monuments that not only belong to different artistic directions, but are also very distant from each other in terms of place of origin.

I. Straight, semicircular, with an even arc, usually reaching to the waist:

Proto-Corinthian Lekythos, Archäologische Zeitung, 1883, plates X, 1 and 2. Heracles shooting arrows at centaurs.

Fragment of the Proto-Corinthian lekite from Aegina, Athenische Mitteilungen, vol. XXII (1897), p. 304, Fig. 29.

Corinthian Aryhallos from Berlin, No. 2955, Jahrbuch d. deutsch. bow. Inst., Bd. I (1886), p. 146, Artemis bogenschießend[471].

II. A straight, semicircular bow, tapering sharply towards the ends, with curled corners at each end. Bow usually with wrapping.

Old Attic amphora with gigantomachia, Gerhard, A. V. 95-96.

Archaic Vulci bowl with Gigantomachia, Gerhard, A. V. 61 and 62.

Black-figure amphora from Paris, de Ridder, Cat. des Vas. peints, Bd. I, P. 133, Fig. 15. Heracles and Athena against Gerionus.

Fragment of an archaic bronze plate, Annali 1880, Tav. H, myth Eberjagd[472].

Carnelian scarab in Berlin, A. Furtwängler, Antike Gemmen, Bd. II, Taf. VII, No. 53. Heracles with bow and club[473].

III. The bow recedes in the middle to form two bulges, reaching only to the waist: Corinthian Alabastron of Samothrace, Athenische Mitteilungen, Bd. XXXIII (1908), P. 112, Fig. 32.

Amphora from Corneto, Antike Denkmäler, I, 22. Apollo and Artemis fire arrows at the Niobids.

Black-figure amphora, Gerhard, A. V. 105-106. Heracles fighting Geryon.

Black-figure bowl, Gerhard, A. V. 133, No. 1. Heracles is about to disembowel the Nemean lion he has just killed.

Black-figure amphora from Paris, de Ridder, Cat. des vas. peints, Bd. I, P. 147, Fig. 19. Heracles in the fight with the Nemean lion.

---

[471] See Etruskische Vase aus Cervetri, Gazette archéol. Bd. VII (1881/82), p. 200, Taf. 28 (Seegefecht). Gerhard, Etruskische Spiegel, Bd. I, Taf 87. See też A. Schaumberg, a. a. O. p. III.

[472] See also de Ridder, Catalogue de Bronzes de la Société bow. d'Athènes, Paris 1894, p. 138, Nr. 799.

[473] See Athenische Mitteilungen, Bd. XXVI (1901), fig. from p. 146. Bulletin corr. Hellén. Bd. XXII (1898), p. 463, fig. 8 und Taf. VI. Lenormant et de Witte, Élite céramograph. Bd. I, Taf. I. Monumenti Antichi, Bd. XVII, Taf. XXIII. O. Benndorf, Griechische und sizil. Vasenbilder, Taf. XII, 6. A. Furtwängler, Olympia, Bronzen, Taf. XXXVIII. Gerhard, Etruskische Spiegel, Bd. I, Taf. 77.

Fig. 51

Gerhard, Auserl. Väsenbilder, Taf. 70, Nr 4

Black-figure Lekythos, de Ridder, Cat. des vas. peints, Bd. I, P. 203, Fig. 34. Heracles with the centaur Pholös.

Black-figure amphora, Mönumenti äntichi, Bd. XVII, Taf. 40. Heracles and the Nemean Lion[474].

About the material or type of information from point III, it can be said that, as with the corresponding geometric group, almost nothing can be cut with complete certainty.

However, the fact that the bend is on the outside of the bow forces us to assume that we are dealing with horn bows.

IV. Bows in which both arches do not originate from one point, but from two places, where both arms of the horns are connected by a bridge (Fig. 51)[475], in them we undoubtedly see a horn bow. This bow shape is very closely related to the previous one, so much so that it can actually only be seen as a further development of the way the horn bow is represented. This is new evidence of the existence and form of the Homeric horn bow, which is of great importance to us due to its faithful reproduction of the weapon. If the form is relatively rare, the fault obviously lies only in the inaccuracy of the artists, whose drawings are sometimes so poor in this respect that we are unable to distinguish whether we are dealing with a horn bow or a Scythian sigma bow.

V. The most common form on monuments is called the S-shaped bow or the Scythian bow. This is a compound – a „double arc” – in the form of a mustache or the Greek sigma sign, as we see in Untersuchung des skytischen Bogens, pp. 54 et seq. (Fig. 52). This Scythian form was apparently unknown in

---

[474] See Gerhard, A. V. 43, 97, 193, 215, 246, 322. B. Graef, a. a. O. Bd. I, Taf. 25, Nr. 425. Archäologische Zeitung, 1846, Taf. XXXIX, 1, Olpe des Amasis. O. Benndorf, Griechische und sizil. Vasenbilder, Taf. LI, 2. A. Conze, Melische Tongefäße, Taf. IV (as far as it is visible).

[475] See Gerhard, A. V. 116, 135. Gerhard, Etruskische und kampanische Vasen, Taf. XV-XXVII, 1. H. B. Walters, Catalogue of the Bronzes in the Brit. Mus. Taf. XVIII.

Fig. 52

Archäologische Zeitung, 1881, Taf. XII, Nr. 1

the Geometric period. We thus have two different forms of the composite double bow, one that is limited to Late Geometric monuments and, among others, it corresponds in shape to the Old Babylonian[476] and Scythian bows, which together form a group and appear in Scythia and on monuments of Greek art, as well as in Etruscan representations of bows[477], clearly under Greek influence.

The so-called Corinthian vase Dodwell, Lau, Greek vases, plate III, 1b.

Amphora from the early Corinthian period Eurytios, Mon. dell' Inst. VI-VII, table 33.

Melian vase, A. Conze, Melische Tongefße, plate III.

Althion amphora with riding archers, Römische Mitteilungen, vol. II (1867), table IX.

Fragment from the Acropolis of unknown production, B. Graef, a. A. O. Plate 25, no. 465 a.

Black-figure pottery of the Acropolis, B. Graef, a. A. O. Table 31, No. 606.

Black-figured hydra in London, Jahrbuch d. deutsch. bow. Inst. Bd., VII (1892), p. 48.

Chalcidian vase, Furtwängler-Reichhold, Griech. Vas. Tap. 101.

Klitiasund Ergotimos vase, Furtwängler-Reichhold, Griech. Vas. Table 13[478].

---

[476] See the bow of King Naram-Sin, fig. 14.

[477] See np. Gerhard, Etruskische Spiegel, Taf. 80, 133, 160.

[478] See dalej Archäologische Zeitung, 1859, Taf. 125; 1878, Taf. X; 1881, Taf. XI. Έφημ. άρχαοολ. 1883, πίν. 3; 1885, πίν. 3. Römische Mitteilungen, Bd. IX (1894), p. 317, fig. 22 (Bronzerelief). Jahrbuch deutsch. Inst., Bd. IV (1889), Taf. 5, 6; Bd. XIII (1898), Taf. 1. Mon. dell' Inst. I, Taf. 51; VI, Taf. 30, 2, 3; IX, Taf. 55. Gerhard, A. V. 69, 70, 113, 114, 119-120; 190-191. M. N. Tod and A. J. Wace, Catalogue of the

γ) Bows depicted since the 5th century

Archaic art already shows a large number of bow forms, but in developed art we find an even richer variety. As art as a whole has progressed, so has the accuracy in faithfully reproducing detail, although sometimes we still encounter depictions of bows that leave us wondering whether such bow forms ever existed in reality or whether they are even possible. We distinguish the following groups of forms:

I. A straight bow, in the shape of a capital letter C, always thickened towards the center, with small hooks at the ends, usually curved outwards[479]. From this list we see that the simple bow shape is most often used by Apollo and Artemis. This statement is interesting because it makes the simple bow look like a real Greek bow, unlike the so-called Scythian arc. This is a form which, as we have already mentioned, is said to have been invented by Apollo.

II. An bow, roughly in the shape of a capital letter D; in fact, the bow is almost straight, only sharply curved inward at the ends (Figs. 53, 54). The bow, unknown to archaic art, retains its shape whether or not it is strung, as evidenced by the curvature of the arms. The ends were not caused by stringing, but rather because the actual bow must have already achieved this shape at the time of manufacture. However, we are unable to see the advantage of this form, which weakens the power of the shot rather than increases it, because the tension force, which would otherwise accumulate in the center next to the handle in other shapes, had to be distributed here between the inwardly curved ends[480].

III. The horn bow, which is shown much more often and more clearly than before in monuments of developed art. The arms of the horns protrude sharply from the connecting central beam[481]. Mention should also be made of the bows from the famous vase of Darius[482], which have a particularly strange shape.

Sparta Mus. Nr. 694, Bleifigürchen aus dem argivischen Heraion. A. Furtwängler, Antike Gemmen, Bd. I, Taf. VI, 35, 58; Taf. VII, 58; Taf. VIII, 36, 38. Collignon-Thraemer, Geschichte der griechischen Plastik, Bd. I, fig. 85, Relief vom Tempel von Assos, Herakles gegen die Kentauren. Jahreshefte d. öst. bow. Inst., VI (1903), p. 185, fig. 108.

[479] See Mon. dell' Inst I, Taf. 20 (Apollo und Idas); II, Taf. 23 (Apollo); X, Taf. 9 (Amazone); Taf. 28 (Herakles); XI, Taf. 33. Gerhard, A. V. 3-4 (Artemis); 28 (Artemis); 78 (Artemis); 165 (Amazone). Furtwängler-Reichhold, Griech. Vas. 112 (Artemis); 127 (Apollo). O. Benndorf, Griechische und sizil. Vasen, Taf 49, 4 (Artemis). Millin, Peintures de Vases, I, 20 (Eros); II, 77 (Artemis und Gefährtinnen). See Annual British School., Bd. III (1896/97), Taf. XIII, Archaistisches Relief in Konstantinopel (Artemis). Brunn-Bruckmann, Denkmäler, Taf. 60.

[480] See Mon. dell' Inst. I, Taf. 9 (Apollo); 23 (Apollo); III, Taf. 12 (Apollo); IX, Taf. 17 (Artemis); X, Taf. 20 (Apollo). See noch Furtwängler-Reichhold, Griech. Vas. Taf. 55 (Apollo); 96 (Apollo); 115 (Artemis). On the other hand, it is extremely rare to find this form in hands other than those of Apollo or Artemis. See Furtwängler-Reichhold, Griech. Vas. Taf. 58 (Amazone). Jour. Hell. Stud. Bd. XXIV (1904), Taf. VIII (Amazone). See Gerhard, A. V. 28, 78, 202 (Artemis). See also Artemis- Terrakotten von Kerkyra, Athenisches Nationalmuseum, Inv. Nr. 1115-1119, 1136. Brunn-Bruckmann, Denkmäler, Taf. 150.

[481] Mon. dell' Inst. I, Taf. 55; II, Taf. 11; V, Taf. 28 (Thronsessel des Apollo); VI, Taf. 21, 27 A. Heuzey-Daumet, Mission bow. en Macédoine, Taf. IV, 2. Roscher, Myth. Lex. I, p. 2157 (Silbermünze aus Metapont); p. 2204 (Heracles riding through Oceanus in a solar chariot). W. Amelung, Die Skulpturen, des Vatikanischen Museums, Bd. II, Taf. 10, Nr. 38. Furtwängler-Reichhold, Griech. Vas. Taf. 108.

[482] Furtwängler-Reichhold, Griech. Vas. Taf. 88.

Fig. 53

Monumenti dell' Instituto, XI, Taf. 40

According to v. Laschan, they show „an astonishing ignorance of the simplest laws of bow construction[483]". However, we believe that this is the result of the artist's efforts to faithfully reproduce everything in the „Persian" style, which results in some errors in the representation of the bow (see Fig. 79).

IV. The most common form is the Scythian sigma bow. It is almost no different from the same form depicted in archaic art, perhaps it has only lost some of its size. While archaic art depicts bows of this type as being slightly higher than waist-high, today they only reach waist-high. Representations of this form differ in various details, but the difference is not fundamental and is limited to the number of curves, different lengths of the arms and the shape the bow takes after drawing and stretching[484].

---

[483] v. Luschan, a. a. O. in Festschrift für O. Benndorf, p. 192.

[484] Furtwängler-Reichhold, Griech. Vas. Taf. 22, 47, 62, 74, 81, 90, 91, 96, 109, 110. Gerhard, A. V. 143, 144. Mon. dell' Inst. II, Taf. 49/50; V, Taf. 11; X, Taf. 53 (Odysseus gegen die Freier); XI, Taf. 28. Lenormant et de Witte, Élite céramogr. Bd. II, 56, 74. A. Furtwängler, Ant. Gemmen, Bd. I, Taf. IX, 20, 21, 23; Taf. XIV,

Fig. 54

W. Klein, Die griechischen Vasen mit Lieblingsinschriften, ryc. 27

There are a few more notes at the end. Some forms should be mentioned which would have no equivalent in ancient art[485]. So we have in Fig. 55 an bow that appears to consist of two parts that are not connected by a simple connector, but rather directly. It should be noted that the arms cannot be made from horn. It is impossible to guess what material the artist had in mind. Another form is shown in Fig. 56. Here the bow is completely straight, and at the ends it has two hooks – bends – which served to hold the string. The handle is unique – ττήχος – clearly standing out from the material of the bow. The bow appears to be made of metal and the handle is made of wood. It is impossible to decide whether this is possible and whether this type of bow was ever used in ancient Greece, in any case we have no other examples. Finally, we mention the bow of Heracles on a bas-relief from Thasos, which only came to us in a drawing by Christides[486]. The shape of this arc is probably incorrectly reproduced. The original probably depicted a simple sigma arc as depicted on Thasian coins[487].

7, 8, 10; Taf. XX, 47, 55 usw. Th. Homolle. Fouilles de Delphes, Bd. IV, Taf. 44-45. O. Benndorf, Gjölbaschi-Trysa, Taf. VII, XXIII, XXIV usw.

[485] Antike Denkmäler, II, Taf. 14.

[486] Studniczka, Jahreshefte öst. bow. Inst., Bd. VI (1903), p. 180, fig. 106-107.

[487] Derselbe, a. a. O. p. 185, fig. 108.

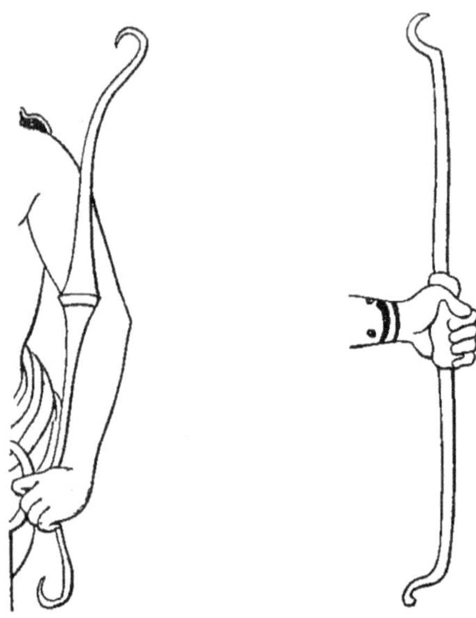

<table>
<tr><td align="center">Fig. 55</td><td align="center">Fig. 56</td></tr>
<tr><td align="center">Lenormant et de Witte, Elite ceramogr. Taf. 46</td><td align="center">Lenormant et de Witte, Elite ceramogr. Tafel 57</td></tr>
</table>

3. Stringing the bow

Attaching the string to the τόξον παλίντονον, or rather attaching the string to the free end of the bow arm, was and still is a difficult feat because, in addition to much and long practice, it requires a lot of strength and skill. The Greeks always referred to the attachment of the string with the expression ἐντανόειν or τανόειν[488]. Homer sometimes explicitly mentions the chord[489], but sometimes he only talks about ἐντανόειν τό τόξον[490].

For the actual „tensioning" Homer always uses τιταινειν, e.g. B. II.V, 97; VIII, 266 or similarly II.IV, 124 τείνειν. Regarding the position XXI, 259 is given by A. Schaumberg, Homer used τιταίνειν instead of: ἐντανόειν. This view, however, is not correct, because Antinous does not mean the attachment

---

[488] v. Luschan, a. a. O. in Festschrift für O. Benndorf, p. 190.

[489] Od. XXI, 97 and 127: νευρήν ἐντανύειν; Od. XXIV, 170-171: οὐδέ τις ἡμείων δυνατό κρατεροῖο βιοιο / νευρήν εντανύσαι .... κτλ.

[490] See Od. XIX, 577; XXI; 92, 114, 150, 171, 174, 185, 247 A. Schaumberg, a. a. O., p. 81 f., denies the possibility of using the expression τόξον (oder βιόν) ἐντανόειν with the word „to the string" and calls for a more „analogous translation". If the chord is mentioned in Homer, then the translation „fixing the bowstring" can certainly be used in the passage in question, but if the chord is not mentioned, as is usually the case, the term „stringing" is best, as for example Od. XXI, 184-185:

(τώ τόξω) ρα νέοι θ'ἀλπόντες ἐπειρώντ', οδδέ δύναντο

ἐντανύσαι, πολλόν δε βιης ἐπιδεοέες ἦσαν.

of the string, but rather refers to archery itself. It is the festival of Apollo and on such a day shooting is not allowed for religious reasons, it is a pity that the inhabitants of Ithaca will not be so numerous, it will mean that due to the festival the exercise will be postponed to the next day. This is Antinous's line of thought in response to Eurymachus' lament.

In the wonderful scene of Odysseus' master shot, there are three tasks: a) to draw the bow, b) to hit the target from any distance, and c) to shoot through twelve axes placed one behind the other with one shot[491].

But the fact that drawing the bow was the most important part of the wager and required great effort is best demonstrated by the fruitless efforts of Telemachus and the suitors. Telemachus takes vain offense at his clumsiness, Od. XXI, 131-133:

> ὦ πόποι, ἦ καὶ ἔπειτα κακός τ' ἔσομαι καὶ ἄκικυς.
> ἠὲ νεώτερός εἰμι καὶ οὔ πω χερσὶ πέποιθα
> ἄνδρ' ἀπαμύνασθαι, ὅτε τις πρότερος χαλεπήνῃ.

The suitors also complain in vain in the words of Eurymachus, Od. XXI, 249 and 253-255:

> ὦ πόποι, ἦ μοι ἄχος περί τ' αὐτοῦ καὶ περὶ πάντων.
> . . . .
> ἀλλ' εἰ δὴ τοσσόνδε βίης ἐπιδευέες εἰμὲν
> ἀντιθέου Ὀδυσῆος, ὅτ' οὐ δυνάμεσθα τανύσσαι.
> τόξον· ἐλεγχείη δὲ καὶ ἐσσομένοισι πυθέσθαι.

Neither fat nor fire could help, only Odysseus managed to attach a string to his bow, Od. XXI, 405-409:

> αὐτίκ' ἐπεὶ μέγα τόξον ἐβάστασε καὶ ἴδε πάντη,
> ὡς ὅτ' ἀνὴρ φόρμιγγος ἐπιστάμενος καὶ ἀοιδῆς
> ῥηιδίως ἐτάνυσσε νέῳ περὶ κόλλοπι χορδήν,
> ἅψας ἀμφοτέρωθεν εὐστρεφὲς ἔντερον οἰός,
> ὣς ἄρ' ἄτερ σπουδῆς τάνυσεν μέγα τόξον Ὀδυσσεύς.

So how did people string their bow? The best answer to this question is monuments. Using a simple Greek bow, one rested one end of the bow on the ground and pressed the inside with the left knee; at the same time, it was necessary to press the other end of the bow to the breast with the left hand, and with the right hand to attach the free end of the string to it, as seen on Neaps' vase (Fig. 57). There, three young men shoot arrows at a rooster placed on a fluted pillar. One of the archers is shown drawing his bow using the method just described. This is the same method we learned about earlier in Egypt. This method was also briefly and precisely described by Ovid[492]:

Lunavitque genu sinuosum fortiter arcum.

---

[491] Gdy W. Reichel, op.cit., p. 117, He thinks that this feat consisted of two tasks (described above as B and C), he is wrong. Indeed, the course of the plant shows that tensioning played the most important role in it.

[492] Ovidius Am. I, 1, 23.

Fig. 57

Museo Borbonico, Bd. VII, Taf. 41

But there must have been another method of winding known in antiquity, since the one described above does not in any way correspond to the winding comparison, a sequence of characters to φόρμιγξ (Od. XXI, 405-409). This issue was already sufficiently explained by W. Reichel[493], and the relevant monuments were collected by P. Hartwig[494]. When Pandaros drew his bow, he placed it on the ground, Il. IV, 112-113:

$$\text{καὶ τὸ μὲν (τόξον) εὖ κατέθηκε}$$
$$\text{τανυσσάμενος ποτὶ γαίη}$$
$$\text{ἀγκλίνας . . . . . . κτλ.}$$

In these verses, the participle ἀγκλίνας was always incorrectly combined with the phrase ποτί γαίτβ. Only Reichel, in his astute comments on this fragment of the Iliad, showed that ἀγκλίνας does not belong to ποτί γαίη, but to τανοσσάμενος, so the order of the words in the translation should be as follows: κατέθηκε ποτ ί γαίη τανοσσάμενος ἀγκλίνας, where the last participle „by bending (that) in up"[495]. The Scythian from the well-known electron vase (Fig. 58) from Kul-Oba shows us how this bending of the arc took place. He places the bow under his left thigh so that its end with the tied string rests on his right thigh. Meanwhile, he bends down and raises the opposite end of the bow with his left hand, and with his right hand he attaches the loop of the

---

[493] W. Reichel, a. a. O. p. 118 f.
[494] P. Hartwig, Die griechischen Meisterschalen, p. 121, Anmerkung 2.
[495] W. Reichel, a. a. O. p. 118.

90

Fig. 58

Kondakoff, Tolstoi, Reinach, a. a. O. ryc. 261

string to the κορώνη. In this case, the lower end of the bow does not touch the floor, but rather the thigh. However, it probably often happened that the end of the bow rested directly on the ground, maintaining the same method of stringing, which is shown in Fig. 59, where you can see the Amazon River being stretched. You can't see the other end of the arc, but you have to imagine it lying on the ground. Once the string was attached, the leg wrapped around the bow and the string had to be pulled from the bow. However, since the drawing was done in a kneeling or at least strongly bent position, the easiest way to free the leg was to place the bow on the ground. This procedure also explains why Pandaros placed the bow on the ground after drawing it.

This type of bow tension must have been very widespread, as evidenced by images on coins and vases[496]. Upon closer inspection, some illustrations show slight deviations from the type of covering last described. Thus, on the vase in the Louvre (Fig. 60) we have a young man who is not drawing his bow in a kneeling position, but standing and leaning heavily. The archer from Gjöl-baschi-Trysa[497] is also depicted in the same pose.

---

[496] Barclay V. Head, Catalogue of Greek coins (Central Greece), London 1884, Taf. XII, 4 und 5. See P. Hartwig, Die griechischen Meisterschalen, p. 121, Anmerkung 2. W. Reichel, a. a. O. S, 118, Anmerkung 1; L. Grasberger, a. a. O. Bd. III, p. 154.

[497] See O. Benndorf und G. Niemann, Das Heroon von Gjölbaschi-Trysa, Taf. XXIV, p. 202. »He stands with his upper body bent forward on his bent right leg, placed one end of his horned bow on his right thigh, grabbed the other with his left hand, guided his left leg hovering over the center of the bow to squeeze it with his knee joint, and is now busy with his closed right arm at the highest end of the bow to fasten the taut (plastic) tendon.« See also W. Reichel, op. cit., fig. 62. Archer at the moment of tension depicted on a vase by J. Bankó, in Festschrift für O. Benndorf, p. 66.

Fig. 59

A. Furtwängler, Aegina, Textband, ryc. 250

This slight difference in the type of draw seems to indicate that the bow offered less resistance to the archer; otherwise, people probably rested their bows on the ground. Homer compared attaching a string to a bow to drawing a string on φόρμιγξ[498]. As long as it was believed that the bow could be strung using the method described at the beginning, the comparison must have remained incomprehensible. But if we use Fig. 58-60, e.g., adopting the presented method, Homer's statement is simple and clear, because „the string on the formin was also strung by clamping it between the legs, by pulling the string clamped under the bridge with one hand and turning the peg at the top with the other[499]."

At this point it is also worth mentioning some statues of Eros, which have so far been mostly misinterpreted. They belong to a widespread type that probably originated in the 4th century[500], when the bow appeared as an attribute of Eros[501].

In these cases, two ways of tensioning can be demonstrated:

Eros either stiffens the bow sideways on his right leg, holds it in the middle with his left hand, and with his right hand rests on the loop of the string at the

---

[498] Od. XXI, 406-408.

[499] W. Reichel, a. a. O. p. 119; For pictorial representation, cf. Furtwängler-Reichhold, Griech. Vas. Taf. 71.

[500] W. Amelung, Die Skulpturen des Vatikanischen Museums, Bd. I, p. 634. Baumeister, Denkmäler des klassischen Altertums, Bd. I, p. 497. A. Furtwängler, Meisterwerke der griechischen Plastik, p. 538 f.

[501] A. Furtwängler in Roschers Lex. Myth. Bd. I, p. 1363 f.

92

Fig. 60

Daremberg et Saglio, Dictionnaire, Bd. I, S. 389, ryc. 472

upper end of the bow[502], or uses the tensioning method, which can be found in Fig. 60: places the bow on the right thigh, pushes the center of the bow back with the left thigh, at the same time, with the left hand, pulls the upper end of the bow to the chest and tries to fasten the string with the right hand[503].

According to Sauer[504], the central figure of Western Olympus – Apollo – „does not stop at holding the bow (in his left hand and resting on the ground), but presses it so that the right hand can comfortably hold the string already held at the ready with the index finger of the left hand." It should be noted that this operation is physically impossible, because firstly, one and the same hand cannot press (bend) the bow and draw the string at the same time, secondly, if this action were possible, Apollo's body would have to have at least a slight inclination to the left – but here he stands completely erect. In our opinion, Treu correctly explained Apollo's[505] operation: the right hand had no attribute, while the lowered left hand held the bow and arrows in such a way that the

---

[502] Friederichs-Wolters, Die Gipsabgüsse antiker Bildwerke, Berlin 1885, p. 636 f. See Clarac-Reinach, Répertoire Stat. Bd. I, fig. 1464, 1471, 1485, 1495. W. Helbig, Führer durch die öffentlichen Sammlungen in Rom, Leipzig 1899, Bd. I, Nr. 437. W. Reichel, a. a. O., p. 118 f., Anmerkung 1. W. Amelung, a. a. O. Bd. I, p. 633 f.

[503] Clarac-Reinach, Répertoire Stat. Bd. I, fig. 1471 A, 1471 B, 1471 C, 1491. S. Reinach, Répertoire Stat. Bd. II, p. 427, fig. 1-7; Bd. III, p. 261, fig. 3 und 5. W. Reichel, a. a. O. p. 118 f., Anmerkung 1. Roscher, Myth. Lex. fig. p. 1363.

[504] B. Sauer, Nachträgliches zum olympischen Westgiebel, Jahrbuch deutsch. bow. Inst., Bd. VI (1891), p. 93 f.

[505] Treu, Olympia-Ergebnisse, Bd. III, p. 69 f., Taf. XXII.

index finger helped to hold the arrows. The motif of holding arrows in the left hand next to the bow was common and well-known in Greece[506].

In this context, Reichel drew attention to a Homeric verse that the poet used in two seemingly different cases[507]. In the Iliad XXI, 176 and in the Odyssey XXI, 125 we read:

τρὶς μέν μιν πελέμιξεν ἐρόσσεσθαι μενεαίνων.

In the Odyssey, this verse depicts Telemachus's futile efforts to hook the string to the neck of his bow, while in the Iliad, it depicts Asteropaios' futile efforts to pull Achilles' spear from the ground. Apparently, although the actions of the young men were different, the main motive behind their efforts was the same: in both cases, the goal was to attract an object to themselves.

However, our comments on bow tension would not be complete if we did not think about a device which, according to some researchers, was intended to be used to attach the string to the free end of the bow[508]. This instrument takes the form of two bronze rings cast together, about the width of a finger, with three, four or more tips above them. The type, shown in Fig. 61 is the most common. Based on its shape alone, this device must seem virtually useless for drawing a bow. Just as we have no information about it in ancient writings, we will not find any trace of it on monuments. On the contrary, everywhere the string[509] is not gripped by the loop, but under it, not with outstretched fingers – this is how the string would have to be held if the stringing ring was used – but with a closed fist. We therefore believe that this assumption, unconfirmed by either monuments or literary records, can be rejected as impossible.

Fig. 61

Daremberg et Saglio, a. a. O. Bd. I, S. 389, ryc. 473

---

[506] See Furtwängler-Reichhold, Griech. Vas., Taf. 13, 22, 26, 27, 90, 110 usw.

[507] W. Reichel, a. a. O. S, 119.

[508] Daremberg et Saglio, Dictionnaire, Bd. I, p. 389. D. N. Anuczin, a. a. O. p. 359.

[509] See fig. 58 i 59. See also Bankó, in Festschrift für Benndorf, p. 66, where the loop is clearly visible.

4. Drawing the bow

After drawing the bow, the archer's next action is to draw and shoot. Unfortunately, the presentation of tensioning on ancient monuments is reproduced on too small a scale, and some illustrations of this process are so poor, often even ambiguous, and show such great differences in the way of presentation that it is almost impossible to precisely distinguish the tensioning method. It can be concluded, as E. Morse has already shown in his study of stringing methods[510], that Greek artists paid little attention to the presentation of this motif.

The power and accuracy of the shot depend on the quick and correct drawing of the bow, because while the Byzantine Anonymous emphasizes εὐστόχως, ἰσχορώς, ταχέως βάλλειν, i.e. an accurate, strong and quick shot as a condition for a good archer, everything depends on the correctly used method of cocking and proper deflation chord[511]. Plato warns[512] to use both hands alternately both when holding and drawing the bow, and Aristotle advises the same, clearly emphasizing: ὅπως ἀμφιδέξιοι γένωνται κατά την μελέτην[513]. However, on monuments, Greek archers always hold the bow with their left hand when shooting and draw it with their right, similarly to the so-called Scythian archers, although, according to Plato, the different use of both hands resulted from a common custom among the Scythians[514].

The mentioned Anonymous from Byzantium describes the types of cocking used by ancient archers[515]: Τών δέ τοξευοντων οι μέν τρισί τοῖς μέσοις δακτυλοις την νευράν ελκοοσι, οι δε δυσί, καί τούτοις οι μέν του μεγίστου επικειμένου τφ λιχανφ, οι δέ τ'ούναντίον, οἵ καί μάλλον την νευράν ελκουσι καί πέμπουσι τδ βέλος σφοδρδτερον.

Then there were two, or actually three, different tensioning methods, depending on how many and what fingers were used during the tensioning:

1. οι μέν τρισί' τοῖς μέσοις δακτυλοις ελκουσι – some people pull the string with their three middle fingers.

2. οι δέ δυσί – the rest use only two fingers, in two ways, a) οι μέν του μεγίστου επικειμένου τφ λιχανώ, in which the largest finger – probably the

---

[510] E. Morse, Ancient and modern methods of arrow release, in Bulletin of the Essex Institute, Bd. XVII (1885), p. 145 ff. See M. Büchner, Das Bogenschießen der Ägineten, Zeitschrift für Ethnologie, Bd. XL (1908), p. 854. v. Lusehan, Über das Bogenspannen, in Zeitschrift für Ethnologie, Bd. XXIII (1891), Verhandlungen p. 670 ff. M. Jähns, a. a. O. p. 292 f. A. Schaumberg, a. a. O. p. 14.

[511] 'Ανωνύμου Βυζαντίου περί τοξείας in Rüstow-Köchly, Griechische Kriegs- schriftsteller, Leipzig 1855, Bd. IIb, p. 198 ff.

[512] Plato, Leges VII, 794 c-VII, 795 a.

[513] Arist. Polit. II, 9, 8.

[514] Plato, Leges VII, 795 a: ἔδειξε δὲ ταῦτα ὁ τών Σκυθών νόμος, οὐκ ἐν ἀριστερα μέν τόξον ἀπάγων, ἐν δεξιά δέ οίστόν προσαγόμενος μόνον, ἀλλ' ομοίως εκατέράις επ' ἀμφότερα χρώμενος.

[515] I, 7 (S. 200 ed. Rüstow-Köchly). It is also worth mentioning the parable of Emperor Julian (Ep. XL, 419 b-c) on occasional wrist exercises, probably due to left-handed aiming: το της ἀρετης παράγγελμα διά πάντων σώζειν, οίον αγαθών τοξότην, ος καν μὴ τον αντίπαλον εχη, πάντίυς ἐς τό καίριον ἀεί την χεῖρα γυμνάζει. See L. Grasberger, a. a. O. Bd. III, p. 153 f.

Fig. 62

Wiener Vorlegeblätter, Serie D, Taf. IX

middle one – rests on the thumb, b) οι δέ τ 'ουναντίον, with the thumb resting on middle finger.

Today's bow experts, who have taken a closer look at modern drawing methods, also distinguish several methods that almost all originate from ancient peoples. First, however, we want to stick to the classification of anonymous people.

I. Three middle finger stringing method; the thumb remains inactive. On the other hand, the string is drawn by three fingers, but the arrow rests slightly pressed to the side, between the index and middle fingers. We call this method the „Mediterranean method". It most often appears on ancient monuments. We also found them in almost all the peoples we have discussed, except the Persians. The slight differences in presentation are understandable, given the difficulty of reproducing the tension motif. The Mediterranean method is best seen in the ancient Attic amphora (Fig. 62), where Heracles grasps the bowstring with his right hand, showing the viewer its interior[516].

II. a) The middle finger rests on the thumb, i.e. the middle finger bends above the thumb (of course, the index finger also bends, but remains inactive when cocked), the arrow is held by two fingers, but the string runs between the

---

[516] See Archäologische Zeitung, 1858, Taf. 114, 2. Mon. dell' Inst. I, Taf. 20; Taf. 40. Furtwängler-Reichhold, Griech. Vas. Taf. 96. de Ridder, a. a. O. Bd. II, fig. 71.

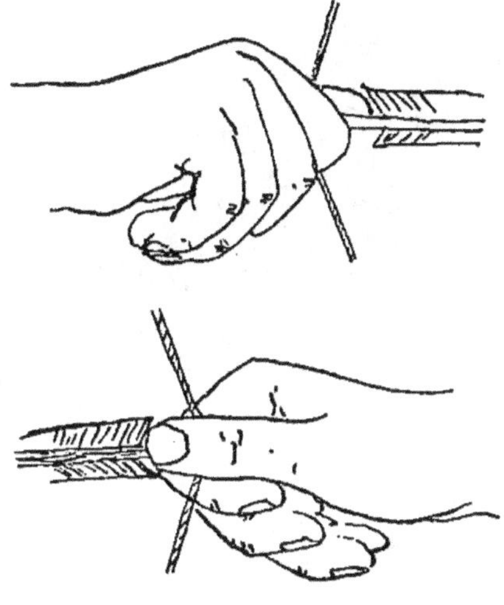

Fig. 63
E. Morse, a. a. O. Bd. XVII, ryc. 1-2

index finger and the thumb. Modern bow experts perceive this method as a combination of the simplest method (mentioned in point III) and the so-called „Mongolian method". According to M. Büchner, this method was used by the so-called Paris from the western aegetic area[517].

II. b) The thumb is placed on the middle finger, the string and the arrow are held in the same way as in II a). This method is rare and difficult to distinguish from method II a). It most closely corresponds to the contemporary „tertiary tension"[518].

III. Moreover, there is the simplest form, not mentioned by Anonymous, in which the arrow and the string are drawn back using the thumb and forefinger (Fig. 63). Occasionally, shooters also use the middle finger[519] as an aid in this method (Fig. 64).

Of course, in a large number of representations the method of stringing remains unclear, so that, as already mentioned, neither one nor the other method can be recognized[520] (Fig. 65). We find a completely incomprehensible method

---

[517] M. Buchner, a. a. O. p. 849, fig. 4, 5. See weiter Archäologische Zeitung, 1884, Taf. IV. Furtwängler-Reichhold, Griech. Vas. Taf. 74, 96, 115. Furtwängler, Olympia, Bronzen, Taf. 40. Nach K. Lange, Die Komposition der Ägineten, Leipzig 1878, p. 33. A hand belonging to the Eastern style also shows the same method.

[518] Mon. dell' Inst. I, Taf. 52. P. Hartwig, Meisterschalen, Taf. 56, 1 (Schale des Onesimos [?]). Gerhard, A. V. 119. The pulling hand is better reproduced by M. Büchner, a. a. O. p. 855, fig. 12. See A. Schaumberg, a. a. O. p. 16.

[519] Mon. dell' Inst. I, Taf. 20, 51; X, Taf. 53. Antike Denkmäler, II, Taf. 21, 3; Taf. 30, 22. Furtwängler-Reichhold, Griech. Vas. Taf. 115. See A. Schaum- berg, a. a. O. p. 17. H. Walters, Catalogue of the Bronzes of Brit. Mus. p. 52, Nr. 337.

[520] Roscher, Myth. Lex. Bd. I2, fig. p. 1655.

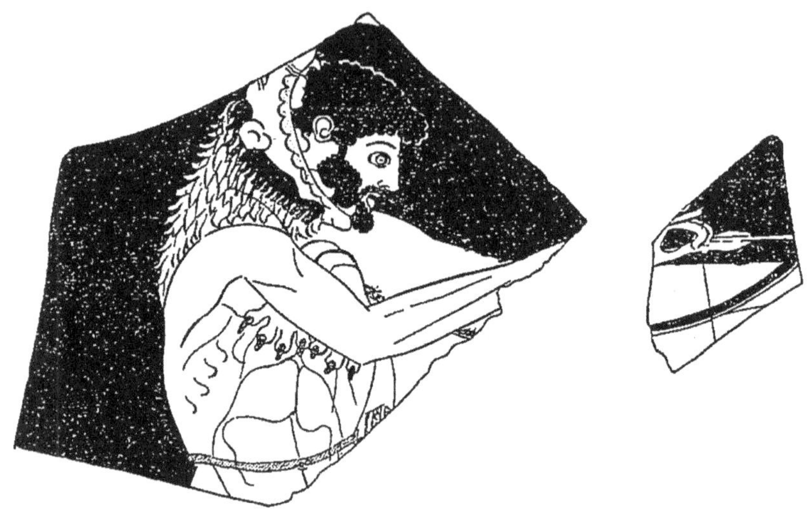

Fig. 64

de Ridder, Catalogue Vas. Bibl. nat. Bd. II, ryc. 71

of tension on a well-known bas-relief from the Carapano collection in the National Museum of Athens[521], depicting a youthful Heracles shooting arrows. A. Emerson doubted the authenticity of the bas-relief[522] and claimed that it was a modern forgery. This opinion was opposed by A. Furtwängler, who was convinced that the bas-relief is not archaic, but archaistic[523] and comes from the 1st century BC. It is not my intention to discuss the bas-relief style here, but one thing we can say is that it is a method of draw that causes the shooter's body to exert a supernatural effort. However, it is difficult to assume such ignorance of the art of shooting on the part of the Greek artist. Therefore, Emerson's doubts about its authenticity seem to us very justified[524].

In his oft-quoted work on the ancient bow, v. Luschan draws attention to the fact that „among the many known and possible methods of drawing an arrow, there is almost none that does not require some device for securing the right hand with a strong bow[525]." The question naturally arises whether such security devices can be found on monuments. We recall here what we said earlier about the gloves found on the Phaistos disk. Xenophon also observed the use of gloves by Persians[526]. In turn, Eustathius refers to the story from Odyssey XXIV, 230, according to which Laertes, Odysseus' father, worked in the gar-

---

[521] O. Rayet, Monuments de l'art antique, Paris 1884, B.d. I, Taf. 23.
[522] A. Emerson, Two modern antiques, Amer. Jour. Arch. Bd. I, (1885), p. 152 ff., Taf. V, 2.
[523] A. Furtwängler, Note on Plate V, 2, of Volume I, Amer. Jour. Arch. Bd. II (1886) p. 52.
[524] See E. Morse, a. a. O. p. 179f.
[525] v. Luschan, a. a. O. in Festschrift für O. Benndorf, p. 195.
[526] Xenoph. Kyrup. VIII, 8, 17.

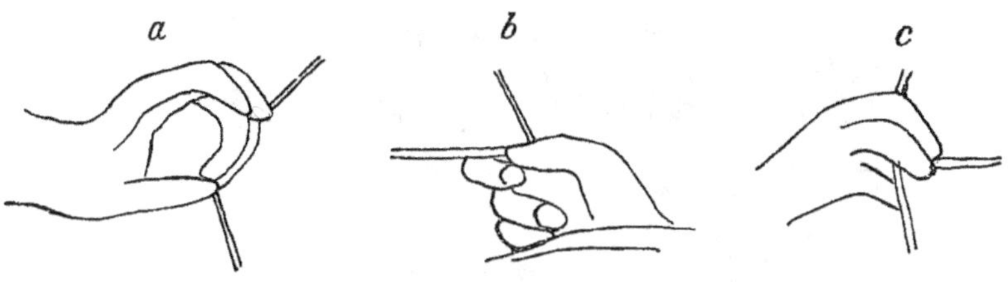

a *b* *c*

Fig. 65

E. Morse, a. a. O. Bd. XVII, ryc. 49-51

den wearing gloves, and that the archers used gloves similar to those worn by Laertes, but without fingers[527].

This custom, however, cannot be found on ancient monuments, but v. Luschan rightly recognized it on some vases with black figures[528]. Their form resembles those seen in Fig. 31, and what is clearly visible in the bas-relief with an archer from Sendshirli[529].

There is no device on any monument that protects the left hand from striking the string, so it seems that the ancient Hellenes were completely unaware of the existence of such a protective device.

Each shot depends on the method of tension and the force with which the string is pulled back. When Pandaros was ready to release, he drew the string to his chest. IV, 123[530]. But the string was also drawn to the ear, or rather to the neck[531]. In later times, when bows lost their size, the string reached only up to the elbow[532] (fig. 66). Anonymous I, 9, also mentions this type of string retraction:

Κάμπτομεν δὲ τὸ τόξον ποτὲ μὲν κατὰ
ὠτός [ποτὲ δὲ κατὰ τραχήλου,] ποτὲ δὲ κατὰ μαζοῦ τὴν νευρὰν ἕλκοντες· φέρεται
δὲ τὸ βέλος ἰσχυρότερον μέν, ὅταν κατὰ ὠτὸς τὴν νευρὰν ἕλκωμεν, εἶτα, ὅταν κατὰ
τραχήλου, ἀσθενέστατον δὲ ὅταν κατὰ μαζοῦ αὐτὴν ἕλκωμεν.

---

[527] Eust. ad Od. XXIV, 230 (p. 1960) ... καί τοξεύοντες γοῦν τινές χειγίσι χρώνται, εἰ καί μή δακτυλωταῖς ... κτλ.

[528] v. Luschan, a. a. O. in Festschrift für O. Benndorf, p. 195 f., fig. auf p. 196. See Gerhard, A. V. 94, 97, 102, 110, 119/120, 134, 141.

[529] See p. 32, fig. 23.

[530] F. Dümmler, Römische Mitteilungen, Bd. II (1887), p. 187, Taf. IX. Loeschcke, Jahrbuch d. deutsch, bow. Inst, Bd. II (1887), p. 278. Gerhard, A. V, 190/191. Mon. dell' Inst. VI, Taf. 33; Antike Denkmäler, II, 21, 3; 30, 22.

[531] Gerhard, A. V. 5, 61, 96, 119/120.

[532] Mon. dell' Inst. I, Taf. 51. de Ridder, a. a. O. Bd. II, fig. 71.

Fig. 66

A. S. Murray, Desings from greek Vases, Taf. I, Nr 3

5. Shapes of arrows and arrowheads

We have already said at the beginning of our study that the arrow in its basic form is in fact a reduced lance and, like this, consists of two parts, the shaft and the point. Naturally, the latter was subject to various development possibilities both in terms of form and material.

Homer knows only brass arrowheads, except Pandaros's iron ones; however, it does not need to be particularly emphasized that in his times stone arrowheads were also used, perhaps even to a greater extent than brass arrowheads, which were much more expensive[533]. In an attempt to group the known material, we must summarize all the fragments that were found in the areas on the Aegean Sea, later inhabited by the Greeks. Of course, it cannot be said that the arrows found in the oldest cultural layers were „Greek". The first arrows on Greek soil, as elsewhere, were certainly cut from a single piece of wood, their shaft sharply sharpened at the upper end. Later, the blade was made from a special piece of another material, initially using bone fragments because this material was easier to work with than any other[534].

The next harder material from which people made arrowheads and other tools necessary for life was stone. The stone arrowheads that came to light on

---

[533] W. Reichel, a. a. O. p. 115.
[534] A. J. Reinach, w Daremberg et Saglio, Dictionnaire, p. v. »sagitta«.

100

Fig. 67

Χρ, Τσούντας, Διμήνιον, πιν. 42

Fig. 68

Perrot et Chipiez, Histoire de l'art., Bd. VI, p. 116, fig. 2

Greek soil were generally made mainly of two types of stone: flint and obsidian[535]. In addition, arrowheads made of pebbles also came to light[536].

Most of the stone points known to us can be divided into two large groups according to their basic shape: A. points with a tongue, B. without a tongue[537]. Within each of these main groups, several subdivisions can then be created: Group A. Stem tongue arrowheads.

I. Tips with a leafy, sharpened upper part and with noticeable notches at the transition to the poorly developed tongue of the shaft (Fig. 67, No. 1)[538].

---

[535] See R. C. Bosanquet, in Excavations at Phylakopi in Melos, London 1904, p. 222 f. Most known stone arrowheads are made of obsidian, which is a dark, glassy, translucent stone of volcanic origin. This stone is provided by the islands of the Greek archipelago. It is well known that the most beautiful obsidian can be found on the island of Melos and it was this island that exported this type of stone everywhere. See H. Schliemann, Tiryns, Leipzig 1886, p. 29; D. Mackenzie, Annual British School, Bd. III (1896/97), p. 79; D. G. Hogarth, Annual British School, Bd. IV (1897/98), p. 1 ff; Chr. Blinkenberg, Archäologische Studien, p. 6, where more information is also given on the properties of the types of stone; R. C. Bosanquet, in Excavations at Phylakopi, p. 216 ff.; G. Finlay, Παρατηρήσεις m της έν Ελβετός και Έλλάδι προϊστορικής άρχαιολογίας, Athen 1869, p. 16 f.

[536] Among the arrowheads made of pebbles (silex), specimens from the tholos of Thorikos should be distinguished, Πρακτικά, 1893, p. 16; z macedońskiego tumulusa, Zeitschrift für Ethnologie, Bd. XXXIV (1907), p. 73; aus Vaphio, Athenisches Nationalmuseum, Nr. 1846.

[537] Χρ. Τσοόντας, Αί προϊστορικά! άκροπόλεις Διμηνίοο και Σέσκλου, Άθ᾽ήναι, 1908, p. 325.

[538] See also Χρ. Τσούντας, a. a. O. p. 325, Taf. XLII, Nr. 1, 3, 4, 8, 9, 10 (obsidian).

101

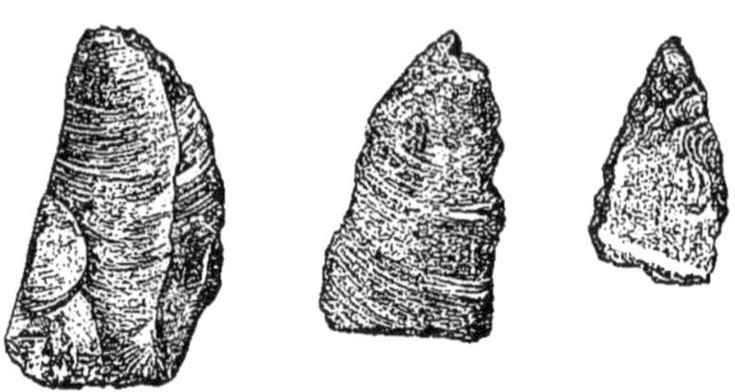

Fig. 69

H. Schliemann, Tiryns, S. 196, Nr 108-110

a   *b*   *c*   *d*

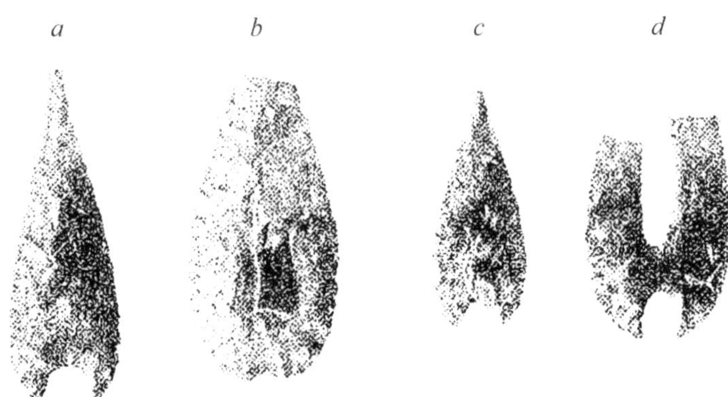

Fig. 70

Athenische Mitteilungen, Bd. XXIV, Taf. XV, Nr 6-9

II. Triangular, sharply ended, with cuts and a clearly marked tongue (Fig. 67, no. 2, 3, 4)[539].

This group of stone points with tongued shafts was probably unknown in the Mycenaean period, has not yet been found together with Mycenaean finds, and may belong to the previously little-known „pre-Mycenaean" period in Greece.

Stone caves of the second group B (without a shaft blade) can be divided into the following subgroups:

I. Roughly made points, in the shape of an elongated tetrahedron, with un-evenly hewn surfaces (Fig. 68)[540].

---

[539] In a prehistoric tomb on the southern slope of the Acropolis, eight arrowheads of this type were found. See Α. Σκιάς, Τύμβος προϊστορικός οπο τήν Ακροπολιν, in Έφημ. άρχαιολ. 1902, p. 123 ff., fig. 3. A. Dumont, Melanges d'archéologie. et d'épigraphie, Paris 1892, p. 25, fig. 15 und danach bei Perrot et Chipiez, a. a. O. Bd. VI, fig. 2, Nr. 3 The arrowhead shown in the photo made of stone (silex) was found in Asia Minor and is probably not Greek. See C. R. Bosanquet, in Excavations at Phylakopi, p. 222, Anm. 2.

[540] H. Schliemann, Tiryns, p. 196, Nr. 111. Perrot et Chipiez, a. a. O. Bd. VI, p. 116, fig. 2 (za G. Finlay, a. a. O. fig. 11, 13).

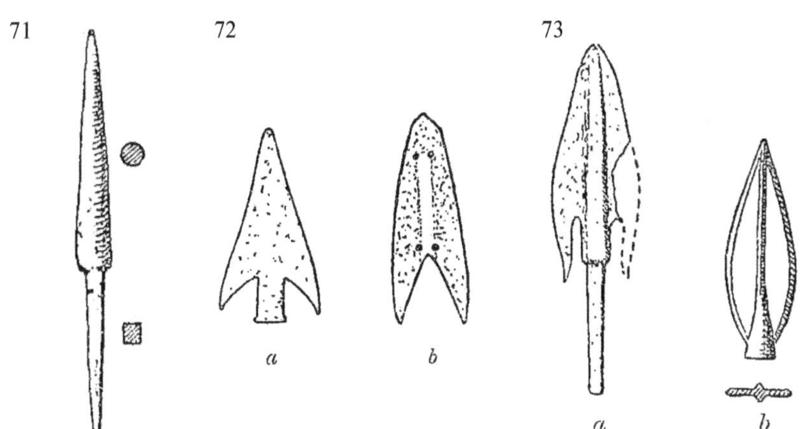

Fig. 71

H. Schmidt, Schliemanns Sammlung trojanischer Altertümer, S. 249, Nr. 6165

Fig. 72

H. Schmidt, a. a. O. S. 256, Nr. 6450, 6451

Fig. 73

H. Schmidt, a. a. O., S. 260, Nr. 6534, 6538

II. Triangular, prismatic narrow chips, with a straight base, roughly struck (Fig. 69)[541].

III. Leafy, pointed, with a rounded base, finely made (Fig. 70 b)[542].

IV. Carefully made, triangular or elongated oval tips, forming a pointed oval in cross-section, with a crescent-shaped or angle-shaped notch at the base, the ends of which end in a sharp, usually sharp and slightly inwardly curved barb (Fig. 70 a, c)[543].

V. Arrowheads similar to those described in IV, but with a hole in the center for attachment to the shaft (Fig. 70 d)[544].

It is impossible to determine with certainty the time when stone arrowheads were created. Those with a molar tongue may come from the Stone Age, i.e. from Dimini and Sesklo, and those from the grave on the southern slope of the

[541] H. Schliemann, Tiryns, p. 88, 196. H. Schliemann, Zeitschrift für Ethnologie, Bd. XVI (1884), p. 85-88 (Marathon).

[542] H. Schliemann, Mykenä, p. 311 (Obsidian und Feuerstein), fig. 435. Kurt Müller, Alt-Pylos, die Funde aus den Kuppelgräbern von Kakovatos, Athenische Mitteilungen, Bd. XXXIV (1909), p. 292, Taf. XV, Nr. 7.

[543] See H. Schliemann, Mykenä, p. 311. (35 obsidian arrowheads were found in the fourth shaft grave, 15 of which are pictured, a. a. O. fig. 435. See auch p. 85. fig. 126.) Kurt Müller, a. a. O. p. 292, Taf. XV, Nr. 1-6, 8. Xp. Τσούντας, a. a. O. p. 325, Taf. XLII, Nr. 11 -13 (Nr. 11 und 13 aus Feuerstein, Nr. 12 Obsidian). Candia Museum, Nr. 283, 284, 281 aus Knossos. Nationalmuseum in Athen, Nr. 1846 (Vaphio).

[544] Kurt Müller, a. a. O. p. 292, Taf. XV, 9. So far, as Dr. K. Müller told us, this species is only represented by the specimen shown in the image.

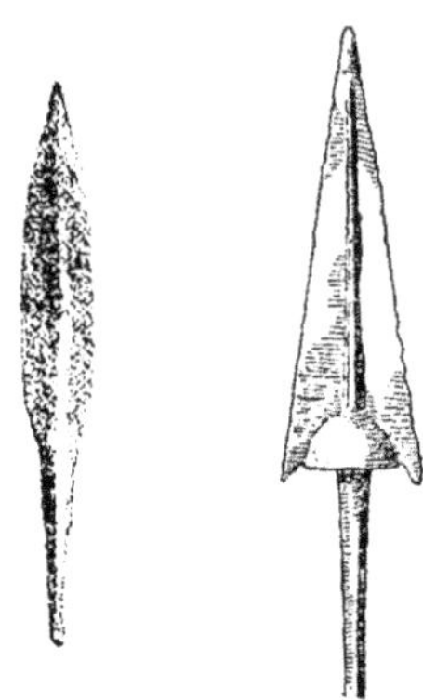

Fig. 74

Bosanquet, Excavations at Philakopi, Taf. XXXVIII, Nr. 6

Fig. 75

Olympia, Bronzen, Taf. 64, Nr. 1093

Acropolis[545]. The remaining types of groups I and II may belong to the same era, although the findings obtained here do not say anything positive. However, the remaining groups were certainly also used in the Bronze Age, as evidenced by finds regarding Mycenaean arrowheads[546].

It is not yet possible to determine when the use of bronze arrowheads first appeared, but it is certain that they were present in Troy[547] and that from then on stone and bronze were used in parallel[548]. Initially, as we will see, the shape of bronze arrowheads, especially in the shape of a pointed leaf with barbs (cf. our Type B, III), was only an imitation of stone arrowheads.

Now let's try to divide the brown arrowheads into groups:

a) Pencil-shaped arrowheads with two distinct parts, of which the upper part – the tip proper – is always round, while the lower part – the tongue of the shaft – is usually square (Fig. 71)[549].

b) Points approximately dagger-shaped, triangular, made of sheet metal, with or without two holes in the blade for better attachment to the handle and with a sharp notch at the base forming spikes (fig. 72 b)[550].

---

[545] Α. Σκιάς, Ἐφημ. ἀρχατολ. 1902, p. 123 ff. C. R. Bosanquet, in Excavations at Phylakopi, p. 222.

[546] See 35 obsidian arrowheads from the tomb of the fourth shaft in Mycenae.

[547] H. Schliemann, Ilios, p. 564, Nr. 931, 933, 942, 944, 946, from the second to the fifth layer. H. Schmidt, a. a. O. p. 249, Nr. 6162-6166.

[548] A. Baumeister, Denkmäler, Bd. III, p. 2017.

[549] H. Schmidt, a. a. O. p. 249, Nr. 6162-6166, from the II-V Trojan layer. (According to Schmidt, maybe an awl). See also H. Schliemann, Ilios, p. 564, Nr. 9317 933, 942, 944, 946.

[550] H. Schmidt, a. a. O. p. 256, Nr. 6451, from the Trojan layer VI; z A. Götze, a. a. O. p. 418, fig. 448a marked as undated,. Χρ. Τσούντας, Ἐφημ ἀρχαιολ. 1888, πιν. 9, Nr. 22. (Gefunden in Mykenä im Kuppelgrab am Löwentor.) Tsountas and Manatt, a. a. O. p. 206, fig. 92. Ἀθήναιόν, Bd. VI (1877), Taf. E, Nr. 69 (from Spata in Attika). A. J. Evans, Annual British School, Bd. X (1903/04), p. 61. Das Kuppelgrab von Menidi, Athen 1880, Taf. IX, 22.

104

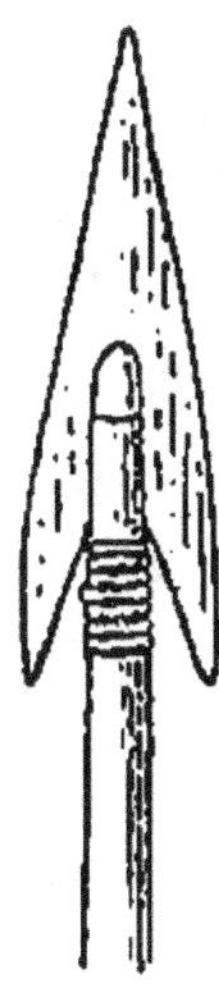

Fig. 76

Reichel, Homerische Waffen, II. Aufl., ryc. 64

c) Sheet metal points with a shape similar to b), with spikes and sharpened edges (fig. 72a)[551].

d) Leaf-shaped points with spines, a central ridge, a tongue and a shank (Fig. 73a)[552].

e) Sharp, leafy, long points like the previous ones, but without thorns, the central spine is strong (Fig. 74)[553].

f) The points are approximately dagger-shaped, with spines, a strong central ridge, a shaft tongue, a shaft shank, very massive (Fig. 75)[554].

---

[551] H. Schmidt, a. a. O. p. 255, Nr. 6448-6450. From Trojan layer VI; from A. Götze, a. a. O. p. 418, fig. 448b Listed as undated. Χρ. Τσοόνυας, Ἐφημ. ἀρχαιολ. 1888, πιν. 9, Nr. 23. Tsountas and Manatt, a. a. O. p. 206, fig. 93. Ἀθήναιον, Bd. VI (1877), p. 167 ff, Taf. E, Nr. 67 (aus Spata in Attika). C. R. Bosanquet and F. B. Welch, in Excavations at Phylakopi, p. 190, Taf. XXXVIII, Nr. 7, 8, 9, J. E. Evans, Prehistoric tombs of Knossos, Fig, 28. L. Savignoni, Monumenti antichi, Bd. XIV, p. 536, 537, fig. 21 (Phaistos). A. J. Evans, Annual British School, Bd. X (1903/04), p. 61. This form is also found in Spain, which is referred to in see H. i L. Siret, Les premiers âges du métal dans le sud-est de l'Espagne, Anvers 1887, Atlas Taf. III, Nr. 15.

[552] H. Schmidt, a. a. O. p. 260, Nr. 6534, 6535, p. 261, Nr. 6535, 6537 (Trojan layers VII-IX); przy A. Götze, a. a. O. p. 418 f. listed as not feasible. See also H. Schliemann, Ilios, p. 675, Nr. 1423. Ἀθήναιον, Bd. VI (1877), p. 167ff., Taf. E', Nr. 68. Nach Ohnefalsch-Richter, Zeitschrift für Ethnologie, Bd. XXXI (1889), Verhandlungen p. 332, barbed arrowheads on Kypros can only be found in tombs from the Hellenistic period Rößler, Zeitschrift für Ethnologie, Bd. XXXI (1899), Verhandlungen p. 266, fig. 33. This type of spearhead is also recorded in Achmaki in Transcaucasia.

[553] C. R. Bosanquet i F. B. Welch, Excavations at Phylakopi, p. 190, Taf. XXXVIII, Nr. 6, Gr. Lge. 0,11. Ridgeway, a. a. O. p. 302 (Nikosia, Kypros), fig. 57. Myresand Ohnefalsch-Richter, Catal. of Cyprus Museum, Nr. 565-571. M. P. Perdrizet, in Fouilles de Delphes, Bd. V, p. 97, fig. 336 c. These tips show a slight deviation from the type described above because they are rounder.

[554] Olympia, Bronzen, Taf. LXIV, 1093-1096. Perdrizet, in Fouilles de Delphes, Bd. V, p. 97, fig. 336 a, b, 338. Carapanos, Dodone et ses ruines, Taf. LVIII, 18. W. Froehner, Collection Gréau, Paris 1885, p. 142 f. Nach A. Furtwängler, Olympia, Bronzen, p. 178, important to this group is that it appears as a motif on coins from the time of Alexander; such arrowheads are also said to have been found in Marion's graves on Kypros.

g) Leafy points with a central ridge and a shaft calyx (Fig. 73b)[555].

h) Points similar to the previous group, but with a hook on the guide[556].

i) Three-edged or multi-edged tips with a guide. (In some cases the cutting edge extends down to sharp points and thus creates spikes)[557].

j) Points of the same type as i), but still with a hook, on the shaft guide[558].

k) Lanceolate, long but narrow points with sharp edges, strong central spine, two barbs[559].

We have highlighted here all known types of bronze points that are suitable for highlighting differences in shapes. In many cases they cannot be separated in time because the discovery reports do not provide sufficient support for chronological findings. Among the bronze tips, the youngest is group k), which became widespread only in the Hellenistic period[560]. Based on the finds, there is no doubt that different types were used side by side. Just as stone arrowheads remained in constant use along with bronze arrowheads, iron arrowheads came into use along with bronze arrowheads beginning in the 6th century; they generally imitated the shapes of bronze arrowheads[561].

At Delphi, several bronze arrowheads were discovered which were still connected to each other when they came out of the mold[562].

The arrowhead was most often made of reed (δόναξ)[563] or very light wood. Equipped with notches or grooves (γλυφίδες) at its lower end[564], it was feathered above the notch (πτερόεις)[565]. If the fletches were intended to better control the flight of the arrow, the notches were intended to allow for a more secure positioning of the arrow on the string and a better grip when shooting[566].

---

[555] Olympia, Bronzen, Taf. LXIV, 1076, 1079. H. Schmidt, a. a. O. p. 260, Nr. 6538 (Trojan layers VII-IX).

[556] Olympia, Bronzen, Taf. LXIV, 1077, 1078. Froehner, a. a. O. p. 142. Perdrizet, a. a. O. fig. 337. C. Friederichs, Kleinere Kunst und Industrie, Düsseldorf 1871, p. 238, Nr. 1113-1114. K. Schumacher, Sammlung antiker Bronzen, Karlsruhe 1890, Taf. XIV, 37-39.

[557] Olympia, Bronzen, Taf. LXIV, 1079, 1082-1084, 1086, 1089. A. Furtwängler, Ägina, Bd. II, Taf. 117, Nr. 42, 44, 46. W. Froehner, a. a. O. p. 142. K. Schumacher, a. a. O. Taf. XIV, 28-34. Zu diesem Typus vgl. P. Reinecke, Die skythischen Altertümer im mittleren Europa, in Zeitschrift für Ethnologie, Bd. XXVIII (1896), p. 21. W. Helbig, Homerisches Epos, 2. Aufl. p. 341, fig. 134. This figure can also be clearly seen on the head of Tytos at Delphi, cf. Athenische Mitteilungen, Bd. XXXIV (1909), Taf. V, 4.

[558] Olympia, Bronzen, Taf. LXIV, 1080, 1085, 1087, 1088, 1092.

[559] Olympia, Bronzen, Taf. LXIV, 1094; Museo Italiano, Bd. II (1888), p. 763 bis 764. Carapanos, a. a. O. Taf. LVIII, 17.

[560] A. Furtwängler, Agina, Bd. I, p. 423, Nr. 258; Bd. II, Taf. 117, Nr. 45.

[561] H. Schmidt, a. a. O. p. 259, Nr. 6502 (from the Ninth Trojan Layer). Carapanos, a. a. O. Taf. LVIII, 14. Baumeister, Denkmäler, Bd. III, p. 2042. Jahrbuch d. deutsch, bow. Inst Bd. XXII (1907), Anzeiger, p. 383. W. M. Flinders Petrie, Naukratis I, London 1886, Taf. XI, 2-4 (aus dem VI. Jahrhundert v. Chr.).

[562] Perdrizet, a. a. O. p. 97, fig. 33g.

[563] Il. XI, 584: ἐκλάσϑη δέ δόναξ, ἐβάρυνε δέ μηρόν.

[564] Il. IV, 122: ελκε δ' ομοῦ γλυφίδας τε λαβών καί νεῦρα βόεια; vgl. auch (Od. XXI, 419) Eust. 452. 11: γλυφίδες δέ τό γλύμμα τού ατράκτου, τό ἐντιϑέμενον τῇ νεύρα. Nonnus Dionys. XV, 331 δάκτυλα μαρμαίοοντα περί γλυφίδεσσι δοκεύων (ed. A. Köchly).

[565] See Il. IV, 117; V, 171. Liv. XLII, 65: huic ad abiegnae breves pinnae tres velut sagittis solent, circumdabantur. See Ovid. Met. VI, 258.

[566] See E. Buchholz, a. a. O. Bd. II, p. 355 f. W. Reichel, a. a. O., p. 115, believes that the shaft is called πηχυς'υηά beruft sich auf Odyss. XXI, 419 τόν ῥ' επί πήχει ελών ελκεν νευρήν γλυφίδας τε. However, as we have shown (p. 79), πηχυς is the name of the bracket on the bow. Ulysses took the bow in his hands, drew it, then felt the sound of the bowstring, took the arrow from the table, seized the bow by the stirrup, and drawed it. (Od. XXI, 404-419).

The tip was mounted in a slot at the upper end of the beam. Triangular spearheads (τριγλώχιν)[567] were attached similarly. The points were made with two burrs (ὄγκοι)[568], which is best described by W. Reichel in the following way[569]: „So that the point, when it hits a hard body, does not tear the gap even further and does not move back into it, it was practical to wrap the radius over the gap between the burrs using a string or tendon (Fig. 76).

If the arrow was stuck in the body, the barbs resisted attempts to pull it rearward, and because they were deliberately broken into thin shavings, they bent when force was applied. Usually the ray also released the point, which remained in the wound and could only be removed by excision[570], unless this was also impossible and the last and most dangerous solution was to force the point to leak with a bandage[571].

We see such a projectile in the Pandaros-Menelaus scene; Pandaros hits Menelaus in the middle of the stomach[572]. The arrow penetrates the skin completely through the half-armor with the front end. Menelaus is scared because he sees that he is bleeding, but he calms down, fig. 76 Feb. Nevertheless, Machaon's attempt to pull the arrow fails because the barbs are already stuck in the half-armor and immediately bend[573], so that there is no choice but to completely undress Menelaus. The two arrows received by Diomedes, Il.V, 97 f. and Il. XI, 375 f., are equally harmless. In both cases, the arrowhead completely penetrates the hit part of the body, so the arrow can simply be pulled out (διαμπερές, Il. V, 112).«

The arrow is called χαλκήρης[574] or χαλκοβαρής[575], on the one hand, because of the metal from which the arrowhead was made, and on the other hand, because of the weight of this bronze arrowhead.

In the much-discussed fragment of Iliad IV, 123, the ending is called simply σίδηρος. (Πάνδαρος) νευρήν μεν μαζώ πέλασεν, τοξω δέ σίδηρον[576].

Here are some details that can be gleaned from Homer's poems about arrows. Let us now turn to ancient depictions of arrows and finds that will also shed some more light on us here.

---

[567] Il. V, 393 δίστῳ τριγλώχινς; Il. XI, 507 ἱῴ τριγλώχινι. W. Helbig, Homer. Epos, p. 341, Translated τριγλώχιν as trisector.

[568] Il. IV, 151; 214: ὀξέες ὄγκοι.

[569] W. Reichel, a. a. O. p. 115 f.

[570] Il. XI, 515; 829; 814, 845 εκ μηρού τάμνε μαχοάρη / οξύ βέλος περιπευκές.

[571] See Il. V, 395-402.

[572] Il. IV, 132 f. αύτή δ'αυτ' ιθυεν όθι ζωστηοος οχηες/χρύσειοι σόνεχον καί διπλόος ηντετο θώρηξ.

[573] I prefer: πάλιν and άγεν, not ἐξελκομένοιο. Bronze sheet does not break like glass. If the barbs broke off, the arrow could be pulled out without further ado (W. Reichels Anmerkung).

[574] We find this term three times in relation to arrows: Il, XIII, 650; 662; Od. I, 262.

[575] Only twice Il. XV, 465; Od. XXI, 423. Other names of arrows, por.τανογλώχιν (Il. VIII, 297), πικρός (Il. IV, n8), ἐχεπεοκές (Il. IV, 129), ὀξύς (Il. XI, 845), περιπευκές (11. XI, 845), οξοβελής (Il. IV, 126), ὠκύμορος (Il. XV, 441) u. v. a. For more information, see E. Buchholz, a. a. O. Bd. II, p. 356.

[576] Homeric scholars agree that this passage should be considered to have been inserted later, since it implies a closer knowledge of iron by the listeners. P. Cauer, a. a. O. p. 285. C. Robert Studien zur Ilias, Berlin 1901, p. 209 f, 435. W. Reichel, a. a. O. p. 115, On the Relationship Between Bronze and Iron in the Homeric Poems, por. G. Beloch, Rivista di Filologia dass. Bd. II (1873), p. 42 ff. Griechische Geschichte, Leipzig 1893, p. 80 f., Anmerkung 4.

First we go back to the arrow shaft. As noted, Homer's poems only mention that the shaft had a notch at the lower end, below the flight feathers. On red-figure vessels, the arrows have notches at the lower end of the shaft, which could in no way have been cut into the shaft itself, as the notches are usually much wider than the radius[577]. It is probably possible, although not documented in the literature, that the radius was reinforced with other, stronger wood or perhaps bone due to its easy splitting, as we see in Egyptian examples[578]. We think we can adopt this process in some depictions of arrows because the part between the fletching and the actual notch appears to be much thinner and as if made of a different material than the shaft itself[579]. With this paste, perhaps the artist wanted to make the base of the arrow stronger and clearer. From a practical point of view, such strengthening was necessary, otherwise the radius would almost always break under greater stress.

It is likely that the flight feathers consisted of three feathers glued vertically at specific intervals, although the depictions do not provide us with sufficient evidence on this point. Feathers are always shown flat. The ancient artist still lacks the necessary training to reproduce the third feather in proper foreshortening.

The arrow in the well-known photo of the Sosias bowl shows either a wrap around the shaft where the shuttle sticks (perhaps to prevent breakage) or there is merely some decoration at the end of the shaft.

The arrows can then be divided into small subgroups, both in terms of notch and fletching. We found:

a) Arrows without fletches, with a notch in the shaft itself[580].

b) Arrows without fletches in which the end of the shaft has a bulbous protuberance at the end, which will probably have a notch cut into it[581].

c) Arrows with fletching, where at the end of the shaft there is a small fork, wider than the shaft itself[582].

If we don't see the notch on the shaft on some monuments, it's because the arrows are usually already mounted on the string. Plumage did not come into common use until the mid-7th century. In developed art, the notch and fletching of free-standing arrows are always reproduced[583].

The Greeks rarely used poisoned arrows. In Homer, poison is mentioned only once, Od. I, 259-264, where Athena says that Odysseus went to the Siren Ilos in the city of Ephyr to get poison for arrows, but she did not give it to him

---

[577] See Friedrich Hauser in Furtwängier-Reichhold, Griech. Vas. Serie III, p. 16 f. zu Taf. 123.

[578] See fig. 8.

[579] See Furtwängler-Reichhold, Griech. Vas. 32.

[580] Fragment of a Protocorinthian vessel, Ath. Mitt. Bd. XXII (1897), p. 304, fig. 29. Dodwellvase, Lau, Griech. Vas. Taf. III, 1b. Korinth. Vase, Jour. Hell. Stud. Bd. V (1884), Taf. zu p. 176. Reliefpithos in Wien, K. Masner, Die Sammlung antiker Vasen und Terrakotten, fig. 12.

[581] Mon. dell Inst. IX, Taf. 55; cf. perhaps also Furtwängler-Reichhold, Griech. Vas. Taf. 16.

[582] Mon. dell' Inst. I, Taf. 55. Furtwängler-Reichhold, Griech. Vas. Taf. 32, 101.

[583] See arrow from the shell of Sosia. Furtwängler-Reichhold, Griech. Vas. Taf. 22, 55, 61, 90, 96. Antike Denkmäler, II, 14; 21, 3. See A. Schaumberg, a. a. O. p. 112 f.

for fear of the gods. He then received poison from Anchialus, king of the Taphians[584]. Pausanias[585] tells us that Heracles took poison from the Hydra for his arrows. He is also said to have used poisoned arrows against centaurs[586]. Perhaps this story has preserved for us the memory of the once common use of poison for arrows.

6. Quiver

An open or lidded quiver was used to store arrows and sometimes a bow. While today we can judge from depictions on ancient monuments that quivers were made of perishable materials, leather or wood[587], this also explains why none have been preserved. In Homer's case, the shooters have a quiver that was equipped with a lid (πῶμα). It is said that when Pandaros wanted to send his arrow at Menelaus, Il. IV, 116:

αύταρ ὁ σύλα πώμα φαρετρης, εκ οελετ' ιόν[588].

We do not learn anything from Homer about its appearance, decorations or the material from which it was made. The terms used by the quiver refer only to the storage of arrows[589].

In the case of a leather quiver, parallel side strips were probably sewn in for reinforcement, so as to maintain the shape at all times. The representations of these quivers also show that they either had painted decorations or decorations made of other leather (Fig. 77), or were covered with decorative metal plates (Fig. 78).

The quiver was worn with a band in four ways:

a) On the back, almost between the shoulders, in such a position that the arrows can be pulled straight over the right shoulder[590].

b) Attached to the belt on the left side at hip level[591]. The strap ran from the right shoulder, across the chest, to the left hip.

c) On the back next to the left shoulder[592].

---

[584] See therefore, Strabo VIII, 3, 5, O. 338 (ed. Meineke).

[585] Paus. II, 37, 4.

[586] Euripides, Herakles, 365, 366 ... εστοουσεν τόξοις φόννίοις. See dazu noch V. 1184 See Verg. Aen. IX, 771, according to which Amycus is particularly adept at poisoning arrows. Otherwise, Virgil mentions poison with arrows Aen. X, 140; XII, 857.

[587] Rüstow-Köchly a. a. O. p. 21.

[588] See Od. IX, 312-315, where it is said that Polyphemus the Giant removed the boulder from the entrance as easily as an archer removes the lid from a quiver.

[589] ίοδοκος 11. XV, 444; Od. XXI, 12, 60; ιών εμπλειος Od. XXII, 3; άμφηοεφής II. I, 45; por. dalej Poll. Onom. X, 142; Auth. Pal. VI, 296.

[590] See Gerhard, A. V. 120, 121, 130, 135; Furtwängler-Reichhold, Griech. Vas. 16; Mon. dell' Inst' III, Taf. 12.

[591] Gerhard, A. V. 95/96, 104, 149; Mon. dell' Inst. I, Taf. 24, 55; VIII, Taf. 6. Furtwängler-Reichhold, Griech. Vas. 26/27, 58, 74; W. Amelung, a. a. O. Bd. I, Taf. XI, 71; Michaelis, Jahrbuch d. deutsch bow. Inst., Bd. I (1886), p. 1 ff.

[592] Gerhard, A. V. 95/96, 97, 100, 101, 105/106, 110.

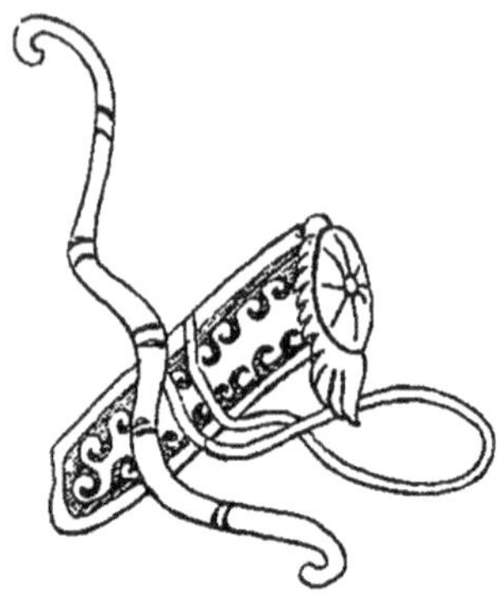
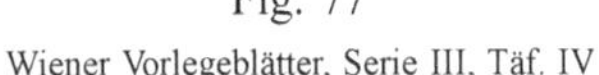

<table>
<tr><td align="center">Fig. 77
Wiener Vorlegeblätter, Serie III, Täf. IV</td><td align="center">Fig. 78
Wiener Vorlegeblätter, Serie V, Taf. VII, Nr. 3</td></tr>
</table>

d) Under the fencing arm[593].

Sometimes, especially in works of archaic art, it cannot be said with certainty whether a quiver (if not attached to a belt) is worn one way or another[594].

It is obvious that the representation of quivers, like bows, is not always true. In general, all quivers can be divided into two large groups:

A. Shape as in Fig. 78, mainly from the Scythians, used by the Amazons and Heracles.

B. Cylindrical form (fig. 79), given by artists to Apollo and his sister Artemis.

Within each of these groups, not only individual types[595] can be distinguished, but also individual phases of the development of their form can be identified.

Group A

a) A quiver without a lid, almost the same width from top to bottom, either without decoration or with very faint decoration on the upper or lower edges[596] (fig. 80).

b) Quiver with a lid, an oblong or conical quiver, with a round lid and as if made of solid material. In archaic representations, usually without decorations[597].

---

[593] Mon. dell' Inst. I, Taf. 20 (Herakles), 23. W. Amelung, a. a. O. Bd; I, Taf. XV, 92 und 108, Taf. XL, 120; Bd. II, Taf. XXXIX, 210.

[594] Mon. dell' Inst. I, Taf. 51; Gerhard, A. V. 121, 130.

[595] See A. Schaumberg, a. a. O. 114 ff.

[596] Lau, Griech. Vas. Taf. III, 1b (Dodwellvase). Archäologische Zeitung, 1883, Taf. X, 1 (protokorinthisch). Jahrbuch d. deutsch. ärch. Inst. Bd. XIII (1898), Taf. 1 (Sophilosscherbe aus Menidi); Bd. IV (1889), Taf. 4 (Andokides). Reliefpithos, Bull. Corr. Hell. Bd. XXII, 1898, p. 463, fig. 8. Antike Denkmäler, II, Taf. XXIX, 9 (Korinth, Pinax). Ἐφημ. ἀρχαιολ. 1883. πιν. 3 (tyrrhenische Amphora). Gerhard, A. V. 100 schwarzf. att. Vas. E. Pottier, Vas. peinis du Louvre, Bd. II, Taf. 89, G. 5 (rotryc.). A. Eurtwängler, Antike Gemmen, Taf. VI, 58.

[597] K. Masner, a. a. O. fig. 12. Mon. dell' Inst. I, Taf. 23, 51; VI-VII, Taf. 27, 33 Gerhard, A, V. 105/106, 190/191, 323. Jahrbuch d. deutsch. bow. Inst Bd. XIII (1898), Taf. 12. Archäologische Zeitung 1881, Taf. XII, 1. B. Graef, a. a. O. Bd. I, Taf. 31, Nr. 606. Furtwängler-Reichhold, Griech. Vas. 101.

110

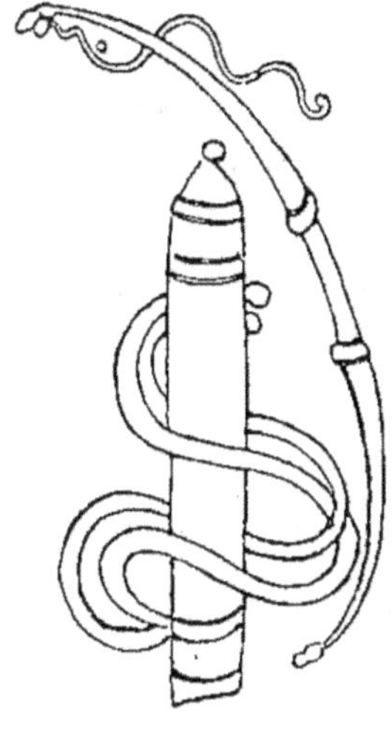

<table>
<tr><td align="center">Fig. 79
Wiener Vorlegeblätter, Serie VII, Täf. VIa</td><td align="center">Fig. 80
Wiener Vorlegeblätter, 1890/91, Taf. IV (Oinochoe des
Nikosthenes)</td></tr>
</table>

c) Quiver, oblong, tapering downwards, usually decorated, with a lid in the form of a shorter or longer flap[598], always worn on a belt.

Group B

a) Cylindrical shape, oblong, equally wide, usually rounded at the bottom, with a lid also round, but tapering slightly towards the height[599].

h) Shape as a), but flat at the bottom, with a petal-shaped lid[600].

We mentioned that quivers were decorated with paintings or specially made metal plates. Although the remains of a quiver have not yet been found on Greek soil, we have an example of the type of decoration of Attic quivers from the 5th century[601], in a well-known gold setting from Nikopol (Fig. 81). The

---

[598] This form is almost always depicted by the bows of the Scythian archers, the Amazons, and in the red-figure painting also Hercules. See Furtwängler-Reichhold, Griech. Vas. 23, 26/27, 58, 74 usw. Murray, Designs from Greek Vas. Taf. I, 3; IV, 15; V, 19. Mon. dell' Inst. I, Taf. 55; VI-VII, Taf. 22; VIII, Taf. 6; X, Taf. 50. Gerhard, A. V. 69, 94, 192 Fouilles de Delphes, Taf. 41 und 44/45 (hängt an der Wand). Furtwängler, Antike Gemmen, Bd. I, Taf. IX, 21; XVIII, 18. Mon. Piot 1897, Taf. IV-V. Jour. Hell. Stud. Bd. VI (1885), Taf. 57 Altertümer von Pergamon, II, Taf. XLIX, 16.

[599] Gerhard, A. V. 29, 95, 119/120, 193, Nr. 4. Furtwängler-Reichhold, Griech. Vas. 88 (Dariusvase). Amer. Jour. Arch. Bd. XI (1907), Taf. XII. Revue bow. Bd. XIII (1889), p. 31. Jour. Hell. Stud. Bd. VI (1885), Taf. 58. Mon. dell' Inst. XI, Taf. 40 (Artemis).

[600] Mon. dell' Inst. I, Taf. 20. Jour. Hell. Stud. Bd. XIII (1892), Taf. III. Gerhard, A. V. 54, 70, 119/120. Overbeck, Kunstmyth. Atlas, Apollo XXIII, 6. Dümrnler, Bonner Studien, p. 72. Antike Denkmäler, I, 22. Lenormant et de Witte, Élite céram. II, 17, 18.

[601] Stephani, Compte Rendu 1864, Taf. 4. Wiener Vorlegeblatter, Ser. B, Taf. 10. Kondakoff-Tolstoi-Reinach, a. a. O. fig. 263 (they believe that it is a work from the beginning of the third century). He doubted the authenticity of B. Graef, Hermes, Bd. XXXVI (1901), p. 86. However, a second specimen was found, Jahrbuch d. deutsch, bow. Inst. Bd. XVIII (1903), Anzeiger, p. 84.

Fig. 81

Kondakoff, Tolstoi, Reinäch, a. a. O. ryc. 263

scene depicted there has been described many times before. Stephani thought the quiver depicted the myth of Alope and Theseus[602].

However, C. Robert was probably more right in explaining this scene as Achilles among the daughters of Lycomedes[603].

In addition to the quiver, the bow was usually carried in such a way that the bow was tied with a belt. There are also temporal differences in the type of bonding. In older art, the bow was always „tied"[604], from the 5th century onwards the string was usually tied on the side[605].

The gorytos was used to hold a bow. So we hear that Penelope takes the bow from the Gorytes to then give it to the suitors for the competition, Od. XXI, 53-54:

$$\ldots\ldots\ldots\ldots\ldots\ldots\ldots\ \alpha\H{\iota}\nu\upsilon\tau o\ \tau\acute{o}\xi o\nu$$
$$\alpha\grave{\upsilon}\tau\tilde{\wp}\ \gamma\omega\rho\upsilon\tau\tilde{\wp},\ \H{o}\varsigma\ o\acute{\iota}\ \pi\varepsilon\rho\acute{\iota}\varkappa\varepsilon\iota\tau o\ \varphi\alpha\varepsilon\iota\nu\acute{o}\varsigma.$$

Although Gorytos was already mentioned in Homer, it was probably little known in Greece, which is reflected in the few representations of Gorytos[606].

---

602 See Kondakoff-Tolstoi-Reinach, a. a. O. p. 302 ff.

603 Jahrbuch d. deutsch, bow. Inst Bd. IV. (1889), Anzeiger, p. 151, und 16. Hall. Winckelmannsprogramm Nekyia, p. 38 (V. Jahrhundert).

604 A. Michaelis, Jahrbuch d. deutsch, bow. Inst. Bd. I (1886), p. 36, też np. Archäologische Zeitung, 1881, Taf. XII, 1.

605 See Fürtwängler-Reichhold, Griech. Vas. Taf. 4, 23, 26/27, 58 usw.

606 Visconti, Museo Pio Clementino, Bd. IV, Taf. 40, 43. Zoega, Bassirilievi antichi, Roma (1808), Bd. II, Taf. 98. W. Amelung, a. a. O. Bd. II, Taf. XXI, 79.

As can be seen in the illustrations, the Gorytos also served as an arrow container. It is well depicted on the well-known electron vase from Kul-Oba. Therefore, it is also likely that Gorytos rarely covered the entire arc, usually only three-quarters of the arc's length[607].

To conclude these observations, we would like to point out that the archers, who had neither quivers nor gorytos, carried arrows in their left hands next to the bow. We cannot say whether this custom was universal; we find them mainly in Heracles, Apollo and Artemis[608].

7. Archer's stance when shooting

The shooting attitude of the shooters naturally depended on the conditions in which the shooting took place. First of all, as far as Homer is concerned, we read about Apollo coming in anger from the heights of Olympus (Il. I, 48): εζετ' επειτα άπανευθε νεών, μετά δ'ιόν εηκεν. None of the great archers of the Iliad, neither Pandaros (Il. IV, 113), nor Teucros (Il. VIII, 267 ff.), nor Alexandros (Il. during the battle they had to seek protection elsewhere, Pandaros and Teukros behind the shields of the other warriors[609], Alexandros behind natural cover. This also explains the attitude of the archers in question. They had to either kneel or at least bend very much, as standing upright was too much of a target for the enemy and their comrade's shield was unable to provide them with sufficient protection from the enemy. And if, for example, we read about Pandaros (Il. IV, 112, 113):

καὶ τὸ μὲν εὖ κατέθηκε τανυσσάμενος ποτὶ γαίῃ
ἀγκλίνας· πρόσθεν δὲ σάκεα σχέθον ἐσθλοὶ ἑταῖροι,

So Pandaros places his bow on the ground for two reasons, firstly, to extend the leg with which he drew the bow. But secondly, to shoot, he either kneels or takes a bent position and has to hide behind the shield. An example of a kneeling archer is the statue of a Scythian from the National Museum of Athens[610] (Fig. 82). The Scythian is almost kneeling on his left knee, his right foot resting on it. With his left hand down, he holds the bow, which is almost lying on the ground, and with his right hand he pulls an arrow from the quiver. The motif of shooting behind a shield has been preserved on a red-figure

---

[607] G. v. Kieseritzky und C. Watzinger, Griechische Grabreliefs aus Südrußland, Taf. XL, 587, 593, 594, 606; Taf. XLI, 575, 597, 599, 600.

[608] Furtwängler-Reichhold, Griech. Vas. 22 (Herakles), 55 (Apollo), 61 (Herakles), 90 (Herakles), 96 (Artemis).

[609] J. H. Krause, a. a. O. Bd. I, p. 604. L. Grasberger, a. a. O. Bd. III, p. 155. See the battle of hoplites with archers on a black-figure amphora in Berlin, Gerhard, A. V. Taf. 63; Furtwängler, Vasensammlung zu Berlin, Nr. 1865.

[610] Καστριωτης, Γλυπτά του Ἐθνικού Μουσείου, Athen 1908, p. 132. A. Brückner, Der Friedhof am Eridanos, Berlin 1909, p. 84. Arndt-Amelung, Einzelverkauf Nr. 623.

Fig. 82

Arndt-Amelung, Einzelverkauf, Nr. 623

bowl[611], on which a Scythian archer is protected by the shield of his accompanying hoplite. One must think about Alexander's behavior during a similar shooting, Fig. XI, 371: στήλη κεκλιμένος. These words do not determine his attitude, as he could have been standing or kneeling, but the fact that he was kneeling seems certain when we read further[612] Il. XI, 378-379:

$$..... \ ὁ \ δὲ \ μάλα \ ἡδὺ \ γελάσσας$$
$$ἐκ \ λόχου \ ἀμπήδησε. ... κτλ.$$

We can name only three monuments in which the archer himself holds a shield. On a red-figure vase in the British Museum we see (Fig. 83) an archer wearing helmet, chiton, armor and greaves; he has a quiver on his left side. Shoots arrows in a crouching position. On his left arm he has a shield covering both hands and almost the entire bow"[613]. In the red-figure volute crater from New York, the Amazon holds a shield and a bow in her left hand[614]. Finally, we see a similar archer with a very large shield on the Präneste[615] box.

Regarding Odysseus' attitude, Penelope says that Odysseus shot στάς arrows in his master shot, Od. XIX, 575: στάς δ'ο γε πολλόν ἀνεουθε

---

[611] P. Hartwig, a. a. O. Taf. 56, Nr. 2: Schale des Onesimos (?).This bowl speaks against K.Wernickemu, Hermes, Bd. XXVI, p. 63, who sees something „extraordinary" in Teukros' way of fighting.

[612] W. Reichel, a. a. O. p. 117 f. A. Schaumberg, a. a. O. p. 85 f.

[613] A. p. Murray, Designs from Greek Vas. Taf. IV, Nr 15.

[614] Furtwängler-Reichhold, Griech. Vas. Taf. 116.

[615] Mon. dell' Inst. Supplbd. XII (1884/85), Taf. XVII und XVIII.

114

Ryc. 83

A. S. Murray, a. a. O., Taf. IV, 15

διαρρίπτασκεν οιστόν. How should this στάς be understood? Certainly not that Odysseus actually stood upright, because then the axes would have to be at the height of an upright man, because, as we know, the target and the eye must be at the same height. Even if the shafts were 1 m high, Odysseus would be very much bent over; and they were probably not even 1 m high[616]. Elsewhere, Homer says that at the moment of the shot, Odysseus is sitting in a chair, Od. XXI, 419-421:

> τὸν ῥ' ἐπὶ πήχει ἑλὼν ἕλκεν νευρὴν· γλυφίδας τε,
> αὐτόθεν ἐκ δίφροιο καθήμενος, ἧκε δ' ὀιστὸν
> ἄντα τιτυσκόμενος . . . . . .   κτλ.

According to Reichel[617], it should be imagined only as a slight support, with the shooter leaning towards the target. Perhaps his seating was intended to demonstrate increased skill, strength, and marksmanship, as well as to create a contrast with his suitors.

The posture that Odysseus adopts as he shoots at the suitors becomes much clearer, Od. XXII, 2-4:

> ἆλτο δ' ἐπὶ μέγαν οὐδὸν ἔχων βιὸν ἠδὲ φαρέτρην
> ἰῶν ἐμπλείην, ταχέας δ' ἐκχεύατ' ὀιστοὺς
> αὐτοῦ πρόσθε ποδῶν . . . . . .   κτλ.

---

[616] Chr. Blinkenberg, Archäologische Studien, p. 41.
[617] W. Reichel, a. a. O. p. 117.

Odysseus threw his arrows at his feet, so he had to either kneel or at least bend down – almost crouch – to shoot at the suitors.

Over time, we have seen some changes in the way archers' posture is depicted in artistic depictions. Leaning strongly forward, in a crouching position that should be considered more like running than crouching, the archer shoots on a well-known soapstone from Crete[618]. The Mycenaean dagger archer occupies almost the same position[619]. The female archer is probably depicted on a Cretan carnelian in a knee-race[620]. A slight difference can be seen in the posture of the archers on the fragment of the silver chalice from the grave of the fourth shaft in Mycenae, because although the torso is also bent forward, the right leg is strongly extended forward, while the left leg is deeply bent, almost at the knee[621]. On a cut stone in the Mycenaean style we see a kneeling shooter hunting a goat[622]. Although archers generally appear in a similar posture in monuments from the Cretan-Mycenaean area, the position is always determined by the given situation[623].

In archaic art, archers are depicted in a way that more closely resembles actual kneeling. This pattern should be understood mainly as a regular running step, as is clear from the topic presented. Thus, the example of Heracles can be cited in the bas-relief from Assos[624] or on the red-colored pithos in Vienna[625]; his attitude should be understood similarly to that of, for example, Achilles, who on horseback chases Troilus on an amphora with a black figure[626], because „here and there the pattern of kneeling symbolizes a stormy attack and a stormy pursuit"[627].

In further development, running on stiff knees turns into a running system in which the legs are very stretched and are no longer bent as deeply as older monuments show[628]. It is worth noting here that on some „Chalcidian vases"[629]

---

[618] Annual British School, Bd. VII, p. 44, fig. 13.

[619] W. Reichel, a. a. O. fig. 61.

[620] A. Furtwängier, Antike Gemmen, Bd. I, Taf. II, 24.

[621] W. Reichel, a. a. O. fig. 17 a.

[622] Perrot et Chipiez, a. a. O. Bd. VI, Taf. XVI, 8.

[623] A. Furtwängler, Antike Gemmen, Bd. III, p. 53, 72, 94.

[624] M. Collignon-Thraemer, Geschichte der griechischen Plastik, Bd. I, fig. 85.

[625] K. Masner, a. a. O. p. 19. On Heracles' pursuit of the fleeing centaurs, see O. Puchstein, Archäologische Zeitung, 1881, p. 240 ff. A. Furtwängler, Archäologische Zeitung, 1883, p. 156 ff. Derselbe, Roschers Mythologisches Lexikon, Bd. II, p. 2193 fr.

[626] Gerhard, A. V. Taf. 185. E. Schmidt, Der Knielauf, in Münchener Archäologische Studien, 1909, p. 291, fig. 18.

[627] A. Kalkmann, Jahrbuch d. deutsch. bow Inst. Bd. X (1895), p. 66. As for Heracles in the battle of the centaurs on the chest of Cypselos, Pausanias only states that he was depicted as τοξεύων (vv. 19, 9). To see kneeling archers, see the following sights: A. Furtwängler, Olympia, Bronzen, Taf. 40. Gerhard, A. V. Taf. 105, Herakles gegen Geryones, por. Studniczka, Jahrbuch d. deutsch, bow. Inst. Bd. II (1887), p. 155. Mon. dell' Inst. I, Taf. 51. Chalkidische Amphora, mit dem Kampf um den Leichnam des Achilles, Paris wegfliehend. Die François-Vase (Jagd auf den kalydonischen Eber). Mon dell' Inst. IV, Taf. 54-58; A. Furtwängler-Reichhold, Griech. Vas. Taf. 13.

[628] Antike Denkmäler, I, 22, vgl. Löschcke, Jahrbuch d. deutsch. bow. Inst, Bd. II, p. 275 ff. (Apollo and Artemis shoot the Niobids). Ἐφημ. ἀρχαιολ. 1883, πιν. 3. (Apollo and Artemis shoot the Niobids). Wiener Vorlegeblätter, Serie D, Taf. IX, Nr. 8 (Herakles vor Prometheus). Archäologische Zeitung, 1883, Taf. X 2 (Protocol Corinthian vase with lion hunting).

[629] Gerhard, A. V., 191, 322. See F. Studniczka, Jahrbuch d. deutsch. bow. Inst. Bd. V (1890), p. 144 fr.

116

the archers have winged feet, which should be considered a sign of their speed[630].

In addition to the older kneeling run, which is sometimes indistinguishable from the running pattern[631], another shooting stance is gradually emerging, namely the proper kneeling[632] in which the weight of the body is mainly supported by the strongly extended hind leg. This pattern, particularly pronounced in Aginete archers[633], is often repeated in archaic art[634]. It is also used by later artists[635], and sometimes a diagram of a knee and a course of knees[636] can be found on the same monument.

On newer monuments we also find archers in the posture known to us from Mycenaean depictions. We see the upper body leaning strongly forward, while one foot is strongly extended forward and the other slightly bent at the knee[637].

This pattern closely resembles the fully upright archer's stance, in which only one foot is forward but the upper body remains mostly upright[638].

To conclude these considerations, we would like to briefly talk about two specific types of archery, chariot and horse archery. Perhaps in the Mycenaean period this first type of fighting must have been common, for we find it on a famous gold ring from a grave in the fourth shaft[639], where an archer standing next to a chariot driver shoots at a deer. This type of fighting may have spread to Cyprus under the influence of the Orient in both the Mycenaean and post-Mycenaean periods[640]. On the other hand, Homer's archers do not seem to have used chariots, which can be inferred from Pandarus's complaints that he

---

[630] See Il. X, 358-359: λαιψηρά γουνατ' ἐνώμα / φεύγεμεναι. A. Kalkmann, Jahrbuch d. deutsch. bow. Inst. Bd. X (1895), p. 67 und Anmerkung 69.

[631] Gerhard, A. V. 95, 96; vgl. dazu F. Studniczka, Jahrbuch d. deutsch. bow. Inst. Bd. I (1886), p. 89 ff.; F. Hauser, Jahrbuch d. deutsch. bow. Inst. Bd. VIII (1893), p. 99 ff. A. Baumeister, Denkmäler, Bd. III, Taf. 88. Dubois-Maisonneuve, Introduction a l'etude de vas. ant. Taf 61.

[632] Mon. dell' Inst. Taf. VI, 33. A. Kalkmann, Jahrbuch d. deutsch, bow. Inst. Bd. X (1895), p. 71, fig. 11.

[633] A. Furtwängler, Ägina, Heiligtum der Aphaia, Taf. 104, 105.

[634] A. Kalkmann, Jahrbuch d. deutsch. bow. Inst., Bd. X (1895), p. 72, Anm. 103. See also Joubin, Bull. Corr. Hellenique, Bd. XVIII (1894), Taf. XVI. Auch F. Studniczka, Jahreshefte d. öst. bow. Inst., Bd. VI (1903), p. 185, fig. 107, 108.

[635] Wiener Vorlegeblätter, 1890/91, Taf. I, 6; II, 1c. Löschcke, Bonner Studien, p. 250, fig. 3. Museo Gregoriano, Bd. II, 27, 2 c. A. Furtwängler, Vasensammlung zu Berlin, Nr. 2263.

[636] See Archäologische Zeitung, 1851, Taf. 31, 1. On either side of the depicted scene is an archer, one kneeling and the other running.

[637] Wiener Vorlegeblätter, 1890/91, Taf. VII, 1a. Mon. dell' Inst. X, Taf. 53; VIII. Taf. 6. P. Hartwig, Meisterschalen, Taf 55.

[638] See Furtwängler, Jahrbuch d. deutsch, bow. Inst. Bd. III (1888), p. 119,Taf. III, 7. Die schönste Darstellung dieser Haltung bietet uns der Apollo vom Belvedere, Amelung, a. a. O. Bd. II, Nr. 92, p. 256 ff, Für diese Haltung auf Vasen vgl. Mon. dell' Inst. I, Taf. 20, 23; II, Taf. 49-50; III. Taf. 50; XI, Taf. 40 u. v. a.

[639] Furtwängler, Antike Gemmen, Bd. I, Taf. 2, Nr. 8. See also ciosany kamień w p. Wide i L. Kjeiberg, Athenische Mitteilungen, Bd. XX (1895),S. 300 f. fig. 20, which, found at Kalarea, probably belongs to the Mycenaean period; Here, too, the archer is depicted on a chariot.

[640] See Ohnefalsch-Richter, Kyptos, Text p. 66, fig. 70 (mykenisch). Murray-Walters, Excavations in Cyprus, Taf. I, aus der Nekropole von Erikomi (spät-mykenisch). Ohnefalsch-Richter, Kypros, Tamassosvase, Text p. 66, fig. 71 (postmykenisch); nach E. Schmidt, Knielauf, a. a. O. p. 366, ist dieses Gefäß andie orientalische Kunst anzuschließen. Kyprisches Vasenbild bei Ohnefalsch-Richter, Kypros, Taf. 158; Perrot et Chipiez, a. a. O. Bd. III, fig. 527, 528. Studniczka, Jahrbuch d. deutsch. bow. Inst. Bd. XX (1907), p. 173, fig. 20.

regrets that he marched on Troy with a bow on foot rather than with a chariot.
Il.V, 197-205:

ἦ μέν μοι μάλα πολλὰ γέρων αἰχμητὰ Λυκάων
ἐρχομένῳ ἐπέτελλε δόμοις ἔνι ποιητοῖσιν·
ἵπποισίν μ᾽ἐκέλευε καὶ ἄρμασιν ἐμβεβαῶτα
200 ἀρχεύειν Τρώεσσι κατὰ κρατερὰς ὑσμίνας ·
ἀλλ᾽ ἐγὼ οὐ πιθόμην, ἦ τ᾽ ἂν πολὺ κέρδιον ἦεν
ἵππων φειδόμενος, μή μοι δευοίατο φορβῆς
ἀνδρῶν εἰλομένων, εἰωθότες ἔδμεναι ἄδην.
ὣς λίπον, αὐτὰρ πέζος ἐς Ἴλιον εἰλήλουθα,
205 τόξοισι πίσυνος . . . .   κτλ.

Chariot archers appear extremely rarely in later Greek art. On a black-figure
vase in Paris, Apollo, standing on a chariot, shoots arrows at two fleeing people (Niobids or Tityos and Ge?). He stands with his legs deeply bent, leaning
heavily on the windowsill[641]. The second example is probably the goddess
from the so-called The frieze of the Western Cnidian Treasury at Delphi[642]
which – as first recognized by R. Heberdey[643] – shoots an arrow while de-
scending from the chariot. Heracles also shoots arrows from his chariot at the
giants on the black-figure vase in the British Museum[644]. The small number of
such representations allows us to assume that this type of fighting was known
among the Greeks of the classical period, but was not as common as among
other peoples, including Egyptians or Assyrians.

Archer riders are not mentioned at all in the Odyssey and only once in the
Iliad, in Dolonei[645], Il. X, 513-514:

καρπαλίμως δ᾽ ἵππων ἐπεβήσετο (Diomedes), κόψε δ᾽ Ὀδυσσεύς
τόξῳ · τοὶ δ᾽ ἐπέτοντο θοὰς ἐπὶ γῆας Ἀχαιῶν.

It cannot be decided with certainty whether the poet Dolonea really knew
mounted archers, or whether the use of horses in the nocturnal adventure of
Diomedes and Odysseus seemed necessary only because of the speed necessary. In any case, archers on horses are rare in archaic art[646]. On a reddish
pithos, probably from the late 7th or early 6th century BC[647], we see five horse
archers in relief[648]; the riders are naked and wear caps similar to Phrygian ones.
The one in our drawing holds a bow in his right hand. In Fig. 84, riders are

---

⁶⁴¹ Mon. dell' Inst. II, Taf. 18. A similar image can be seen on an Etruscan gold ring, formerly in the
Campan collection, Müller-Wieseler, 4. Edition, provided by K. Wernicke und B. Graef, Apollo, Taf. xxvi, 5.
However, in addition to Apollo, the griffin is missing here.

⁶⁴² Th. Homolle, Fouilles de Delphes, Bd. IV, Taf. VII-VIII.

⁶⁴³ R. Heberdey, Das Schatzhaus der Knidier in Delphi, Athenische Mitteilungen,Bd. XXXIV (1909),
p. 159 f., Taf. V, 3. Gegen diese Erklärung Courby, Rev. bow. Bd. XVII (1911), p. 214 f.

⁶⁴⁴ Roscher, Mythologisches Lexikon, Bd. I, Figur auf p. 1655. See, in this regard, Euripides, Herakles,
177 ff.; Gerhard, A. V. 5.

⁶⁴⁵ P. Cauer. a. a. O. p. 501.

⁶⁴⁶ A. de Ridder, Amphores Beotiennes à reliefs, in Bull. Corr. Hellén. Bd. XXII (1898), p. 462.

⁶⁴⁷ de Ridder, a a. O. p. 519, Taf. VI.

⁶⁴⁸ See de Ridder's more detailed description, a. a. O. p. 459.

Ryc. 84

Bulletin de correspond. Hellénique, Bd. XXII, S. 463, ryc. 8

shown with a bow[649], the upper end of which rests on the shoulder, and the horse is steered with the left hand. On his back he has a quiver slung on a strap that runs over his left shoulder and under his right armpit. Another example is the Chalcidian vase from Vulci[650], which also depicts two archers on horses.

Often, in depictions of barbarians, we only encounter horse archers[651]. If we have already pointed out the Eastern origin of this custom in the case of chariot archers, this applies even more to horse archers, which, being common and widely known in the East, was not native anywhere in Greece[652].

---

[649] Based on the lower end of the bow shown, which is open towards the target, you can think of a composite bow.

[650] Gerhard, A. V. 190-191.

[651] de Ridder, a. a. O. p. 465. See in this regard Lysias, Κατά Ἀλκιβιάδου, II, §. 6 = 15, 6 ed. C. Scheibe. Xenoph. Memor. III, 3, 1.

[652] Archers' cavalry on the so-called „Cypriot" bowls, cf. Perrotet Chipiez, a. a. O. Bd. III, fig. 544 (Caere); fig. 547 Amathus auf Kypros. Mon. dell' Inst. X, Taf. 33 (Präneste). See also Americ. Journ. Arch. Bd. XII (1908), Taf. 14. In any case, it should be noted that archers on horseback appeared to the later Greeks as a formation characteristic of the Orient (Plut. Apophtheg. T. Quinct. 3 p. 197 C; Diodor, XIX, 29. 2), but still originating in Crete, as Plato claims Leg. VIII, 834 D, hervorgeht. See about it E. Reisch, in Pauly-Wissowas Real Enzyklopädie, Bd. I, p. 2721.

8. The role of the bow in agonism and education of young people

Although the bow has been known since ancient times, it does not occupy a place corresponding to its importance in agonistics and general gymnastics. This is all the more striking because, as we noted earlier in the Ethiopian king's response to Cambyses' spies, the drawing or drawing of the bow was also considered evidence of general fitness[653].

Also in the Odyssey, drawing a bow is a sign of overall strength. The first point of the competition for Penelope's hand is to draw Odysseus's bow. But neither Telemachus nor any of the suitors are able to string the bow. At the beginning of the shooting competition, Antinous says that there is no man in the assembly as strong and capable as Odysseus; and that drawing the bow will no longer be so easy (Od. XXI, 90-95). When Telemachus unsuccessfully tries to draw his bow, he says mournfully (Od. XXI, 132-133):

> . . . . . οὔ πω χερσὶ πέποιθα
> ἄνδρ' ἀπαμύνασθαι, ὅτε τις πρότερος χαλεπήνῃ.

His inability to draw his bow is a sign that he is too weak to defend himself if someone insults him.

When Leiodes also proves to be too weak to draw the bow and announces death by bow to the suitors, Antinous tells him (Od. XXI, 172-173):

> οὐ γάρ τοι σέγε τοῖον ἐγείνατο πότνια μήτηρ,
> οἷόν τε ῥυτῆρα βιοῦ τ' ἔμεναι καὶ ὀιστῶν.

Leibodes is generally a weak man, made only for the Mantics; can't compete with strong people. Eurymachus feels the shame of weakness even more than others. It's not that he cares so much about marrying Penelope, but that he turns out to be so weak compared to Odysseus. Od. XXI, 249-255:

> ὦ πόποι, ἦ μοι ἄχος περὶ τ' αὐτοῦ καὶ περὶ πάντων.
> 250 οὔ τι γάμου τοσσοῦτον ὀδύρομαι ἀχνύμενός περ·
> εἰσὶ καὶ ἄλλαι πολλαὶ Ἀχαιίδες, αἱ μὲν ἐν αὐτῇ
> ἀμφιάλῳ Ἰθάκῃ, αἱ δ' ἄλλῃσιν πολίεσσιν.
> ἀλλ' εἰ δὴ τοσσόνδε βίης ἐπιδευέες εἰμὲν
> ἀντιθέου Ὀδυσσῆος, ὅ τ' οὐ δυνάμεσθα τανύσσαι
> 255 τόξον, ἐλεγχείη δὲ καὶ ἐσσομένοισι πυθέσθαι.

The excuse that it is Apollo's holiday allows players to postpone the shooting competition to the next day. – For fear of disgrace, they initially do not want to let Odysseus try to draw the bow (Od. XXI, 285-286):

> . . . . . . οἱ δ' ἄρα πάντες ὑπερφιάλως νεμέσησαν
> δείσαντες, μὴ τόξον ἐύξοον ἐντανύσειεν.

---

[653] In this regard, it is necessary to recall once again the task which Heracles entrusted to his sons in the country of the Scythians, gab, p. 51 ff.

This fear that the stranger may turn out to be stronger than the suitors is expressed by Eurymachus's response to Penelope's demand to give Odysseus his bow (Od. XXI, 323-329):

ἀλλ' αἰσχυνόμενοι φάτιν ἀνδρῶν ἠδὲ γυναικῶν,
μή ποτέ τις εἴπῃσι κακώτερος. ἄλλος 'Αχαιῶν·
325 ἢ πολὺ χείρονες ἄνδρες ἀμύμονος ἀνδρὸς ἄκοιτιν
μνῶνται, οὐδέ τι τόξον ἐύξοον ἐντανύουσιν·
ἀλλ' ἄλλός τις πτωχὸς ἀνὴρ ἀλαλήμενος ἐλθὼν
ῥηιδίως ἐτάνυσσε βιόν, διὰ δ' ἧκε σιδήρου.
ὣς ἐρέουσ', ἡμῖν δ' ἂν ἐλέγχεα ταῦτα γένοιτο.

When Odysseus bent his bow and shot, he says with derision (Od. XXI, 424-430):

Τηλέμαχ', οὔ σ' ὁ ξεῖνος ἐνὶ μεγάροισιν ἐλέγχει·
425 ἥμενος, οὐδέ τι τοῦ σκοποῦ ἤμβροτον, οὐδέ τι τόξον
δὴν ἔκαμον τανύων · ἔτι μοι μένος ἔμπεδόν ἐστιν,
οὐχ ὥς με μνηστῆρες ἀτιμάζοντες ὄνονται.
νῦν δ' ὥρη καὶ δόρπον 'Αχαιοῖσιν τετυκέσθαι
ἐν φάει, αὐτὰρ ἔπειτα καὶ ἄλλως ἐψιάασθαι
430 μολπῇ καὶ φόρμιγγι · τὰ γάρ τ' ἀναθήματα δαιτός.

Pausanias tells us another story, no less instructive for us in this respect, about the Pancratiast Timantesus Cleon[654], whose statue he made at Olympia on the occasion of the Olympic victory[655]. In later years he gave up the sport, but every day he checked whether his strength was still intact by stretching a large bow. However, when he went on a long journey and neglected his daily exercises, he returned home and tried to regain his strength with his bow, but he was unable to draw the string as usual. Saddened by this loss of strength, he built a pile of wood, set it on fire and threw himself into the flames. Pausanias describes his actions as madness – μανία – but in our opinion it was only a consequence of the previously mentioned opinion widespread in ancient times: whoever could not draw or draw a bow was considered a weak person, opposed to violence, unable to defend himself against the enemy and generally it wasn't very effective.

Homer knows about regular shooting competitions. Archery is also among the competitions organized in honor of the deceased Patroclus. The shooters' task was to hit a pigeon tied to the mast with a thin ribbon[656]. In Virgil's imitation of these Homeric games, Aeneas also invites his friends and companions to a shooting competition on the occasion of the commemorative games in honor of Anchises[657].

---

[654] Pausanias, VI, 8, 4. The same story told according to Pausanias p.v. Τιμάνθηςauch Suidas.- See H. Krause, a. a. O. Bd. I, p. 600. L. Grasberger, a. a. O.Bd. III, p. 151 f.

[655] About the time of his victory, Lt.H. Hitzig i H. Bluemner, in Pausaniaeedit. Bd. II2, p. 574, Anm. zu p. 473, 18.

[656] Il. XXIII, 859-858.

[657] Verg. Aen. V, 485 528. See also J. H. Krause, a. a. O. Bd. I,.S. 602. f.

As is commonly known, in historical times there was no place for the bow during the main festivals on the Greek mainland. Although Apollo killed the dragon Python with his arrows, and the Pythian games were erected in memory of this deed, there was no place for archery during the Pythian Agony[658].

Nevertheless, the bow must have been in constant use on the islands (Crete, Ceos, Salamis) and in places where the Greeks came into contact with archery peoples. It is impossible to determine whether it has always been used to the same extent there since ancient times. However, what is certain is that archery flourished at the end of the 3rd and 2nd centuries, as evidenced by inscriptions[659]. For example, archery is part of the competition in the town of Koressos on the island of Keos[660]. In the relevant text it is first written: The organizer of the games should employ a school student whose task it will be, ποιεῖνλαμπάδα / των νεωτέρων τηι εορτήι καί τάλλα επιμ ε λεί σθαι τά κατά τό γο /μνάσιον, καί ἐξάγειν είς μελέτην ακοντισμού καί το ξικη ς καί / καταπαλταφεσιας τριςτοῦ μηνός[661]. It is further decreed that the winner of the tournament receives a bow and a quiver of arrows worth 15 drachmas as a prize. The second prize is also a bow, but worth 7 drachma[662].

Archery was also part of the agony on the island of Samos, as seen from a Sámi inscription that mentions „Ασκληπιάδης Δημοκράτου as the victor in archery[663].

In this context, we are interested in two inscriptions from Larissa in Thessaly[664], which describe three types of archery competitions. One of the inscriptions says that a certain „Αλέξανδρος Κλέωνος was σκοπφ πεζών victorious, Ὀνόμαρχος Ἡρακλείδου only τόξφ infinitely" Αρι στομένης ‘Ασα[ν]δρίδου again σκοπφ ιππέων. Then we are dealing with three types of archery, i.e. shooting at a target from a horse while riding: σκοπώ ιππέων[665], the same shooting while running: σκοπφ πεζών and finally ordinary shooting from standing in a fixed place: τοξω[666].

These inscriptions only talk about victory in general terms. But we also have news that gives us more information about the archers' performances. On a stone found in Olbia, currently in the Odessa Museum[667], we can find de-

---

[658] Pausanias, X, 6, 3. See Delphi Inschriften Bull. Corr. Hellenique, Bd. XVII (1893), p. 574; Bd. XVIII (1894.), p. 352. Only once did Apollodorus (III, 6, 4, 4) hold a shooting contest at the mythical first Nemean Games, which is said to have been won by a certain Parthenopaios.

[659] A. J. Reinach, in Daremberg et Saglio, Dictionnaire, p. v. sägitta, p. 1005.

[660] IG XII5 Nr. 647 = Dittenberger, Sylloge, 522.

[661] Ver. 23-25 Dittenberger, Sylloge, 522.

[662] V. 26-29 Dittenberger, Sylloge, 522.

[663] Dittenberger, Sylloge, 673. Cf. also ibid., 672 from Tralles and 674 also from that city.

[664] Dittenberger, Sylloge, 670-671.

[665] Shooting horses was common in Crete, as witnessed by Plato, Leg. VIII, 834 D: τοξότης δέ ἀὰφ' ἵππων Κοής ούκ ἀχρηστος ... usw. See też E. Reisch, in Pauly-Wissowas Realenzyklopädie, Bd. I, p. 2721 f.

[666] See Dittenberger, Sylloge, 670, Anm. 6.

[667] E. v. Stern, Der Pfeilschuß des Olbiopoliten Anaxagoras, Jahreshefte d. Öst.bow. Inst. Bd. IV (1901), Beiblatt p. 57 ff.

tailed information about the shooting distance achieved during archery competitions.

Φημὶ διακοσίας τε ./ καὶ ὀγδοήκοντα ὀργυιάς
Καὶ δύο τοξεῦσαι / κλεινὸν ᾿Αναξαγόραν,
῾Υιὸν Δημαγόρεω · / Φίλτεω δὲ παῖδα ὀργυιάς . . . .

We give here the explanation published by E. v. Stern, the editor of this inscription: „The stela is erected in honor of the inhabitants of Olbia, who apparently achieved the best results in archery competitions during the festival, which is confirmed in various places, and the first mentioned prize was won by Anaxagoras, son of Demagoras, with his shot at a distance of 282 orgies [a measure of length, approx. 2 steps (transl.'s note)] = 501 m[668].

The result of the competition was considered worthy of immortalization, just as the shooting scores recorded on the small marble columns at the Ok-meidân in Constantinople transmit the achievements of previous sultans to their contemporaries and posterity"[669]. Strabon[670] gives us another piece of information about the range of the shot when he says that Mithridates fired an arrow from the corner of the roof of the temple of Artemisium in Ephesus, which flew a little to the distance of the stadium [approx. 185 m][671].

Among the officials and officers of Attic Ephebia, we always find in the fifth place on the stones τοξότης, the teacher of archery[672]; when a man named Neandros is at the end of the list; interestingly, he is Cretan[673]. Contrary to what we hear, the bow was not always properly appreciated[674], hence Plato felt compelled to highly recommend archery to his fellow citizens[675]. Over time, however, this art developed more strongly, which can be seen in the previously mentioned agonistic letters of the winners, as well as in inscriptions about teaching teachers. The already mentioned inscription from Teos states that an archery teacher should earn 250 drachmas[676]. Also a beautifully described inscription from Sestos[677] tells about archery lessons, and Aristotle also emphasizes this aspect of ephebe learning[678]. We can see how shooting practices took place in Luciano's story, where it is reported that beginner archers (τόῖς

---

[668] After Nissen, Griechische und römische Metrologie, Handbuch, T. V. Müller, Bd. P, p. 837; Hultsch, Metrologie, 2. Auflage, Tab. III, p. 689 calculates the value of Orgyia at 185 m; also 282 Orgyien = 5217 m.

[669] E. V. Stern, a. a. O. p. 58. See regarding the shooting results on Ok-meidân, J. Karabacek, Nachträgliches zu dem Aufsatz von E. v. Stern, Jahreshefte d. öst.bow. Inst. Bd. IV (1901), Beiblatt, p. 61 ff.

[670] Strabo XIV A, 23 p, 641 C: της δ' ασυλίας τους ορους άλλαγηναι συνέβη πολλάκις,᾿Αλεξάνδρου μεν επί στάδιον ἐκτείναντος, Μιθριδάτού δέ τόξευμα άφέντος από της γωνίας τουκεράμου κάι δόξαντος υπερβαλεσθαι μικρά τό στάδιον .... κτλ.

[671] See also O. Benndorf, in Forschungen in Ephesos, Bd. I, p. 35.

[672] See A. Dumont, Essai sur l'éphébie attique, Paris 1876, Bd. I, p. 192.

[673] A. Dumont, a. a. O. Bd. II, Taf. I.

[674] W. Dittenberger, De ephebis atticis, Gottingae 1863, p. 55. J. H. Krause,a. a. O. Bd. I, p. 559.

[675] Plato, Alk. II, 145 C; Leg. VII, 794 C und VII, 795 B; VII, 813 D; VII, 815 A; VIII, 834 A; Pol. IV, 439 B. In the ideal polity of Atlantis, each of the 60,000 plots into which the empire is divided should have eight soldiers, two of whom are archers, Kritias, 119 A.

[676] See p. 9. Dittenberger, Sylloge, 523.

[677] See p. 9, Anm. 2. Dittenberger, Or. Graec. inscript. sel. 339.

[678] Aristoteles, Ath. Polit. 42.

τοξεύειν μελετῶσιν) placed a bundle of hay on a pole and shot from a short distance[679]. When someone hits the target, everyone screams with great joy, as if something extraordinary had happened (ανέκραγον εὐθύς ὡς τι μέγα ποιήσαντες). But according to Lukianos, this is not a great achievement compared to the achievements of the Scythians or Persian archers, firstly when riding horses (αυτοί κινούμενοι ἀφ' ἵππων), and secondly, behind a moving target (τά τοξευόμενα κινε ῖσθαι αξι ουσ ιν). So they shoot at wild animals, and some of the arrows even hit birds in flight. However, if shooters want to test the power of their shot on a stationary target, they take either a target covered with fresh stiff leather (ασπίδα ὠμοβοΐνην) or a wooden target (ξύλον ἀντίτυπον). If someone shoots through one of these targets, he can be sure that the arrow will even penetrate the armor (καὶ οὕτω πιστεύουσι κᾶν δι' ὅπλων σφίσι χωρῆσαι το ὺς ὀιστούς).

In art, we only have a few depictions of target shooting. In a vase painting from Naples, we saw three young men directing their arrows towards a rooster placed on a pillar[680] (Fig. 58).

***

Despite all the exercises, bets, schools and warnings, the Greeks always preferred close combat, fighting with shield and spear. Only the „Romans" of the Byzantine Empire took first place among bow weapons. Time will tell whether the reason for this preference for the bow is a decline in general courage or a constant struggle with Asians. The fact is that the bow became the most important and valued weapon in the Byzantine Empire. But even then there must have been people who were against the bow and praised the ancient Greeks for their personal courage in hand-to-hand combat and with the shield, as confirmed by the words of Procopius of Caesarea[681] in the introduction to his work „The Persian Wars".

---

[679] Lukianos, Hermot. 33. See also L. Grasberger, a. a. O. Bd. III, p. 156.

[680] Real. Mus. Borb. VII, Taf, 41. Heydemann, Mus. nazion. Nr. 922. Inghirami, Vas. fittil. Nr. 69. See also the Madrid vase depicting the archery competition between Heracles and Eurytus. Half of the target (?) is already on the ground, the other half is still beaten by arrows. P. Bieńkowski, Jahreshefte d. öst. bow. Inst. III (1900), p. 66, fig. 6.

[681] Prokop v. Caes. I, 1.

III. The bows of the nations of the West

For geographical completeness, we include a brief overview of the use of the bow among the nations of the European West. Only the monuments of Sardinia require more detailed discussion, as they provide us with very interesting depictions of archers. These are well-known bronze statuettes from the 8th century BC depicting warriors with bows. We encounter two forms of bows here:

1. A straight bow, about the height of a man, strongly bent at the ends, the string being attached to one end by a tie and to the other by a loop[682];

2. A bow about the height of a man, open towards the target, also strongly curved at both ends, in which the string runs parallel to the ends of the bow[683].

There is almost nothing specific that can be said about carrying a bow. Some warriors carry it on their left shoulder, grasping it from below with their left hand[684], others holding it in front of them with only their left hand[685].

We learn how the bow was strung by looking at the statuette of a warrior who grabs the bow with his left hand approximately at the upper end and intends to press the lower end of the bow to his right thigh, while grasping the free end of the string with his right hand and fixing it on the lower part of the bow[686].

However, Sardinian archers, when drawing, do not draw the string to the right breast or ear, as was the case with other peoples, but to the left breast, which we have not observed anywhere else[687].

As a side note, it is also worth noting that one of the warriors holds the bow with his right hand and draws the string to his right chest with his left hand[688].

Although the warriors carry an oblong quiver on the right side of their back[689] which narrows sharply down[690], we also see archers holding arrows in their hands. This can only be observed among those warriors who also hold

---

[682] See Perrot et Chipiez, a. a. O. Bd. IV, p. 67, fig. 53; p. 72 f., fig. 63; p. 88, fig. 87. Notizie degli scavi, 1878, Taf. VIII, fig. 25, 26, 27; 1904, p. 233, fig. 5, 6. See też A. Schaumberg, a. a. O. p. 97.

[683] Notizie degli scavi, 1904, p. 231, fig. 3, 4.

[684] Notizie degli scavi, 1904, p. 233, fig. 5 i 6. Perrot et Chipiez, a.a. O. Bd. IV, p. 73, fig. 63; p. 88, fig. 87.

[685] Notizie degli scavi, 1904, p. 231, fig. 3, 4.

[686] Perrot et Chipiez, a. a. O. Bd. IV, p. 67, fig. 56.

[687] Perrot et Chipiez, a. a. O. Bd. IV, p. 67, fig. 55; p. 73, fig. 64. Notizie degli scavi, 1878, Taf. VIII, fig. 25 and 26.

[688] Notizie degli scavi, 1878, Taf. VIII, fig. 25.

[689] Perrot et Chipiez, a. a. O. Bd. IV, p. 97, fig. 95. Bullettino bow. Sardo, 1884, Taf. IV, fig. 3.

[690] Notizie degli scavi, 1904, p. 233, fig. 6. Perrot et Chipiez, a. a. O.Bd. IV, p. 88, fig. 87.

a shield in front of them – then the left hand always holds the arrows and the shield at the same time[691].

Finally, it is worth mentioning here that Sardinian archers knew how to use an ordinary glove to protect their left hand from the blow of the returning string (Fig. 85). This custom may have been widespread, as it is found on almost all bronze statuettes[692].

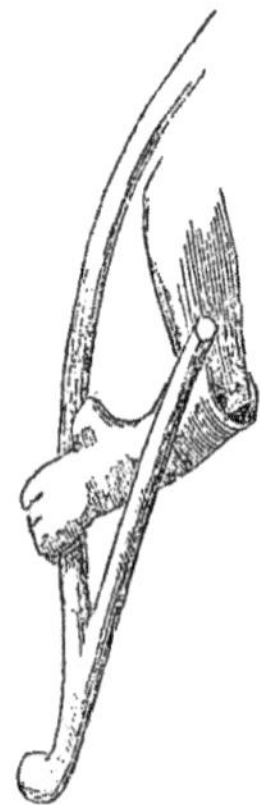

Fig. 85

Perrot et Chipiez, a. a. O., Bd. IV, S. 97, ryc. 96

In Italy, as monuments testify, the bow was common already in prehistoric times[693]; The Etruscans[694], Umbrians[695], Lucanians[696] and others used these weapons, but probably only until Roman rule ended the freedom of these peoples.

As for the Romans, it must be said that the bow has never played a more important role as a weapon of war in the Republican army. The bow was no longer used in the army, even as auxiliary weapons, although it had always been popular as a hunting weapon[697]. Only at the beginning of the imperial period did it begin to be used again as a weapon of war among the „sagittarii", composed of dependent peoples[698]. Also very significant is the fact that during

---

[691] Perrot et Chipiez, a. a. O. Bd. IV, p. 15, fig. 5; p. 67, fig. 54.

[692] Perrot et Chipiez, a. a. O. Bd. IV, 97. Notizie degli scavi, 1904, p. 231 ff.

[693] Monumenti antichi, Bd. XIII (1903), p. 334 f. On the Development of Arrowhead Types see A. J. Reinach, in Daremberg-Saglio, Dictionnaire p. v. sagitta.

[694] See Aen. X, 168. Mon. dell' Inst. V, Taf. 25; VI, Taf. 30, 77; X, Taf. 3, 31. Annali, 1850, p. 259. J. Martha, L'art etrusque, Taf. IV.

[695] See R. Garrucci, Le monete dell' Italia ant. Roma 1885. Taf. LVI.

[696] See R. Garrucci, a. a. O. Taf. CII. See also the statuettes of hippos that adorned the lid of the bronze vessel, Mon. dell Inst. V, Taf. 25 (zob. Annali, 1851, p. 36 ff.).

[697] Suetonius, Domit. 19.

[698] See Cichorius, in Pauly-Wissowa, Real-Enzyklopädie p. v. cohors. R. Cagnat, in Daremberg et Saglio, Dictionnaire p. v. sagittarii.

the Roman wars with the Celts and Germanic peoples, the bow lost its value among the latter[699]. The reason for this is probably that the core of the Roman army consisted of armored legions, to which arrows could not do much damage[700]. But we don't want to say that it has completely fallen out of use. Tacitus in „Germania" does not mention anything about its use, but this does not exclude the possibility of its use, and we have some evidence that closely related peoples of Gaul used the bow at the same time[701].

***

In southern and central Europe, arrowheads are rare in the La Tène period[702].

In turn, in Scandinavia, or rather in Northern Europe, the bow reigns supreme in this era[703], but here too it is increasingly becoming an ordinary hunting weapon[704].

The times of migration brought a new and appropriate quality of ancient small arms. However, it was only in the Middle Ages that the bow gained the highest respect in the European army and, above all, and for a long time among the English. As a common weapon of war, the ancient bow has survived almost into our period in Eastern Europe and among almost all the peoples of Western Asia[705].

---

[699] O. Schräder, Reallexikon der indogermanischen Altertumskunde, p. 620. M. Hoernes, Die Urgeschichte des Menschen, p. 142.

[700] See O. Schräder, Sprachvergleichung und Urgeschichte, Bd. II, p. 105.

[701] Caes. De Bell. Gall. I, 46; IV, 33; VII, 31. Strabo, Geogr. IV, 4, 3. Veget. de re mil. I, 20. L. Lindenschmit, Handbuch der deutschen Altertumskunde, Braunschweig 1880-1889, p. 155. M. Jähns, a. a. O. p. 310 f. A. Demmin, Die Kriegswaffen in ihren geschichtlichen Entwicklungen, Leipzig 1893, p. 99.

[702] M. Hoernes, Urgeschichte der Menschheit, p. 150. M. Hoernes, Natur- und Urgeschichte des Menschen, Bd. II, p. 275.

[703] O. Montelius, a. a. O. S.. 104. M. Hoernes, Natur- und Urgeschichte des Menschen, Bd. II, p. 276.

[704] C. Weichold, Altnordisches Leben, Berlin 1856, p. 205.

[705] At the beginning of the 19th century, it was still used in the Russian army. See D. N. Anuczin, a. a. O. p. 355.